official guides to quality

somewhere special
2005

visit **Britain**
publishing

Contents

Welcome to Somewhere Special	5
How to use this guide	6-7
Regional breakdown	8
The National Quality Assurance Standard	9-12
The regions	13-182
Further information contents	183
Useful information	184-187
Index	188-192
Key to symbols	inside back cover flap
England at a glance	back cover flap

This guide is divided into **8 sections** (see opposite)

VisitBritain

VisitBritain is the organisation created to market Britain to the rest of the world, and England to the British. Formed by the merger of the British Tourist Authority and the English Tourism Council, its mission is to build the value of tourism by creating world-class destination brands and marketing campaigns.

It will also build partnerships with – and provide insights to – other organisations which have a stake in British and English tourism.

Above: Hotels up the hill, Lynmouth, Devon

Right, from top: Shepherd and Dog hotel, Fulking, West Sussex; Seaham Hall Hotel, County Durham; Easton Grey, Malmesbury, Wiltshire

How to use this guide

Guide is designed to **inspire** your choice of quality accommodation

Browse through *Somewhere Special* to find that special place to stay – whichever part of the country you are planning to visit. Even if you're not sure where to go, the guide is designed to inspire your choice.

The guide is divided into four sections: England's North Country, England's Heartland, England's West Country, and South and South East England.

Overleaf, you'll find a breakdown of which county is in which region, together with an accompanying 'England-at-a-glance' map.

Regional listings

Entries are listed by their geographical position, so you'll find that the places you are interested in are usually close to each other in the guide. Serviced establishments (hotels and B&B guest accommodation) are listed separately from self-catering properties and appear first within each regional section. Each of these sub-sections is preceded by a full-colour regional map which clearly plots by the number the location of all the *Somewhere Special* entries, as well as positions of major roads and towns. If you know the area you want to visit, first locate the possible establishments on the regional map and then turn to the appropriate pages in the regional section.

Other features of Somewhere Special

In addition to the accommodation entries, you'll find lots of informative features on a wide variety of subjects scattered throughout the guide. The four detailed introductions to the regions start on pages 14, 58, 96 and 148. For detailed information and advice about booking accommodation, turn to page 184. You are strongly recommended to read this before committing yourself to a firm booking – noting that the published details are supplied directly from the proprietors. Finally, for a complete alphabetical index to all the establishments featured in the guide and the page number on which they appear, turn to page 188.

Left: East Lodge County Hotel, Rowsley, Derbyshire

The **official guide** to award-winning serviced and self-catering accommodation

Welcome...

Go on – spoil yourself with a well-earned break, you deserve it. That's where *Somewhere Special 2005* – celebrating its first decade – comes in. Because we know your holiday time is so precious, VisitBritain has created the definitive guide for the discerning traveller. All featured hotels, B&Bs, inns, farmhouses, guest accommodation and self-catering properties in England offer something a little bit special – just right for a memorable stay.

The guide is easy to use – the detailed entries are all cross-referenced to full-colour maps. Features and helpful hints to each region are included to inspire you. Whatever your budget, and whether you want a short getaway or a longer break, *Somewhere Special* offers a choice of accommodation that promises a warm welcome and an experience that's extraordinary.

Your sign of quality

As in other VisitBritain guides, all accommodation included in this essential guide has been assessed and awarded a rating for quality by VisitBritain (see page 9). In *Somewhere Special*, however, you are promised something extra, as every single entry has achieved a top quality star or diamond rating or a Gold or Silver Award (see pages 10-12). This means that in terms of comfort, service and individuality, your experience will be of the highest quality.

The definitive guide

A decadent luxury break, a long weekend in a cosy cottage or an intimate bed and breakfast: whatever you're looking for, *Somewhere Special* meets your needs. The criterion for inclusion in *Somewhere Special* is excellence rather than the range of facilities available – though of course you'll be able to see at glance exactly what's on offer.

So, go on, flick through and choose your perfect break. It's time to indulge yourself. Then relax – you've already done the hard part!

Left, from top: Jars of pickles at Malmaison Hotel, Newcastle upon Tyne; conservatory lounge overlooking Lake Windermere at Linthwaite House Hotel, Cumbria; Obsidian bar, lounge and restaurant at Arora Hotel, Manchester

The National Quality Assurance Standard

When you're looking for a place to stay, you need a rating system you can trust. VisitBritain's ratings give you a clear guide to what to expect, in an easy-to-understand form. Properties are visited annually by trained, impartial assessors who award ratings based on the overall experience of their visit. There are strict guidelines to ensure every property is assessed to the same criteria, so you can have the confidence that your accommodation has been thoroughly checked and rated for quality before you make your booking. After all, meeting customer expectations is what makes happy guests.

Gold and Silver Awards

Look out for the Gold and Silver Awards that are exclusive to VisitBritain.

They are awarded to **hotels** achieving the highest levels of quality within their star rating. While the overall rating is based on a combination of guest services, facilities and quality, the Gold and Silver Awards are based solely on quality, with an emphasis on service and hospitality.

They are awarded to **guest accommodation** establishments that not only achieve the overall quality within their diamond rating, but also reach the highest level of quality in those specific areas that guests identify as being really important for them. They will reflect the quality of comfort and cleanliness you will find in the bedrooms and bathrooms and the quality of service you'll enjoy throughout your stay.

A note about hotels

There is no restriction on any property that provides serviced accommodation using the word hotel in the title. Hotels with a star rating meet all the requirements for the 1 Star hotel standard and will usually have a drinks licence and offer meals in addition to breakfast. Hotel establishments with a diamond rating meet the minimum entry requirements for the Guest Accommodation standard but do not automatically meet the Hotel 1 Star requirements.

An assessor calls

Before a quality rating is awarded, one of our qualified assessors visits the establishment to make an independent assessment. For serviced accommodation, the assessor books in advance as a normal guest and does not reveal his or her identity until after settling the bill following an overnight stay. Self-catering properties are generally assessed on a day visit arranged in advance with the owner.

Each assessment will involve a thorough tour of the property together with the proprietor. At the end of the tour, they discuss the conclusions, with the assessor making suggestions where helpful.

Only after the visit does the assessor arrive at a conclusion for the quality rating – so the assessment is 100% independent and reliable.

The four-star hotel at Lucknam Park (see page 113)

Stars for Hotels

Star ratings are your sign of quality assurance, giving you the confidence to book the accommodation that meets your expectations. Based on the internationally recognised rating of one to five stars, the system puts great emphasis on quality and is based on research that shows exactly what consumers are looking for when choosing a hotel. Ratings are awarded from one to five stars – the more stars, the higher the quality and the greater the range of facilities and level of services provided.

Remember that only star rated hotels with a Gold or Silver Award **qualify** for *Somewhere Special*

Top: The Rye Lodge Hotel (see page 170)
Above: Swan Hotel (see page 76)

Hotel star ratings explained

At a ★ hotel you will find:

Practical accommodation with a limited range of facilities and services, and a high standard of cleanliness throughout (75% of rooms will have en suite or private facilities). Friendly and courteous staff. Dining room/eating area offering breakfast to you and your guests. Alcoholic drinks served in a bar or lounge.

At a ★★ hotel you will find:

In addition to what is provided at ★

Good accommodation offering a personal style of service with additional facilities. More comfortable bedrooms (all with en suite or private facilities and colour television). Food and drink is of a higher standard.

At a ★★★ hotel you will find:

In addition to what is provided at ★ and ★★

Very good accommodation with more spacious public areas and bedrooms, all offering a significantly greater quality and higher standard of facilities and services. A more formal style of service with a receptionist. A wide selection of drinks, light lunch and snacks served in a bar or lounge, with greater attention to quality. Room service for continental breakfast and laundry service.

At a ★★★★ hotel you will find:

In addition to what is provided at ★, ★★ and ★★★

Accommodation offering excellent comfort and quality. All rooms with en-suite facilities. Strong emphasis on food and drink. Experienced staff responding to your needs and requests. Room service for all meals; light refreshments and snacks available 24 hours.

At a ★★★★★ hotel you will find:

In addition to what is provided at ★, ★★, ★★★ and ★★★★

A spacious and luxurious establishment offering accommodation, extensive facilities, services and cuisine of the highest international quality. Professional, attentive staff, exceptional comfort and a sophisticated ambience.

Diamonds for Guest Accommodation

The diamond ratings for Guest Accommodation reflect visitor expectations of this sector – a wide variety of serviced accommodation, embracing B&Bs, inns, farmhouses and guest accommodation, for which England is renowned.

The quality of what is provided is more important to visitors than a wide range of facilities and services. Therefore, the same minimum requirement for facilities and services applies to all guest accommodation from one to five diamonds, while progressively higher levels of quality and customer care must be provided for each rating.

Somewhere Special does not **include** establishments with less than three diamonds

Guest Accommodation diamond ratings explained

At ♦♦♦ guest accommodation you will find:

A very good overall level of quality in areas such as comfortable bedrooms, well maintained, practical décor, a good choice of quality items at breakfast, customer care and all-round comfort. Where other meals are provided these will be freshly cooked from good quality ingredients.

At ♦♦♦♦ guest accommodation you will find:

In addition to what is provided at ♦♦♦

An excellent level of quality in all areas. Customer care showing very good attention to your needs.

At ♦♦♦♦♦ guest accommodation you will find:

In addition to what is provided at ♦♦♦ *and* ♦♦♦♦

An exceptional overall level of quality – for example, ample space with a degree of luxury, a high-quality bed and furniture, excellent interior design and customer care which anticipates your needs. Breakfast offering a wide choice of high-quality fresh ingredients. Where other meals are provided, these will feature fresh, seasonal, and often local ingredients.

Left: Northam Mill (see page 119)
Below: Jeake's House Hotel (see page 171)

Stars for Self-Catering

The star ratings for self-catering reflect the quality that you're looking for when booking accommodation. All properties have to meet an extensive list of minimum requirements to take part in the scheme. Ratings are awarded from one to five stars – the more stars, the higher the quality. Establishments at higher rating levels also have to meet additional requirements for facilities. Some self-catering establishments have a range of accommodation units in the building or on the site and the individual units may have different star ratings. In such cases the entry shows the range available.

Below: Tiverton Castle (see page 141)
Bottom, left: Oswald Cottage (see page 44)
Bottom, right: Arundel Oast (see page 181)

Self-Catering star ratings explained

At a ★★★★ property you will find:

An excellent overall level of quality with very good care and attention to detail throughout. Access to a washing machine and drier if it is not provided in the unit, or a 24-hour laundry service.

At a ★★★★★ property you will find:

In addition to what is provided at ★★★★

An exceptional overall level of quality with high levels of décor, fixtures and fittings, with personal touches. Excellent standards of management efficiency and guest services.

Only four and five star properties **qualify** for entry in *Somewhere Special*

England's North Country

Top right: Castle Howard from the ornamental pond and fountains in South Yorkshire

Above: Outside the Cavern Club in Liverpool

Right: Couple shopping in Corn Exchange in Leeds

England's North Country

Experience an exhilarating mix of history, culture, industry and nature in England's North. **Discover** a proud industrial heritage at Beamish, and wonder at the enduring Roman legacy along Hadrian's Wall and in Chester. **Explore** rugged and romantic landscape that has inspired centuries of writers and poets. You're in the land of sporting legend, where the beautiful game attracts millions of fans from around the world. **Relax** or hit the town in some of the country's most hip and vibrant cities – Leeds, Manchester, Liverpool and Newcastle.

The Northern highlights

Inspiring landscape

Let the landscape inspire you, just as it did Emily Brontë. For a brilliant metaphor for Cathy and Heathcliffe's intense passion, look no further than the raging tempests of the Yorkshire Moors. Wander lonely as a cloud in the Lake District – where William Wordsworth and Samuel Taylor Coleridge both lived. Find England's highest mountain, Scafell Pike, and its deepest lake, Wastwater. You're spoilt for choice for National Parks. The Forest of Bowland, an Area of Outstanding Natural Beauty, is one unspoilt gem, while Yorkshire alone has 1,000 square miles to explore. Blow the cobwebs away along miles and miles of Northumbria's sandy beaches. Choose from an A-Z of outdoor pursuits at Kielder Water.

Roman Britain

Pace along Hadrian's Wall just as soldiers did nearly two millenniums ago. The wall was a huge

Windswept moors and breathtaking coastlines. Mirrored glass lakes and the magnificent cathedrals of York and Durham. The urban wonders of the Gateshead Millennium Bridge and Urbis in Manchester. There is all-year-round fun and games at Blackpool. It's all just part of an ordinary day in England's proud and historic North.

Above right: Alnwick Castle, Northumberland
Below: The Old Trafford home of Manchester United

England's North Country

undertaking – 73 miles long and built in six years. Explore the many forts, milecastles and turrets that dot the wall's length. For an insight into life as a Roman soldier, visit Housesteads Fort, the most complete base. Find more Roman remains in the walled city of Chester, Britain's best-preserved Roman town – complete with partially excavated amphitheatre. The Dewa fortress – buried beneath the town – now lives on through the Dewa Roman Experience. Imagine the sights, sounds and smells of 2,000 years ago. Turn from history to shopping. Discover The Rows – two-tiered galleries packed with unique and tempting shops.

This sporting life

Get caught up in the passion of the North's great footballing tradition. Drop by the beautiful game's temples of Old Trafford, Anfield and St James' Park. A must for football fans is the National Football Museum at Preston. Experience the agony and ecstasy of GoalStriker, an interactive penalty shoot-out experience. Other obsessions include rugby league and cricket – Geoffrey Boycott, Fred Trueman and Andrew Flintoff are three Northern-born legends. In March don't miss The Grand National at Aintree, near Liverpool. Feel the excitement as you witness this highlight of racing's National Hunt season. Terrifying jumps such as Beechers Brook and The Chair test the skills of runners, riders and punters alike.

Master builders

Be uplifted by the spiritual and physical presence of two of England's most impressive churches. York Minster, the largest medieval Gothic church in Northern Europe, rose phoenix-like after it was severely damaged by fire in 1984. Arrive at Durham by train and be greeted by the magnificent sight of the 900-year-old cathedral perched high above the city. Not to be outdone, many other buildings match its grandeur. Fountains Abbey, Britain's largest monastic ruin, and adjacent Studley Royal Water Garden, are must-sees. Are your walls at home a bit bare? This wasn't a problem at Castle Howard where Canalettos, Holbeins and Gainsboroughs are just some of the art treasures on display. How about some nice wallpaper? William Morris did a good line – see for yourself in Liverpool's half-timbered Speke Hall. Telly addicts will recognise Lyme Park in Cheshire as the home of Mr Darcy in *Pride and Prejudice*. Movie magic also transformed Alnwick Castle and Garden into a location for the Harry Potter films.

A proud industrial heritage

Where did the Industrial Revolution gather pace? In the North Country, of course! Wool cloth in Yorkshire and cotton in Lancashire. Hectic mills powered by fast-flowing rivers. Learn about the days of early industrialisation at Quarry Bank Mill in Cheshire and the Armley Mills Industrial Museum in Leeds. Collieries also once dominated the North's physical and economic landscape. They may have gone, but the coal mining heritage is still very alive. Hear vivid tales at the National Museum of Coal Mining in Wakefield, and the award-winning Beamish Open Air Museum. Another legacy is the North's vast transport network. Relax as you float along a canal past breathtaking countryside and urban heartlands. Steam engines, too, were once a familiar sight. The world's first public passenger steam railway opened between Stockton and Darlington. Experience once more the romance of steam on the Settle-Carlisle or East Lancashire Line, or wonder at the giant locomotives at the National Railway Museum in York.

City slickers

You can't ignore the vibes of north England's dynamic cities – Leeds, Newcastle, Bradford and Sheffield. Regeneration has helped them give London a run for its money. Vibrant Leeds: by day it's a shopping Mecca, by night, it's a buzzing entertainment centre. Stay in chic boutique hotels and splash out in the restored Corn Exchange. Enjoy the renaissance of Newcastle and Gateshead. Be enchanted by the stunning architecture of the Gateshead Millennium Bridge. Shop till you drop at the MetroCentre, Europe's biggest indoor shopping centre or be awe-inspired by the amazing Angel of the North. Sheffield's Winter Gardens is also a place you won't want to miss. What's more, this is a region that is culturally rich. Check out new artists at the Baltic in Gateshead, the Centre for Contemporary Art, and listen to a favourite score at Opera

Above right: Gateshead's Millennium Bridge
Below: York Minster, North Yorkshire

England's North Country

North. Enjoy a performance at the West Yorkshire Playhouse, Leeds, or spend hours at the National Museum of Photography, Film & Television in Bradford, the most visited museum outside London.

A musical movement
Explore the cities of Liverpool and Manchester, both with music beating through their veins. Liverpool, named European Capital of Culture 2008, is famed as the birthplace of The Beatles. You can follow in their footsteps, from the world-famous Cavern Club, to John Lennon's childhood home, Mendips, now in the care of the National Trust. If the visual arts interest you, you'll love Tate Liverpool – an exciting contemporary art space. Manchester also led a musical revolution – this time in the 90s. Remember the Stone Roses and The Inspiral Carpets? Head for Salford Quays and the paintings of LS Lowry – his cityscapes are synonymous with Greater Manchester's industrial age. These areas, criss-crossed by canals, are now a thriving arts and entertainment centre. Choose between 50 free museums and art galleries in the Greater Manchester area, or spice up your life on the 'Curry Mile'. Shopping is first rate: the Trafford Centre and Harvey Nicks offer plenty of opportunities to help you spend your money.

Contact

England's Northwest
www.visitenglandsnorthwest.com

Yorkshire Tourist Board
www.yorkshirevisitor.com

One Northeast Tourism Team
www.visitnorthumbria.com

At-a-glance symbols are explained on the flap inside the back cover

England's North Country — Hotels and Guest Accommodation

Hotels and Guest Accommodation — England's North Country

England's North Country — **Hotels and Guest Accommodation**

Splendid country house hotel recommended in the Good Hotel Guide 2005

1 : Belford, Northumberland

WAREN HOUSE

★★★ Silver Award

Waren Mill, Belford, Northumberland NE70 7EE
Tel: 01668 214581 • **Fax:** 01668 214484
Web: www.warenhousehotel.co.uk

This traditional country house hotel is set in six acres of wooded grounds and walled garden on the coast at Budle Bay. Waren House provides excellent accommodation and food and is recommended in the 2005 Good Hotel Guide. There is a tempting 250-plus bin of reasonably priced wines to tempt the palate too. There are miles of glorious sands on this stretch of the Northumbrian coast and majestic castles dot the landscape from Bamburgh to Warkworth and mighty Alnwick, with its superb gardens. There is something for everyone, from golf to sea trips, and from history to merely enjoying the glorious scenery. And Waren House is the ideal base to start from.

Bed & Breakfast per night:
Double room from £130.00–£205.00

Dinner, Bed & Breakfast per person, per night: £86.00–£129.50

Bedrooms: 5 double/3 twin/4 suites

Bathrooms: 12 en suite

Parking: Available

Cards accepted: Mastercard, Visa, Switch, American Express, Delta, Diners, Euros

Directions: 2 miles off A1 on B1342 midway between Alnwick and Berwick-upon-Tweed.

Hotels and Guest Accommodation | **England's North Country**

2 : Beadnell, Northumberland

Beach Court ◆◆◆◆◆ Silver Award

Harbour Road, Beadnell,
Northumberland NE67 5BJ
Contact: Carole Ann Field
Tel: 01665 720225 • **Fax:** 01665 721499
Web: www.beachcourt.com
E-mail: info@beachcourt.com

Carole and Russell welcome you as house guests to Beach Court, their honey-stone, turreted beachside home, overlooking the tiny 18th century, west-facing harbour. Visit us at any season of the year; perhaps take a winter break when you might savour the crystal clear air, before returning to deep leather armchairs in front of a roaring log fire? All our rooms are double glazed and centrally heated, with huge bathrooms; the tide laps gently under your snug window seat, from which you can catch up on all your reading, paint, or simply unwind as you gaze across the vast stretch of golden sands which form Beadnell Bay. Secure courtyard parking. Self-catering also available.

Bed & Breakfast per night:
Single room from £54.50–£74.50
Double room from £79.00–£119.00

Bedrooms: 1 double/1 twin/1 suite
Bathrooms: 3 en suite
Parking: Available
Cards accepted: Mastercard, Visa, Switch, American Express

Directions: Follow A1 to north of Alnwick. Take B6347 to Beadnell. Follow signs for Beadnell Harbour.

3 : Alnwick, Northumberland

West Acre House ◆◆◆◆◆ Gold Award

West Acres, Alnwick,
Northumberland, NE66 2QA
Contact: Jeannette Hewison
Tel: 01665 510374
Web: www.westacrehouse.co.uk
E-mail: info@westacrehouse.co.uk

West Acre House is a very imposing and elegant Edwardian detached villa set in one acre of beautiful gardens on the very edge of Alnwick, quietly tucked away in a leafy suburb next to open countryside. The garden is available for guests at any time and we encourage you to make yourself at home. You are welcome to browse our library of hundreds of books and maps, or view any of our videos and DVDs in your room. Our bedrooms are spacious and elegant, with private facilities, and are equipped with hospitality trays, radio, TV/video and DVD players. Close to Alnwick Garden, Castle, Cragside and Wallington Hall. Five minutes from the coast.

Bed & Breakfast per night:
Double room from £62.00–£66.00

Dinner, Bed & Breakfast per person, per night:
£47.00–£49.00

Bedrooms: 3 double/1 twin
Bathrooms: 4 en suite
Parking: Available
Cards accepted: None

Directions: From A1 at junction signed for Alnwick, travel to roundabout, turn right then second turn on left. West Acre House is the second detached house on right.

England's North Country — **Hotels and Guest Accommodation**

Fine accommodation and cuisine set amidst the beauties of Northumberland

4 : Hexham, Northumberland

De Vere Slaley Hall

★★★★ Silver Award

Slaley, Hexham, Northumberland NE47 0BY
Tel: 01434 673350 • **Fax:** 01434 673962
Web: www.devereonline.co.uk • **E-mail:** slaley.hall@devere-hotels.com

De Vere Slaley Hall is just 30 minutes away from Newcastle upon Tyne, but it feels like a million miles away, with the Northumberland hotel surrounded by stunning panoramic scenery offering guests luxurious surroundings and spectacular views across 1000 acres of forest and moorland. Guests have a choice of 139 individually designed rooms and a selection of suites in the new or old hall, some with jacuzzi baths and separate lounges and bedrooms. There is a pick of different eating venues, too, including 'the restaurant at Slaley Hall', the Clubhouse, and private dining rooms. There are two 72 par championship golf courses to test your skills, while the Slaley Spa offers relaxing and pampering treatments and therapies. The leisure club has everything to keep you fit and trim, as well as on-site activities ranging from off-road driving to human table football.

Bed & Breakfast per night:
single room from £100.00–£105.00
double room from £75.00–£85.00

Dinner, Bed & Breakfast per person, per night: £95.00–£105.00

Bedrooms: 75 double/47 twin/17 suites

Bathrooms: 139 en suite

Parking: Available

Cards accepted: Mastercard, Visa, Switch, Delta, American Express, Diners

Directions: A1 from the south to A68 link road, follow signs for Slaley Hall. From the north, take the A69 to Corbridge, then follow the A68 south and signs for Slaley Hall.

5 : Barnard Castle, County Durham

Pound House   ♦♦♦♦ Silver Award

The Hagg, Cotherstone, Barnard Castle,
County Durham DL12 9QJ
Tel: 01833 650724
E-mail: jeanwoodpoundhouse@tiscali.co.uk

Pound House is a five-bedroom Norwegian cedarwood house in its own delightful gardens and set in a beautiful haven where guests can enjoy peace and quiet in this historic corner of south Durham. This is an area of outstanding natural beauty, with the bonus that all around there are wonderful things to be seen, including the fascinating Bowes Museum. From Pound House access is easy to North Yorkshire, the North East coast, Northern Lake District and Hadrian's Wall. Jean Wood is an excellent host renowned for making guests feel at home. Enjoy!

Bed & Breakfast per night:
Single room from £30.00–£30.00;
Double room from £60.00–£60.00

Bedrooms: 2 double (double may be used as single, with no supplement, but £30 per night)

Bathrooms: 2 en suite

Parking: Available

Cards accepted: None

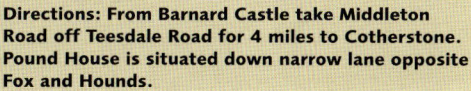

Directions: From Barnard Castle take Middleton Road off Teesdale Road for 4 miles to Cotherstone. Pound House is situated down narrow lane opposite Fox and Hounds.

Early Quakers

Governed by an authoritarian Church and State, 17th century England allowed its people little freedom of expression. But George Fox (1624-91), the son of a Leicestershire weaver, sought to challenge this, convinced by a series of revelations and visions, that he should spread the word of the 'inner light' of Christ's salvation.

Eschewing the rigid framework of the established Church, Fox travelled the country, preaching his simple message to all who would listen. In one vision, while on Pendle Hill north of Burnley, he saw a multitude gathered together 'in worship of God in a place by a river'.

The spring of 1652, found him in Dentdale, north-west Yorkshire (now Cumbria). On Whit Saturday he stayed the night at Brigflatts, a couple of miles west of Sedbergh, before attending a large gathering of a like-minded sect known as 'the Seekers' on the Sunday. This congregation was, according to his diary, the fulfilment of Fox's vision on Pendle Hill.

At Sedbergh's Hiring Fair the following week, he preached to a congregation of over a thousand gathered on Firbank Fell, a hill not far from Brigflatts, now known as Fox's Pulpit. The event played a major part in the setting up of the worldwide movement and the local area has an active group of Friends to this day.

It is at Brigflatts that in 1675 one of the earliest Friends' Meeting Houses was built. Quakers and others seek out this whitewashed stone building beside the River Rawthey, almost unchanged in 300 years.

In nearby Kendal, the 19th century Friends Meeting House is the permanent home of the Quaker Tapestry, a work of art created by more than 4,000 people. It depicts the beliefs and events of the Quaker movement from the time of George Fox's first sermons.

Quaker Tapestry Exhibition, Kendal
Tel: 01539 722975, www.quaker-tapestry.co.uk

England's North Country — Hotels and Guest Accommodation

Superb Jacobean mansion standing in the rolling countryside of lower Teesdale

6 : Darlington, County Durham

Headlam Hall

★★★ Silver Award

Headlam, near Gainford, Darlington, DL2 3HA
Tel: 01325 730238 • **Fax:** 01325 730790
Web: www.headlamhall.co.uk • **E-mail:** admin@headlamhall.co.uk

The superb 17th century Jacobean mansion, Headlam Hall, stands in four acres of beautiful walled gardens, surrounded by its own golf course and rolling farmland in lower Teesdale. Family-owned and run for the past 26 years it has an excellent reputation as one of the region's leading country house hotels. All 34 bedrooms enjoy high quality decor, some with period furnishings and rich fabrics, others more cottage-like with country colours. The restaurant is divided into four rooms, each offering a distinctive style, but with the same high quality cuisine throughout. Amenities include golf, indoor pool, sauna, gym, tennis, croquet and coarse fishing. Nearby are Barnard Castle, Bowes Museum and High Force.

Bed & Breakfast per night:
Single room from £80.00–£120.00
Double room from £100.00–£140.00

Dinner, Bed & Breakfast per person, per night: £65–£69 (minimum 2 nights)
Bedrooms: 24 double/6 twin, 4 family
Bathrooms: 34 en suite
Parking: Available
Cards accepted: Mastercard, Visa, Switch, Delta, American Express, Diners

Directions: 8 miles west of Darlington on A67 and 2 miles north of Gainford.

Hotels and Guest Accommodation — England's North Country

7 : Northallerton, North Yorkshire

Little Holtby ♦♦♦♦ Silver Award

Leeming Bar, Northallerton
North Yorkshire DL7 9LH
Tel: 01609 748762 • **Fax:** 01609 748822
Web: www.littleholtby.co.uk
E-mail: littleholtby@yahoo.co.uk

With its origins in the Domesday Book, Little Holtby has one foot in the past and the other firmly in the land of 21st century comfort. All our spacious guest rooms have glorious views and are tastefully furnished and fully-equipped. Our generous country breakfasts with free-range eggs and organic produce are a fortifying start to the day, whether you intend to enjoy the many sports and attractions nearby or take a gentle meander through this historic region. Little Holtby gives you chance to pamper yourself a little as our regular guests have already found out.

Bed & Breakfast per night:
Single room from £27.50–£30.00
Double room from £25.00–£27.50

Dinner, Bed & Breakfast per person, per night:
£37.50–£40.00 (minimum 2 nights)

Bedrooms: 2 double/1 twin

Bathrooms: 1 en suite, 1 en suite shower room, one public bathroom

Parking: Available

Cards accepted: None

Directions: 50 metres off the A1 between Bedale and Richmond

8 : Masham, North Yorkshire

Swinton Park ★★★★ Gold Award

Masham, Ripon, North Yorkshire HG4 4JH
Tel: 01765 680900 • **Fax:** 01765 680901
Web: www.swintonpark.com
E-mail: enquiries@swintonpark.com

A luxury castle hotel set in 200 acres of parkland in the Yorkshire Dales. Lavishly furnished, this ancestral home combines the best of tradition with modern luxury. Excellent cuisine is served, drawing heavily on fresh produce sourced from the walled garden and surrounding estate. Country pursuits include golf, fishing, riding, falconry and shooting, while many other sports, including archery, croquet and boules are catered for. For that ultimate feeling of well-being, a wide range of beauty treatments and massages is available during your stay. For something really special, join the celebrity chef Rosemary Shrager in her state-of-the-art cookery school in the converted Georgian stables.

Bed & Breakfast per night:
Double room from £120.00–£250.00

Bedrooms: 4 double/21 twin/5 suites

Bathrooms: 30 en suite

Parking: Available

Cards accepted: Mastercard, Visa, Switch, American Express, Delta, Diners, Euros

Directions: Take B6267 off the A1, 25 miles north of Leeds, follow signs to Masham, go through town centre and follow signs to hotel.

England's North Country — **Hotels and Guest Accommodation**

Charming Victorian cottage offering home comforts in picturesque Helmsley

9 : Helmsley, North Yorkshire

No 54

54 Bondgate, Helmsley, North Yorkshire YO62 5EZ
Tel: 01439 771533 • **Fax:** 01439 771533
Web: www.no54.co.uk • **E-mail:** lizziewould@hotmail.com

Situated in picturesque Helmsley on the edge of the North York Moors National Park, No 54, an early 1850s cottage, has three tastefully appointed ground floor en suite rooms facing a pretty courtyard. Fabulous and hard to leave, No 54 has all you need for time out. Luxurious bedding, tasty delights and comfort abound. Enjoy a hearty Yorkshire breakfast or tuck into a hamper full of continental breakfast delights. In the evening rest and relax after a day's enjoyment with a delicious home-cooked dinner. No 54 is a superb base to explore Yorkshire, with Castle Howard, the North York Moors Railway and Rievaulx Abbey all close by.

Bed & Breakfast per night:
Single room from £29.50
Double room from £74.00
Bedrooms: 2 double/1 single/1 twin
Bathrooms: 3 en suite
Parking: Available
Cards accepted: None

Directions: From Helmsley market square follow the A170 towards Kirbymoorside/Scarborough. No 54 is approximately 500 metres from the square on the right of the road.

Hotels and Guest Accommodation — **England's North Country**

10 : Ampleforth, North Yorkshire

Shallowdale House

West End, Ampleforth,   ◆◆◆◆◆ **Gold Award**
North Yorkshire YO62 4DY
Contact: Phillip Gill/Anton Van Der Horst
Tel: 01439 788325 • **Fax:** 01439 788885
Web: www.shallowdalehouse.co.uk
E-mail: stay@shallowdalehouse.co.uk

Every room at Shallowdale House enjoys stunning panoramic views of the surrounding unspoilt countryside through huge picture windows. Owners Phillip Gill and Anton van der Horst run the house with unassuming style, while making every effort to match the wonderful setting with relaxing comfort, carefully prepared home-cooked food from top quality local produce, and meticulous attention to detail. Shallowdale House holds the Good Hotel Guide Cesar Award for Yorkshire Guest House of the Year 2005 on top of many other major awards. It is a superb base for visiting North Yorkshire, with Castle Howard and Rievaulx Abbey very close by.

Bed & Breakfast per night:
Single room from £57.50–£67.50
Double room from £77.50–£95.00

Dinner, Bed & Breakfast per person, per night:
£68.25–£77.00

Bedrooms: 1 double/2 twin-king
Bathrooms: 2 en suite
Parking: Available
Cards accepted: Mastercard, Switch, Visa, Delta

Directions: At the western end of Ampleforth on the turning to Hambleton.

11 : Easingwold, York

The Old Vicarage ◆◆◆◆ **Gold Award**

The Old Vicarage, Market Place,
Easingwold, York YO61 3AL
Contact: JC Kirman
Tel: 01347 821015 • **Fax:** 01347 823465
Web: www.oldvicarage-easingwold.co.uk
E-mail: kirman@oldvic-easingwold.freeserve

Standing in the Georgian market square, yet surrounded by half an acre of garden, with croquet lawn and ample parking, our 18th century home provides a tranquil haven easily accessible to the Yorkshire moors and dales. Tastefully furnished, well-appointed bedrooms have some little, unexpected extra touches. An extensive buffet and traditional English breakfast, using local produce, is served in the east-facing dining room, while the drawing room, which is exclusively for our guests' enjoyment features a well-used grand piano. The Old Vicarage has been noted in *The Guardian* for its attention to detail and superb breakfasts.

Bed & Breakfast per night:
Double room from £65.00–£80.00

Bedrooms: 3 double/1 twin
Bathrooms: 4 en suite
Parking: Available
Cards accepted: None

Directions: From the north take A1 to Dishforth then the A168 to Thirsk and A19 to Easingwold. From the south take M1 then A64 to York, take A123 North York bypass then A19 to Thirsk exiting to Easingwold after 10 miles.

England's North Country | **Hotels and Guest Accommodation**

12 : Knaresborough, North Yorkshire

Gallon House ♦♦♦♦ Gold Award

47 Kirgate, Knaresborough,
Harrogate, North Yorkshire HG5 8BZ
Contact: Susan and Rick Hodgson
Tel: 01423 862102
Web: www.gallon-house.co.uk
E-mail: gallonhouse@ntworld.com

Situated overlooking Knaresborough's beautiful Nidd Gorge, Gallon House offers charming accommodation and delicious locally-sourced food prepared by well-known Yorkshire chef, Rick Hodgson. Guests enjoy stunning views from a pretty veranda, the use of a delightful sitting room and conservatory, with meals being taken in the oak-panelled dining room. Gallon House is tastefully furnished to complement the eccentric architectural style of the building. The compliment of a recent guest sums up the Gallon House experience – "wonderful service and delicious food".

Bed & Breakfast per night:
single room from £70 .00
double room from £90.00
Bedrooms: 2 double/1 twin
Bathrooms: 3
Parking: Available
Cards accepted: None

Directions: A59 from Harrogate and A1.

Yorkshire Dales Barns

Man has played his own part in creating the magnificent landscape of the Yorkshire Dales. Barns, which in northern Dales such as Swaledale (pictured) and Arkengarthdale, are liberally dotted in almost every field, add to the glorious impression these valleys create.

These barns – it is estimated that there are over a thousand in Swaledale and Arkengarthdale alone – also reflect a vanishing form of agriculture. In the 17th, 18th and 19th centuries, when most of these barns were built, farms were small and numerous. Many who tended the land also worked in the local lead and coal mines, and so had little time to devote to farming. The summer harvest was the most labour-intensive time of year, and so an agricultural system of building barns was evolved to allow a more even spread of work. By constructing barns in the field where the hay was growing, it was not only easier for the farmers to store the hay, but also to feed their cattle and for the herds to fertilise the same field with their manure.

Modern life's quest for efficiency has meant that farms are now few and large. This no longer fits in with the traditional system, leaving many outlying field barns redundant. In Swaledale and Arkengarthdale, a conservation scheme run by the national park has saved countless of them from becoming derelict; some are still used by their owners, while others have found new life as 'bunkhouse barns'. These offer basic accommodation to walkers and are often on or near long-distance footpaths. At Hazel Brow, Low Row, visitors may go inside a traditional Dales barn as part of the open farm scheme.

For details of accommodation in bunkhouse barns, contact the Youth Hostelling Association. Tel: 0870 770 8868, www.yha.org.uk

Hotels and Guest Accommodation | **England's North Country**

13 : Knaresborough, North Yorkshire

Staveley Grange   ◆◆◆◆◆

Near Knaresborough, Harrogate,
North Yorkshire HG5 9LD
Tel: 01423 340265 • **Fax:** 01423 340539
Web: www.s-h-systems.co.uk/hotels/staveley.html
E-mail: staveleygrange@onetel.com

A warm welcome awaits you in this elegant 18th century house set in a beautiful Yorkshire conservation area. The three guest bedrooms – double or twin – are all en suite, individually furnished and fully-equipped. In summer the sun terrace is a highlight of the grounds and garden; in winter the open log fire will tempt you to the guest lounge. There is a heated swimming pool and croquet lawn, and you can start the day with a full English or continental breakfast, with fresh produce from our garden or locally grown.

Bed & Breakfast per night:
Single room from £55.00–£60.00;
Double room from £75.00–£80.00

Dinner by arrangement: From £26

Bedrooms: 3 double or twin

Bathrooms: All en suite

Parking: Available

Cards accepted: Mastercard, Visa, Switch/Delta, American Express/Euros

Directions: Leave A1(M) junction 48 (Boroughbridge, Dishforth, Ripon). Take A6055 to Minskip. In Minskip turn right signed Staveley 2. In Stavely turn right at junction. 200 yards on right before low stone wall with iron railings turn right into Staveley Grange drive.

14 : Knaresborough, North Yorkshire

Newton House   ◆◆◆◆

Newton House, York Place,
Knaresborough, North Yorkshire HG5 0AD
Tel: 01423 863539 • **Fax:** 01423 869748
Web: www.newtonhouse.com
E-mail: newtonhouse@btinternet.com

Guest comfort is the order of the day at this lovingly restored double-fronted property, built reputedly, from the stones of Knaresborough Castle. Just a short walk from the town centre, Newton House offers charmingly furnished and decorated bedrooms which are fully equipped – some with four-poster or king-size beds. The guest sitting room/bar is spacious and comfortable too. A good place to relax after breakfast, perhaps. Newton House breakfasts come from an impressive menu, using fresh, local produce, and individually prepared. From traditional English to vegetarian, a great start to the day.

Bed & Breakfast per night:
single room from £45.00–£65.00
double room from £80.00–£90.00

Bedrooms: 5 double/1 single/2 twin/2 family/1 suite

Bathrooms: 10 en suite

Parking: Available

Cards accepted: American Express, Mastercard, Switch, Visa

Directions: Follow the A1(M) to junction 47, follow the A59 to Harrogate and Knaresborough. Turn right towards Knaresborough at first roundabout. Newton House is on the right hand side just before the top of the hill.

England's North Country — Hotels and Guest Accommodation

15 : Bridlington, East Yorkshire

Sunflower Lodge ♦♦♦♦

24 Flamborough Road,
Bridlington, East Yorkshire YO15 2HX
Contact: Rosie Banks
Tel: 01262 400447
Web: www.smoothhound.co.uk (enter Sunflower Lodge in search engine)
E-mail: rosie4info@sunlodge.wanadoo.co.uk

Ideally situated, our elegant Victorian Villa nestling by the sea has a relaxing ambience, with just the right balance of informality and loving care. Arrive to a welcome tray of tea. We'll accompany you to your stylish, luxurious bedroom, with sumptuous feather bedding, tactile fabrics and fresh flowers. Unwind with a film from our library on your TV/DVD or chill out with favourite music on CD/radio. Thoughtful extras include a personal refrigerator, hot chocolate and cookies, bath pearls, fluffy towels and bubbles in your deluxe en suite bath and shower room. In the morning indulge in a leisurely, late breakfast with a comprehensive and delicious choice of foods.

Bed & Breakfast per night:
Single room from £35.00–£50.00
Double room from £52.00–£70.00

Bedrooms: 2 double/2 family
Bathrooms: 4 en suite
Parking: Outside hotel
Cards accepted: Mastercard, Switch, Visa

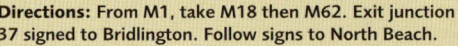

Directions: From M1, take M18 then M62. Exit junction 37 signed to Bridlington. Follow signs to North Beach.

16 : York, North Yorkshire

Barbican House ♦♦♦♦ Silver Award

20 Barbican Road, York, North Yorkshire, YO10 5AA
Tel: 01904 627617 • **Fax:** 01904 647140
Web: www.barbicanhouse.com
E-mail: info@barbicanhouse.com

Welcome to Barbican House our beautifully restored Victorian Villa overlooking the famous medieval walls and York Minster. All City centre attractions are within a ten-minute stroll, so guests invariably leave their cars in our floodlit car park. All bedrooms are en suite and non-smoking, and are decorated to complement the charm and character of our Victorian home. Four superior rooms (one ground floor) have king-sized or twin beds and TV/DVD players, in addition to a complimentary decanter of sherry and fresh flowers we include with our three double rooms.

Bed & Breakfast per night:
Single room from £60.00–£64.00;
Double room from £68.00–£76.00

Bedrooms: 6 double/1 twin
Bathrooms: 7 en suite
Parking: Available
Cards accepted: Mastercard, Visa, Switch/Delta

Directions: Keep on the A64 until you come to the SELBY and YORK A19 slip road (don't follow the A19 THIRSK sign). On the A19 proceed north through Fulford. Follow the fork right sign for Barbican Leisure Centre. This will take you along Cemetery Road, which changes to Barbican Road after the first set of traffic lights. Barbican House is about 100 yards on, on the right hand side just before the next set of traffic lights.

17 : York, North Yorkshire

Holmwood House ◆◆◆◆ Silver Award

114 Holgate Road,
York YO24 4BB
Contact: Rosie Blanksby
Tel: 01904 626183 • **Fax:** 01904 670899
Web: www.holmwoodhousehotel.co.uk
E-mail: holmwood.house@dial.pipex.com

This luxuriously converted Grade II listed Victorian town house backs onto a pretty, tree-lined residential square, with views of York Minster and in easy walking distance of the city centre. Your friendly and enthusiastic hosts will be happy to help you with guidance and information to explore York and its treasures. Holmwood House offers a restful ambience after your exertions, with a guest lounge with open fire and en suite rooms with bigger beds, four-poster beds, coronet/canopy beds en suite spa baths and power showers. Our breakfasts are a wonderful way to start the day, from full English to vegetarian or special diet.

Bed & Breakfast per night:
Single room from £50.00–£90.00
Double room from £65.00–£120.00

Dinner, Bed & Breakfast per person, per night:
£35.00–£60.00

Bedrooms: 14 double/4 twin/1 single/1 family/4 suites
Bathrooms: 14 en suite
Parking: Available
Cards accepted: American Express, Mastercard, Delta, Visa, Switch

Directions: On A59 Harrogate to York Road, 400 yards past the Fox pub in built-up York. See website for maps and instructions on how to find us.

18 : Bolton Percy, York, North Yorkshire

Glebe Farm ◆◆◆◆

Glebe Farm, Bolton Percy,
York YO23 7AL
Contact: Joan Penty
Tel: 01904 744228

An elegant, family run Victorian farmhouse set within a working farm and offering excellent accommodation within easy reach of York. The moors, dales and coast can all be reached within an hour. Guests enjoy a self-contained unit with a twin-bedded en suite room and conservatory. The unit is tastefully furnished and well-equipped. Glebe Farm breakfasts are a great start to the day. The historic village of Bolton Percy has an outstanding 15th century Gothic church, and there are good dining pubs here and in surrounding villages. The farm, itself, concentrates on beef cattle, sheep and chickens, offering tranquillity in a traditional English country setting.

Bed & Breakfast per night:
Single room from £25.00–£30.00
Double room from £50.00–£60.00

Bedrooms: 1 twin
Bathrooms: 1 en suite
Parking: Available
Cards accepted: None

Directions: 4 miles from Tadcaster or go through village from York, via Bishop Thorpe.

England's North Country — **Hotels and Guest Accommodation**

Voted Best Bed & Breakfast of the Year by Northwest Tourism

19 : Blackpool, Lancashire

Seabreeze Guest House

◆◆◆◆ Silver Accolade

1 Gynn Avenue, North Shore, Blackpool FY1 2LD
Contact: Mrs Ann Murgatroyd • **Tel:** 01253 351427 • **Fax:** 01253 310713
Web: vbreezy.co.uk • **E-mail:** info@vbreezy.co.uk

Seabreeze is Northwest Tourism's Best Bed & Breakfast of the Year 2004/2005 and Lancashire and Blackpool Tourism's best as well. It has four diamonds and a silver accolade from VisitBritain in addition to other well-merited awards. But that doesn't say it all. This is a warm, relaxed and comfortable guest house which makes a special effort to welcome everyone – including those with mobility problems, wheelchair users and guests who are vegetarian or have other dietary preferences. Seabreeze is in the quieter North Shore area of town, but only minutes away from the Promenade, the Tower and the trams. All bedrooms are en suite with shower and have television, DVD/CD player, bathrobe and slippers, hairdryer, a comprehensive hospitality tray with home-made biscuits, and complimentary chocolates.

Bed & Breakfast per night:
Single room from £25.00–£35.00;
Double room from £50.00–£70.00
Bedrooms: 3 double/1 twin, 1 single
Bathrooms: En suite
Parking: Guaranteed
Cards accepted: Mastercard, Visa, Switch/Delta

Directions: Drive to the end of the M55. This leads straight on to Yeadon Way towards South Shore. At the end of Yeadon Way is a T junction, turn left. At traffic lights turn right and after 2 miles turn right at Hilton. Take first right after Hilton, then first left. Seabreeze is first on the right.

Cheshire Salt

Two hundred million years ago, the Cheshire Plain, an area of flat, fertile farmland between Chester and Macclesfield, was at the bottom of a shallow, salty sea. As the water evaporated, the salt formed into vast deposits of solid sodium chloride – or rock salt. Water flowing through this layer of rock salt reaches the surface as brine – and it was this that attracted the Romans, who arrived to tap the rich resource of an estimated 400 billion tons of salt.

In the 17th century, coal began to be used to evaporate the brine in large iron pans, and the efficiency of salt production was hugely improved. To improve the transport of coal to the works and salt from them, the navigable stretch of the River Weaver was extended to Winsford. The Trent and Mersey Canal was completed in 1777, allowing salt works to open at Northwich, Middlewich, Wheelock and Lawton. By the late 19th century over one million tons of white salt were sailing down the Weaver Navigation each year.

Of the area's modern commercial plants, the Lion Salt Works at Marston, near Northwich, stuck with the traditional 'open pan' system of evaporation, largely unchanged since Roman times. Following its closure in 1986, it is now open to the public in the afternoons and, together with the Salt Museum in the old Northwich Workhouse, makes an intriguing exploration of Cheshire's industrial past. Perhaps most fascinating of all is the Anderton Boat Lift, a vast monument to the Victorian era's engineering achievements. For over a century this 'wonder of the waterways' just north of Northwich, built in 1875, hauled boats from the Weaver Navigation up 50ft (15m) and into the Trent and Mersey Canal above. Closed in 1982, the Boat Lift was once more brought back to life in March 2002, following a £7 million restoration.

www.lionsaltsworkstrust.co.uk
Tel: 01606 41823

www.saltmuseum.org.uk
Tel: 01606 41331

www.andertonboatlift.co.uk
Tel: 01606 786777

20 : Preston, Lancashire

The Priory Hotel ◆◆◆◆

The Square, Scorton,
Preston, Lancashire PR3 1AU
Contact: Julie Collinson
Tel: 01524 791255 • **Fax:** 01524 793563
Web: www.theprioryscorton.co.uk
E-mail: collinsonjulie@aol.com

Legend has it that Cromwell's men liked The Priory so much they didn't burn it down when they left! All to the good for today's guests who enjoy en suite bedrooms, all fully equipped and decorated and furnished to a very high standard. Farmers and growers around the scenic village of Scorton supply The Priory with local fresh produce for the highly-regarded restaurant, where Lancashire hotpot is a firm favourite. Stouts Bar which is part of the hotel, specialises in local ales. Breakfast at The Priory is a meal to savour before you set off to enjoy the highlights of the region.

Bed & Breakfast per night:
Single room from £30.00–£45.00
Double room from £55.00–£65.00

Dinner, Bed & Breakfast per person, per night:
£65.00–£75.00

Bedrooms: 7 double/1 twin/1 single/1 family
Bathrooms: 8 en suite
Parking: Available

Cards accepted: Mastercard, Visa, Switch, American Express

Directions: The nearest motorway junctions are M6, 32 and 33. Follow the A6 to Garstang and look out for the signs to Scorton and The Priory.

England's North Country — **Hotels and Guest Accommodation**

Genuine 14th century castle set close to Hadrian's Wall with excellent restaurant

21 : Hexham, Northumberland

Langley Castle Hotel

 Silver Award

Langley on Tyne, Hexham, Northumberland NE47 5LU
Tel: 01434 688888 • **Fax:** 01434 684019
Web: www.langleycastle.com • **E-mail:** manager@langleycastle.com

A genuine 14th century fortified castle set in its own woodland estate. All rooms have private facilities, four poster beds and window seats set into the 7ft thick walls. Castleview, within the grounds, offers a further ten rooms and suites – all with private facilities, draped canopies and wonderful views of the castle.

The magnificent drawing room with its blazing log fire complements the intimate Josephine Restaurant, where imaginative menus tempt the most discerning diner. Langley Castle is the perfect base to discover Hadrian's Wall, Holy Island, Northumberland and the Scottish borders.

Bed & Breakfast per night:
Single room from £99.50–£169.50
Double room from £115.00–£229.00

Dinner, Bed & Breakfast per person, per night: £62.50–£125
(minimum 2 nights)

Bedrooms: 15 double/3 suites, 3 family

Bathrooms: 18 en suite

Parking: Available

Cards accepted: American Express, Delta, Diners, Mastercard, Switch, Visa, Euros

Directions: Follow A69 from either A1M or M6 to Haydon Bridge and then 2 miles south on A686.

Lady Anne Clifford and Her Monuments

'They that shall be of thee shall build the old waste places' reads the quotation (from Isaiah 58:12) above the door of Outhgill church near Kirkby Stephen. The message, carved at the instigation of Lady Anne Clifford who restored the church in the 17th century, was one that she took to heart. When at the age of 60, she inherited lands in Cumberland, Westmorland and Yorkshire, she embarked upon a frenzy of building, repairs and restoration with a near-religious zeal. This legacy finally ended years of frustration when she was overlooked by her father's will in favour of her uncle and cousin.

Neglect and the Civil War had taken their toll on her many castles. Those of Appleby, Skipton, Brough, Brougham, Pendragon and Barden Tower had all fallen into decay, but during the next two decades, Lady Anne restored them to their original splendour.

She also repaired churches at Skipton, Brough, Brougham and Appleby and built almshouses and monuments, a display of wealth that perhaps jarred a little in puritan Commonwealth England. To celebrate the restoration of her inheritance, Lady Anne commissioned a remarkable painting – depicting herself and all the major characters from her eventful life. Known as the Great Picture, this now hangs in the keep of Appleby Castle. In the town, she also built the St Anne's almshouses and the white pillars at either end of the main street, while her tomb, and that of her beloved mother, Margaret, Countess of Cumberland, lies in St Lawrence's church.

Skipton Castle (pictured), lovingly restored by Lady Anne, remains one of the most complete and best-preserved medieval castles in England. But, despite all her efforts, Barden Tower and the castles of Pendragon, Brough and Brougham are all ruins once more. A 100-mile (160km) walk, Lady Anne's Way, takes in all the buildings and monuments associated with this redoubtable lady.

Skipton Castle
Tel: 01756 792442, www.skiptoncastle.co.uk

England's North Country — Hotels and Guest Accommodation

22 : Keswick, Cumbria

Lakeside ◆◆◆◆◆ Silver Award

Lakeside Country House, Bassenthwaite Lake, Dubwath, near Keswick, Cumbria CA13 9YD,
Tel: 017687 76358
Web: www.lakesidebassenthwaite.co.uk
E-mail: info@lakesidebassenthwaite.co.uk

Sharon and Arnold Helling invite you to savour the quality accommodation and outstanding food at their upmarket country guest house, just 50 metres from the shore of Bassenthwaite Lake. The house retains many of its original features, including the oak-panelled hallway and marvellous stained glass. Bedrooms are well-furnished and equipped and the guests' lounge and dining room both enjoy glorious views of the lake and mountains. Cuisine here is of excellent quality and value with, five star chef Arnold using the freshest local produce. All this, and you are in Wordsworth country, too. What more could you ask?

Directions: From Junction 40 of the M6 take the A66 to Keswick. Bypassing Keswick itself, continue on the A66 for 8 miles with Bassenthwaite Lake on your right. 400 metres after the dual carriageway prepare to turn right at the sign for the Castle Inn, Dubwath and Embleton on to the B5291 and turn right again.

Bed & Breakfast per night:
Single room from £35.00–£40.00
Double room from £56.00–£80.00

Dinner, Bed & Breakfast per person, per night:
£53.50–£58.70

Bedrooms: 4 double/1 single/2 twin/1 family
Bathrooms: 7 en suite
Parking: Available
Cards accepted: Mastercard, Visa, Switch

23 : Ambleside, Cumbria

Far Nook ◆◆◆◆◆ Silver Award

Rydal Road, Ambleside,
Cumbria LA22 9BA
Contact: Lesley Anne Higgins
Tel: 015394 31605
Web: www.farnook.co.uk
E-mail: lesley@farnook.co.uk

Ideally situated in the centre of the Lake District National Park, Far Nook is a gentle five-minute stroll from the village centre. A detached lakeland stone property in its own gardens and dating from the 1930s, the totally modernised house provides a high degree of comfort, with quality decor and furnishings in a non-smoking environment. You are welcomed with tea and home-made cake. The large breakfast selection, which is cooked to order, includes fish and a vegetarian option, as well as the full grilled breakfast preceded by a buffet of various fruits, juices, cereals and yoghurts.

Directions: North from Ambleside on the A591 passing the health centre and Greenbank Road junction to your right. Far Nook is the second house on the right with two large coach lamps at the driveway entrance.

Bed & Breakfast per night:
Double room from £59.00–£72.00

Bedrooms: 2 double/1 twin
Bathrooms: 3 en suite
Parking: Available
Cards accepted: None

Hotels and Guest Accommodation — **England's North Country**

24 : Ambleside, Cumbria

Rothay Manor ★★★ Silver Award

Rothay Bridge, Ambleside,
Cumbria LA22 0EH
Tel: 015394 33605 • **Fax:** 015394 33607
Web: www.rothaymanor.co.uk
E-mail: hotel@rothaymanor.co.uk

Rothay Manor is a Regency country house hotel set in its own grounds, just a short walk from Ambleside and quarter of a mile from Lake Windermere. The hotel is well-known for its relaxed, comfortable and friendly atmosphere, while the award-winning restaurant has an excellent reputation for food and wine. Personally managed by the Nixon family for over 35 years, the hotel has 16 individually designed rooms and three suites, two of which are in the grounds. Two rooms are adapted for disabled guests. Family rooms and suites are available. Throughout the year there are special interest breaks and parties.

Directions: From south leave M6 at J36, follow A591 to Ambleside, follow signs for Coniston, turn left at lights and then left again 1/4 mile later. From north take J40 of M6 on to A66 for Keswick and A591 to Ambleside.

Bed & Breakfast per night:
Single room from £70.00–£120.00
Double room from £120.00–£190.00

Dinner, Bed & Breakfast per person, per night:
£85.00–£120.00

Bedrooms: 6 double/5 twin/1 single/4 family/3 suites
Bathrooms: 19 en suite
Parking: Available
Cards accepted: American Express, Mastercard, Delta, Visa, Switch

Kielder Water and Kielder Forest

Tucked away in Northumberland, close to Hadrian's Wall and the Scottish borders, Kielder Water, the largest man-made lake in Europe, lies at the heart of Kielder Forest. With 150 million trees, this is the biggest single wooded area in Britain and is home to red squirrels, deer and rare birds. Formerly a sheep-farming and coal-mining area; the first sitka spruces were planted in the late 1940s when these industries became uneconomic.

Today, the Kielder area is Northumberland's most popular tourist attraction, drawing around 100,000 visitors a year. The transformation is thanks largely to the controversial construction of the reservoir. Seventy homes were drowned and eight archaeological sites lost. However, a reliable water supply for the homes and industry of the North East was created, and a host of recreational facilities soon followed Kielder Water's completion in 1982.

Watersports may be the most obvious attraction of the Kielder area, but there is a whole host of other activities available for all the family within the forest. You can fish for trout or for salmon just downstream from the dam; hire canoes, dinghies, sailboards and motor boats from Leaplish Waterside Park; receive expert tuition in yachting, windsurfing and rowing or even waterski in the separate 120-acre area. Alternatively, cruise the lake on board the Osprey – a trip used by many as a means of reaching the north shore to walk on glorious paths far from the nearest car. Experienced walkers can set aside a full day to complete the Kielder Water Challenge Walk. This strenuous route circumnavigates the reservoir's 27-mile (43.5km) shoreline in just 26 miles (42km) – possible if a few corners are cut – the equivalent of a full marathon. Shorter walks, mountain biking, bird-watching (and, if you're lucky, otter-watching), orienteering, horse-riding and a 12-mile (19km) forest drive are land-based options on offer throughout the year.

Kielder Water and Kielder Forest
Tel: 0870 2403549, www.kielder.org

Piel Island

Just offshore from Barrow-in-Furness, lies Piel Island, a small rocky outcrop with a ruined castle. Its position, separate from the mainland, made Piel a useful haven in troubled times. From the 14th century, it was the centre of a lively smuggling trade largely orchestrated by the monks of Furness Abbey. They built the impressive castle (pictured) as a fortified warehouse to keep their cargoes safe from raiders and the prying eyes of the customs men.

The most noteworthy moment in the island's colourful history was the arrival, in June 1487, of Lambert Simnel, pretender to the English throne. Simnel was an impostor, a baker's son claiming to be the Earl of Warwick (then imprisoned in the Tower of London) who, backed by Margaret of Burgundy, gathered a crew of German mercenaries and Irish recruits to take the throne by force. Leaving Piel with his 8,000 men, he set off across Furness towards London, but was defeated at the Battle of Stoke on 16 June.

In contrast, the 18th century brought more prosperous and settled times to the island, with Piel's busy harbour servicing Furness's thriving shipping and iron industries. Built at this time was The Ship Inn, a hostelry that still attracts sailors and daytrippers. The landlord is traditionally known as the King of Piel, a reference, it is supposed, to Lambert Simnel's claim to the throne. Those who sit in a particular old wooden chair become a Knight of Piel and must carry out certain duties – including buying everyone a drink.

The ferry from Roa runs from April to October, 11am–5pm, weather permitting, making the island an easy day trip. Facilities are minimal (the island has neither electricity nor telephone) but for those wishing to stay longer, camping is permitted anywhere on the island by arrangement, on arrival, with The Ship Inn.

25 : Ambleside, Cumbria

Smallwood House Hotel ◆◆◆◆

Compston, Ambleside, Cumbria LA22 9DJ
Contact: Christine Harrison
Tel: 01539 432330 • **Fax:** 01539 433764
Web: www.smallwoodhotel.co.uk
E-mail: enq@smallwoodhotel.co.uk

Ideally situated in the centre of Ambleside, Smallwood House Hotel has one rule – that you enjoy yourself. You will forget the pressures of everyday life amid the peace and serenity that surrounds us here. The relaxed atmosphere and friendly service reflects the tasteful and comfortable accommodation in this refurbished 19th century house, with its en suite rooms equipped with TV, tea and coffee making facilities and hairdryers. We are open all year round for you to enjoy the changing seasons of the English Lakes. Leave the car in our private car park and take a stroll to enjoy some of the most beautiful countryside in England.

Bed & Breakfast per night:
Single room from £25.00 – £45.00
Double room from £50.00 – £90.00

Dinner, Bed & Breakfast per person, per night: from £33.00 – £61.67

Bedrooms: 6 double/2 single/2 twin/2 family
Bathrooms: 12 en suite
Parking: Available
Cards accepted: Mastercard, Delta, Switch, Visa, Euros

Directions: From the south, take M6, exit junction 36 take A591 to Ambleside and you will pass the front door. From the north, enter Ambleside one-way system. Turn right at White Lion pub, and right again at the end.

Hotels and Guest Accommodation — **England's North Country**

26 : Seascale, Cumbria

Cumbrian Lodge Hotel

Gosforth Road, Seascale, Cumbria CA20 1JG
Contact: David J Morgan **Tel:** 01946 727309 • **Fax:** 01946 727158
Web: www.cumbrianlodge.com • **E-mail:** cumbrialodge@btconnect.com

Recently renovated, the hotel has a relaxing, contemporary, interior design. The rooms are decorated in subtle tones and the hotel bar is crafted from maple, with bespoke faux suede benches and original abstract artwork. For added luxury, the bedrooms have opulent Siberian goose down duvets, flat screen TVs, luxuriously thick ultra soft towels and fine complimentary toiletries. Our 30-seater restaurant offers many delights, finely produced from fresh produce. The wine list has been carefully selected to complement the menu and represents good value, whether you are enjoying the house Cabernet Sauvignon or a fine Bordeaux.

Bed & Breakfast per night:
Single room from £62.50–£80.00
Double room from £70.00–£90.00

Dinner, Bed & Breakfast per person, per night: £74.50–£92.50

Bedrooms: 4 double/1 twin/1 family
Bathrooms: 6 en suite
Parking: Available
Cards accepted: Mastercard, Visa, Switch, Delta

Directions: From the A595 at Gosforth, take the B5344 towards Seascale. The hotel is on the left after two miles.

27 : Bowness-on-Windermere, Cumbria

Lindeth Howe ★★★ Silver Award

Country House Hotel, Lindeth Drive, Longtail Hill, Bowness-on-Windermere, Cumbria LA23 3JF.
Tel: 015394 45759 • **Fax:** 015394 46368
Web: www.lindeth-howe.co.uk
E-mail: hotel@lindeth-howe.co.uk

Beatrix Potter loved Lindeth Howe – she even bought it for her mother. It's not difficult to see why. This is a gem of a property nestling in six acres of its own grounds and gardens in the heart of the Lake District. The 36 en suite rooms are well-equipped, some with stunning views. The restaurant is rosette standard and there are lounges with welcoming fires, a cosy bar and enticing facilities for relaxing, including a pool, sauna, solarium and fitness room. Lindeth Howe is an ideal base for exploring the beauty of one of England's most enchanting regions.

Bed & Breakfast per night:
Single room from £57.00–£99.00
Double room from £114.00–£199.00

Dinner, Bed & Breakfast per person, per night:
£84.00–£69.00

Bedrooms: 20 double/10 twin/3 single/3 family

Bathrooms: 36 en suite

Parking: Available

Cards accepted: Mastercard, Visa, Switch/Delta, American Express

Directions: We are situated on Longtail Hill (B5284) one mile south of Bowness on Windermere.

28 : Windermere, Cumbria

Gilpin Lodge Hotel Gold Award

Crook Road, Windermere,
Cumbria LA23 3NE
Contact: John Cunliffe
Tel: 015394 88818 • **Fax:** 015394 88058
Web: www.gilpinlodge.com
E-mail: hotel@gilpinlodge.com

This is an elegant and stylish hotel, set in 20 tranquil acres of woodland, moors and country gardens almost opposite Windermere golf course and at the heart of the area's wealth of sightseeing and history. There are sumptuous bedrooms, many with spa baths, four-poster beds and split-level sitting areas. The food is exquisite with fine wines in the three AA Rosettes restaurant. The hotel has been owned and run meticulously for 17 years by the Cunliffe family and they and their dedicated staff ensure a friendly and exemplary attention to all guests.

Dinner, Bed & Breakfast per person, per night:
£115.00–£150.00

Bedrooms: 8 double/4 twin/2 suites

Bathrooms: 14 en suite

Parking: Available

Cards accepted: American Express, Delta, Diners, Mastercard, Switch, Visa

Directions: Leave M6 at junction 36. Take A590/A591 to roundabout north of Kendal. Take first exit B5284 signposted Crook and Hawkhead via ferry. Hotel is 5 miles on right.

29 : Windermere, Cumbria

Linthwaite House ★★★ Gold Award

Crook Road, Windermere,
Cumbria LA23 3JA
Contact: Reservations
Tel: 015394 88600 • **Fax:** 015394 88601
Web: www.linthwaite.com
E-mail: admin@linthwaite.com

Linthwaite House Hotel surmounts a hilltop with spectacular views of Lake Windermere. It is set in its own 14 acres of peaceful gardens, complete with a private tarn for fishing. This is stylish country house living, but with the bonus of unstuffy staff whose aim is to make your stay as a enjoyable as possible. There are log fires, comfy sofas, fine wine and gourmet food and, if you drag yourself away, Linthwaite is ideally placed for cycling, walking or touring the Lake District – including Beatrix Potter's 'Hilltop' and Wordsworth's homes. "If I was any more relaxed," said one guest, "I'd fall over." Come and see.

Bed & Breakfast per night:
Single room from £120.00–£135.00
Double room from £135.00–£310.00

Dinner, Bed & Breakfast per person, per night:
£85.00–£175.00

Bedrooms: 20 double/4 twin/1 single/1 family/ 1 suite
Bathrooms: 27 en suite
Parking: Available
Cards accepted: American Express, Delta, Diners, Mastercard, Switch, Visa

The following are offsite:

Directions: From junction 36 of M6 follow dual carriageway past Kendal. At large roundabout take first exit left. We are 7 miles on left, 1 mile past Windermere Golf Club.

30 : Grange-over-Sands. Cumbria

Clare House   Silver Award

Clare House, Park Road,
Grange-over-Sands LA11 7HQ
Contact: DS Read
Tel: 015395 34253 • **Fax:** 015395 34310
Web: www.clarehousehotel.co.uk
E-mail: info@clarehousehotel.co.uk

Hospitality is the key to the success of Clare House, with the Read family ensuring that all their guests receive the very best in personal service – not least the meals, which have earned the hotel an AA rosette. The ambience is of elegance, comfort and spaciousness, reminiscent of times gone by. Yet Clare House is fully-equipped with modern facilities and amenities to ensure that your stay in this beautiful part of the northern coastal country is one you will remember – and want to return to!

Dinner, Bed & Breakfast per person, per night: £66.00

Bedrooms: 4 double/3 single/10 twin
Bathrooms: 16 en suite
Parking: Available
Cards accepted: Mastercard, Visa, Switch/Delta,

Directions: Junction 36 from the M6. Head towards Barrow. B5277 to Grange-over-Sands.

England's North Country — Self-Catering

Self-Catering — England's North Country

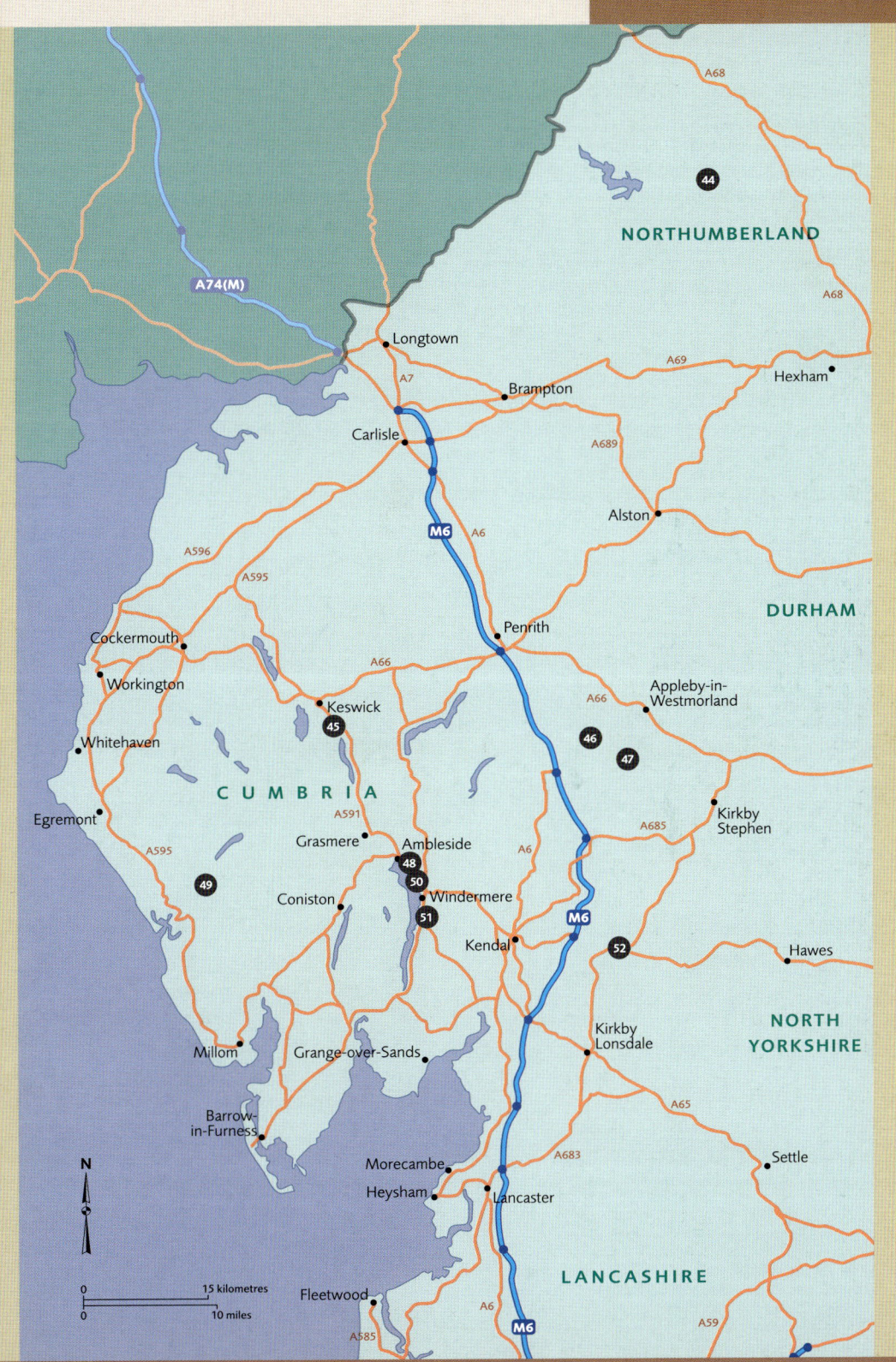

At-a-glance symbols are explained on the flap inside the back cover

England's North Country — Self-Catering

31 : Belford, Northumberland

Outchester & Ross Farm ★★★★

Belford, Northumberland NE70 7EN
Contact: Mrs Shirley McKie
Tel: 01668 213336 • **Fax** 01668 219385
Web: www.@rosscottages.co.uk
E-mail: enquiry@rosscottages.co.uk

Outchester and Ross Cottages lie in one of the most beautiful parts of Britain, between Bamburgh with its impressive castle and sweeping sands and Lindisfarne, the holy island of St Cuthbert and the Lindisfarne Gospels. This is Grace Darling country, too, where the national heroine rowed to rescue the stricken passengers of the Forfarshire. We have a variety of cottages, all of them tastefully furnished, cosy and fully-equipped. They each have their own garden, parking for two cars and a secure area for cycles. We supply delicious, local home-made freezer food – and Lindisfarne oysters from our own beds as a special treat! Sorry, no pets.

Low season per week: £219.00–£390.00
High season per week: £336.00–£649.00
Short breaks: from £153.00–£229.00
16 cottages
Cards accepted: None

Directions: A map and instructions are posted to customers upon booking.

32 : Corbridge, Northumberland

Oswald Cottage ★★★★

10 Front Street, Corbridge, Northumberland
Contact: Hannah Harriman, Swarden House, Kyloe House Farm, Eachwick, Northumberland NE18 0BB
Tel: 01661 852909 • **Fax:** 01661 854106

Oswald Cottage is an exceptional 18th century double fronted large stone cottage. The carved external Latin inscription above the front door, 'To the good all things are good', reflects the interior ambience, beams and open log fire. Situated in the heart of the historic village of Corbridge. A stone's throw from the river and superb local shops. Lovely patio garden, perfect winter or summer. Oswald Cottage is ideally located for Hadrian's Wall, Alnwick Castle and gardens and the wonderful Northumbrian coastline.

Low season per week: £300.00–£400.00
High season per week: £400.00–£550.00
Short breaks: from £150.00–£250.00
1 cottage
Cards accepted: None

Directions: Take A1 north. Pass MetroCentre. Follow A69 West towards Hexham. On A69 you approach a large roundabout. Take second left into Corbridge. Pass Angel pub on right. Take the right turning before the bridge on to Front Street.

Self-Catering — England's North Country

33 : Forest-in-Teesdale, County Durham

Laneside

★★★★

Laneside, Forest-in-Teesdale,
County Durham
Contact: Mrs N Liddle
Tel: : 01833 64029 • **Fax:** 01833 640963
Web: www.rabycastle.com
E-mail: teesdaleestate@rabycastle.com

Laneside is a superb self-catering holiday cottage on the Raby Estates in Upper Teesdale. The surrounding farm and moorland is in an Area of Outstanding Natural Beauty in the North Pennines, where subtle changes in the landscape can be seen throughout the seasons. In an idyllic position where tranquillity is assured, it is a haven for walkers, cyclists, birdwatchers and botanists and for those who choose simply to relax. There is action – from fishing and golf to off-road driving tuition, as well as walking the many bridleways, footpaths and riverside paths. Laneside is a fine base for touring the Dales and visiting historic Durham City itself.

Low season per week: £230.00–£280.00
High season per week: £360.00–£460.00
1 cottage: Sleeping 8 people
Cards accepted: None

Directions: Travelling from A1(M) take A688 to Barnard Castle. Take B6278 to Middleton-in-Teesdale, County Durham. Then B6277 to Forest-inTeesdale.

34 : Middleton-in-Teesdale, County Durham

Daisy Cottage

★★★★

5 Dent Bank, Middleton-in-Teesdale, County Durham DL12 0UY
Contact: Michele Leigh, Orchard Terrace, Chester Le Street, County Durham DH3 3JU
Tel: 07974 961620 • **Fax:** 07092 814098
E-mail: graemeleigh41@aol.com

Dating back to 1840, this delightful former lead miner's cottage has recently been refurbished to provide a cosy character cottage. With open fire and flagged floors this charming and homely cottage with views of the River Tees is perfect for that romantic break. Set in an area of outstanding natural beauty and perfectly located for the Pennine Way, it is a walker's paradise, but within easy reach of Middleton with its shops, tea rooms and pubs serving meals. Daisy Cottage, which sleeps four, is tastefully decorated and fully-equipped throughout, including patio furniture and two cycles ready for guests to explore this beautiful area.

Low season per week: £230.00–£280.00
High season per week: £345.00–£395.00
Short breaks: from £165.00–£220.00
1 cottage
Cards accepted: None

Directions: From the village of Middleton-in-Teesdale follow the signs for High Force. Daisy Cottage is situated approximately 1 mile from the village centre on the B6277.

England's North Country — Self-Catering

35 : Great Ayton, North Yorkshire

Ingleby Manor ★★★★

Ingleby Greenhow, Great Ayton,
North Yorkshire TS9 6RB
Contact: Christine Bianco
Tel: : 01642 722170 • **Fax:** 01642 722170
Web: www.inglebymanor.co.uk
E-mail: christine@inglebymanor.co.uk

The Essence of England:
* Ingleby Manor is a Grade II* historic Manor House, once the home of a courtier of Henry VIII
* Rose garden, walled garden with croquet lawn, 50 acres of woodland with trout stream and wild deer, in a hidden valley in the North York Moors National Park
* Four spacious, totally self-contained apartments and a four bedroom detached house all carefully furnished with antiques (and all modern comforts)
* In the heart of Herriot Country, easy access to the Moors, Lyke Wake Walk and Cleveland Way
* Tudor Kitchen for home-made refreshments.

Low season per week: £244.00–£445.00
High season per week: £380.00–£895.00
Short breaks: from £120.00–£597.00
4 apartments: Sleeping 2–6, 1 house: Sleeping 8 people
Cards accepted: Mastercard, Visa, Euros

Directions: South: From A19 take A172 Stokesley. B1257 Helmsley. At Gt Broughton turn left signposted Ingleby. In Ingleby Greenhow follow road till church. Sharp right. At fork keep right. North: A19, A174 Whitby. A172 Stokesley (Thirsk). Follow as above from B1257 Helmsley.

36 : Richmond, North Yorkshire

High Oxnop ★★★★

Gunnerside, Richmond,
North Yorkshire DL11 6JJ
Contact: Annie Porter
Tel: 01748 886253 • **Fax:** 01748 886253

High Oxnop is situated in the Yorkshire Dales National Park – Herriot Country – an environmentally sensitive area renowned for its stone walls, barns picturesque villages and flora. The holiday cottage has four bedrooms – two twin, one double and one family room, all beautifully furnished and having wonderful views over the surrounding countryside. One bedroom features an original garderobe (wardrobe). The house is centrally heated with a multi-fuel burner. Inside, the finely converted 18th century Dales farmhouse is light and tastefully furnished. Outside, the large garden has a large patio, with seats and a barbecue. Oxnop is ideally situated to explore this historic and beautiful region.

Low season per week: £500.00–£900.00
High season per week: £900.00–£1200
2 houses 1 cottage
Cards accepted: None

Directions: Just off the B6270 between the villages of Gunnerside and Muker.

37 : Kirkbymoorside, North Yorkshire

Monket Cottage ★★★★

Monket House, Farndale West, Kirkbymoorside,
North Yorkshire YO62 7LA
Contact: Vicki Mitchell
Tel: 01751 432402
Web: www.monkethouse.co.uk

This spacious stone-byre conversion sleeps four to six people in delightful and comfortable accommodation set in the famous Daffodil Dale within the North Yorkshire Moors National Park. The large living room with its wood-burning fire and exposed beams is enticing, as is the well-equipped kitchen/diner. There is one twin bedroom and one en suite double bedroom both of which are tastefully furnished and well-equipped. A large raised deck area to the rear of the building gives access to spectacular views across the valley – an ideal setting to plan your days exploring the moors or the coast.

Low season per week: £250.00–£350.00
High season per week: £380.00–£460.00
Short breaks: From £150.00–£200.00
1 cottage
Cards accepted: None

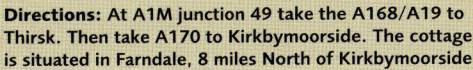

Directions: At A1M junction 49 take the A168/A19 to Thirsk. Then take A170 to Kirkbymoorside. The cottage is situated in Farndale, 8 miles North of Kirkbymoorside.

The Mouseman of Kilburn

The small town of Kilburn, nestling at the southern fringes of the North York Moors, is the home to a furniture-making company of international repute. It was established at the turn of the century by Robert Thompson, a local carpenter, who, inspired by the exquisite medieval wood-carvings in Ripon Cathedral, was determined to revive the craftman's skills and emulate the medieval masters.

Thompson worked in oak, naturally seasoned in the open air, and carved by hand, often making use of a medieval tool, the adze, to create a rough-hewn look on table-tops and other surfaces. His hallmarks of quality, sturdy durability and loving attention to detail were recognised by Father Paul Neville, headmaster of nearby Ampleforth College, who commissioned Thompson to carve a memorial cross for the cemetery there.

This was a turning point for Thompson, for the subsequent commission to refurbish the school and make additions to the church both provided him with a steady supply of work and established his reputation. By the time of his death in 1955, Robert Thompson's carpentry workshop was world-famous. Now run by his grandsons and great-grandsons, it still operates from the Thompson family home, while a visitor centre has been established in the old carpenter's shop.

Robert Thompson's reputation as the Kilburn Mouseman stems from his trademark, a little mouse, which was – and is – carved on every piece of furniture produced by the workshop. According to Thompson, the idea came about when he was working in a church roof with a craftsman who grumbled that they were as poor as church mice. The story goes that Thompson immediately carved a mouse on one of the beams and later adopted it as his trademark. The truth of this story is uncertain, for the original church mouse has never been located.

Mouseman Visitor Centre
Tel: 01347 869100
www.robertthompsons.co.uk

England's North Country — Self-Catering

38 : Scarborough, North Yorkshire

Wrea Head Country Cottages

Barmoor Lane, Scalby, Scarborough,
North Yorkshire YO13 0PG ★★★★
Contact: Steve Marshall
Tel: 01723 375844 • **Fax:** 01723 500274
Web: www.wreahead.co.uk
E-mail: steve@wreahead.co.uk

A rural heaven, charming, tranquil and full of character. Ideally situated just outside Scalby village, surrounded by countryside, yet only two miles from Scarborough and the Heritage Coastline. These nine award-winning cottages have been sympathetically and attractively converted from red brick farm buildings and retain many original features, including oak-beamed ceilings and pantile roofs. The cottages are surrounded by landscaped gardens and the children's play area features the popular Teddy Bears' cottage. The indoor pool, jacuzzi, and sauna are open all year, exclusively for our guests. This is an England for Excellence national award winner.

Low season per week: £255.00–£550.00
High season per week: £545.00–£1375.00
Short breaks: from £140.00–£385.00
9 cottages: Sleeping 2-9 people
Cards accepted: Mastercard, Delta, Switch, Visa

MW DW

Directions: A171 from Scarborough to Whitby passing through Scalby. Turn left at end of houses, down hill and past the duck pond. Continue uphill for quarter of a mile and turn left at our signage down the private drive.

39 : Skipton, North Yorkshire

Dales Holiday Cottages

★★★★/★★★★★

Carleton Business Park, Carleton New Road,
Skipton, North Yorkshire BD23 2AA
Tel: : 0870 9099500 • **Fax:** 01756 797012
Web: www.dales-holiday-cottages.com
E-mail: info@dales-holiday-cottages.com

Full details are in our brochure

Dales Holiday Cottages has a fine selection of quality holiday accommodation in some of the most beautiful countryside from the Derbyshire Dales to the Scottish borders. Each cottage has been personally inspected and with more than 20 years in the business, that means you can book with the confidence that you will find beautiful, well-equipped accommodation for your holiday. No matter what your choice, these four and five star properties are an ideal base to explore some of the UK's most outstanding areas, from the Derbyshire Dales and Yorkshire Moors to the rugged beauty of north Northumberland. Prices vary across the range of cottages and are available on request. As the exact specification for our cottages varies we do not apply the usual symbols here. But our brochure gives full details.

Directions: From Derbyshire to Scottish borders.

England's North Country — Self-Catering

42 : Blackpool, Lancashire

The Beach House
★★★★★

204 Queens Promenade,
Blackpool, Lancashire FY2 9JS
Tel: 01253 352699 • **Fax:** 01253 591164
Web: www.thebeachhouseblackpool.co.uk
E-mail: info@thebeachhouseblackpool.co.uk

The Beach House – the first Five Star accommodation of its kind in Blackpool – has six luxurious and fully-equipped apartments, one of which is suitable for guests with disabilities. The apartments occupy a first-class position on Queens Promenade, near the select area of Bispham, with beautiful sea views. The 21st century facilities include hypoallergenic bedding for our guests' total comfort. Nearby are excellent restaurants and shops, while the North Shore Golf Club is in easy reach. The Beach House apartments offer superb peaceful accommodation, at the same time giving access to all the fun and excitement of Blackpool.

Low season per week: £292.00–£520.00
High season per week: £365.00–£650.00
Short breaks: From £140.00–£310.00
6 apartments
Cards accepted: Mastercard, Delta, Switch, Visa, Euros

Directions: At junction 32 of the M6 turn onto the M55. Leave the M55 at junction 4 and follow the A583 towards Blackpool, following signs for the Promenade. Turn right on to the Promenade, carry on down past the large roundabout. The Beach House is on the right-hand side just before the main traffic lights at Bispham.

43 : Whitby, North Yorkshire

Shoreline Cottages
★★★★/★★★★★ Silver Award

PO Box 135, Leeds LS14 3XJ
Contact: Sue Brooks
Tel: 0113 244 8410 • **Fax:** 0113 244 9826
web: www.shoreline-cottages.com
E-mail: reservations@shoreline-cottages.com

Our 18 properties range from cosy fisherman's cottages to larger country houses in Whitby and the surrounding area. There are several on the harbour or in the nearby cobbled streets. Inside, the cottages look like they've been styled for the latest interiors magazine. Abbey View has, as the name suggests, views of Whitby Abbey, while the slightly grander Sorrel Cottage, a Grade II listed building in the village of Sneaton three miles from Whitby, boasts a walled garden. All our guests are welcomed on arrival and shown round and staff are available 24 hours a day if any assistance is needed.

Low season per week: £400.00–£800.00
High season per week: £540.00–£1230.00
Short breaks: From £330.00–£555.00
18 cottages
Cards accepted: Mastercard, Delta, Switch, Visa, Euros

Directions: From the south, take the A1(M) to the A64 York and Malton, then the A169 to Pickering and Whitby. From the north take the A1(M) or A19 to Middlesbrough, then the A171 to Whitby.

44 : Hexham, Northumberland

Riverdale Court ★★★★

Riverdale Hall Hotel, Bellingham, Hexham, Northumberland NE48 2JT
Contact: John Cocker
Tel: 01434 220254 • **Fax:** 01434 220457
Web: www.riverdalehall.demon.co.uk
E-mail: iben@riverdalehall.demon.co.uk

The four apartments at Riverdale Court nestle beside Riverdale Hall Hotel with its Les Routiers gold plate restaurant, the only one in the North. All apartments have southerly views over the North Tyne river and Dunterley Fell on the Pennine Way. One apartment sleeps two, one sleeps four, and two sleep six. Children are welcome. Guests can enjoy free use of the swimming pool, cricket field and selected salmon beats. Nearby are historic Hadrian's Wall, the beautiful Kielder Water and the fascinating market town of Hexham with its shops, pubs and restaurants. Guests are sure of a warm welcome at Riverdale which has been run by the Cocker family for 27 years.

Low season per week: £230.00–£290.00
High season per week: £360.00–£420.00
Short breaks: from £120.00–£210.00
4 apartments: 1 sleeps 2 people, 1 sleeps 4 people, 2 sleep 6 people
Cards accepted: American Express, Mastercard, Switch, Visa

Directions: From South: A1, A69, A68. From North A68. From East: A69–A68. From West: A69 leave at Greenhead for Hadrian's Wall Road.

45 : Keswick, Cumbria

Derwent Cottage Mews ★★★★★

Portinscale, Keswick, Cumbria CA12 5RF
Contact: Derwent Cottage, Portinscale, Keswick, Cumbria CA12 5RF
Tel: 017687 74838
Web: www.derwentcottage.co.uk

Derwent Cottage Mews is a spacious one-bedroomed first floor apartment, part of the old stable block that abuts Derwent Cottage. It is decorated and furnished to a high standard and is fully equipped for two people to enjoy. From its own entrance and staircase the Mews opens out into an open plan lounge/dining room with a part-glazed stable door giving access to the garden. The traditional pine kitchen complements the pine furniture in the living area. The en suite bedroom is tastefully furnished to match the beamed ceiling. The Mews is just a mile from Keswick and set back from the road in its own grounds.

Low season per week: £320.00–£320.00
High season per week: £420.00–£460.00
Short breaks: from £50.00–£70.00 per day
1 apartment
Cards accepted: Mastercard, Delta, Switch, Visa

Directions: From Junction 40 of the M6 head west towards Keswick and Cockermouth on A66 for 17 miles. Turn left into Portinscale, Derwent Cottage can be found on the right at a small crossroads past the village pub called The Farmers.

Self-Catering | England's North Country

40 : Ilkley, West Yorkshire

Westwood Lodge Ilkley Moor

Westwood Drive, Ilkley, ★★★★/★★★★★★
West Yorkshire LS29 9JF
Contact: Tim Edwards and Paula Hunt
Tel: 01943 433430 • **Fax:** 01943 433431
Web: www.westwoodlodge.co.uk
E-mail: welcome@westwoodlodge.co.uk

Set on the very edge of the world famous Ilkley Moor in Wharfedale, we are ideally situated for a town and country break at any time of the year. We have miles of adjacent open access land, to enjoy walking, riding and mountain biking. The Yorkshire Dales National Park, Brontë Country, York and Leeds are all in easy reach. Westwood Lodge is our carefully restored Victorian mill owner's country retreat. The Listed historic house has been fully refurbished as apartments and courtyard cottages. Each is individually designed, decorated and furnished to the highest standards and fully-equipped. There is also a sauna, spa, workout room, children's play area and large gardens.

Low season per week: £325.00–£575.00
High season per week: £425.00–£1095.00
Short breaks: From £239.00–£649.00
4 cottages plus 3 apartments in main house
Cards accepted: Mastercard, Visa, Delta, Maestro, Euros

Directions: About 30 minutes from M1, M62, M65, and A1. We are about three quarters of a mile from Ilkley town centre.

41 : York, North Yorkshire

Homefinders Holidays ★★★★

11 Walmgate, York YO1 9TX
Contact: Helen Jones
Tel: 01904 632660 • **Fax:** 01904 651388
Web: www.homefindersholidays.co.uk
E-mail: agents@homefindersholidays.co.uk

We have a range of holiday flats and houses available throughout the historic city of York. Most of them are rated four star and some five, and are registered with VisitBritain. All are within easy reach of the historic city centre with its ancient wall, host of fascinating churches, the Minster and other attractions like the world-famous Norvik Centre. All our accommodation is well decorated, equipped and furnished to provide a relaxing base from which to explore the city and its outlying areas.

Low season per week: £245.00–£335.00
High season per week: £355.00–£650.00
Short breaks: Various
3 cottages, 1 house, 8 flats
Cards accepted: Mastercard, Delta, Switch, Diners Visa, American Express

Directions: Properties can all be reached from A59, A19, M1 Junction 45, A64.

England's North Country | **Self-Catering**

46 : Penrith, Cumbria

Chestnuts

★★★★

Maulds Meaburn,
Penrith, Cumbria CA10 3HN
Contact: Annie Kindleysides
Tel: 01931 715168 • **Fax** 01931 715434
Web: www.cumbria-bed-and-breakfast.co.uk
E-mail: meaburnhillfarm@pentalk.org

Chestnuts was created within this traditional Cumbrian barn, dated 1753, with all living accommodation on the first floor to maximise the terrific views over the village green, Lyvennet Beck and the hillside beyond. There is a ramped access for guests who don't like stairs. The owner, Annie Kindleysides was AA Landlady of the Year in 2004, and welcomes guests to the farm where she was born, with a fund of knowledge on local walks, cycle rides and drives to the Lakes, Dales and Pennine foothills. The accommodation is spacious and tastefully furnished. And, while the kitchen is fully-equipped, award-winning cuisine is available from the farmhouse kitchen next door.

Directions: Exit M6 at junction 39. Follow signs for Shap. Turn right for Crosby Ravensworth. Left at t-junction in village. Chestnuts is second left after cattle grid.

Low season per week: £200.00–£300.00
High season per week: £350.00–£450.00
Short breaks: From £170.00–£350.00
1 cottage: Sleeps 2-4 people
Cards accepted: None

Salts Mill

Pre-eminent among Bradford's textile mills until its closure in the 1980s, Salts Mill was built in 1853 by Titus Salt (pictured) for his worsted manufacturing business. Now the vast Italianate-style mill is a Grade II listed building, still surrounded by the terraced sandstone houses and community buildings of the village Salt planned to cater for his workers' every need.

In 1987, Salts Mill was bought by locally-born Jonathan Silver and since then has been undergoing a sympathetic restoration. It is now home to several businesses (employing some 1,400 people in fields such as electronics and manufacturing) and a clutch of cultural enterprises. Of the latter, the most notable are the galleries devoted to the work of artist David Hockney, another of Bradford's sons. The 1853 Gallery was the first of the three Hockney galleries to open. On its walls hang 350 original works, a permanent exhibition of cartoons, prints, paintings and computer-generated images from Hockney's childhood years to recent times. A second gallery is to be found in an old wool-sorting room, next to Salts Diner on the second floor. This is an experimental space and exhibitions change regularly: the past few years have, for example, seen pictures of Hockney's dachshunds and his opera sets. The third and newest gallery, above the Diner, is a more intimate space, displaying images that have a particular meaning for David Hockney personally.

In addition to the galleries, browse a number of upmarket shops, whose goods range from contemporary furniture and high-quality household objects to designer clothes. The civilised, relaxed atmosphere that pervades the galleries carries through to Salts Diner, where you can pick up a newspaper to read while you enjoy good, reasonably priced food and drink.

Salts Mill: 01274 531185; www.saltsmill.org.uk

Self-Catering — England's North Country

47 : Appleby, Cumbria

Scalebeck Cottages ★★★★

Great Asby, Appleby,
Cumbria CA16 6TF
Contact: Keith Budding
Tel: 01768 351006 • **Fax:** : 01768 353532
Web: www.scalebeckholidaycottages.com
E-mail: mail@scalebeckholidaycottages.com

Set in the beautiful Eden Valley, amidst 12 peaceful acres of designated SSSI countryside with a stream and abundant wildlife, these three cottages have been created from the superb conversion of a 17th century barn. Spacious and comfortable, they enjoy ground-floor bedrooms and lovely views across open fields. Fully-equipped with central heating, colour TV and CD/radio – the cottages have open plan living room/dining and kitchen areas with exposed beams. There is a games room, outdoor play area and a wildflower meadow. There is easy access to the Lakes – Dales and National Parks, while nearby is Appleby, famous for its award-winning inns and restaurants.

Low season per week: £228.00–£290.00
High season per week: £320.00–£440.00
Short breaks: from £114.00–£308.00
3 cottages: Sleeps 2-5 people
Cards accepted: None

Directions: From Junction 38 of M6, follow B6260. We are situated approximately 5 miles south-east of Appleby between the villages of Drybeck and Great Asby.

48 : Ambleside, Cumbria

Cuckoo's Nest ★★★★★

Compston Road, Ambleside,
Cumbria LA22 9JD
Contact: Christine Harrison
Tel: 01539 432330 • **Fax** 01539 433764
Web: www.cottagesambleside.co.uk
E-mail: enq@cottagesambleside.co.uk

This luxuriously furnished hideaway offers everything you'll need for an extra special and enjoyable lazy break. Cuckoo's Nest is cosy and comfortable and ideally situated for shops, post office and public transport, though the hustle and bustle does not intrude on the privacy and romantic atmosphere inside. There is a luxury bathroom with jacuzzi, underfloor heating and twinkling lights. The lounge is extremely comfortable and well-appointed and the kitchen/diner is equipped with everything you need. As well as being ideal as a touring base, Cuckoo's Nest comes with free use of the Low Wood Leisure Club.

Low season per week: £275.00–£395.00
High season per week: £450.00–£510.00
Short breaks: from £275.00
1 cottage
Cards accepted: Delta, Mastercard, Switch, Visa, Euros

Leisure club membership

Directions: Take the M6 to junction 36 then follow A591 into Ambleside. Compston Road is part of the one way system. We are on the right hand side.

England's North Country — Self-Catering

49 : Holmrook, Cumbria

3 Randle How ★★★★

Eskdale Green, Holmrook,
Cumbria CA19 1UA
Contact: S Wedley, Long Yocking How,
Eskdale, Holmrook, Cumbria CA19 1UA
Tel: 01946 723126 • **Fax:** 01946 723490
E-mail: js.wedley@btopenworld.com

3 Randle How is a cosy 18th century cottage in Eskdale Green at the heart of the Esk Valley. The two-bedroomed (one double, one twin) cottage is furnished to a high standard and is well-equipped, with an open fire in the sitting room and oil-fired central heating. There is a large established garden, with furniture – ideal for children who are welcome at Randle How. The village shop and pub are within half a mile and the cottage is ideally situated as a base to explore the western Lake District, right to the coast at Ravenglass. The Ravenglass and Eskdale Railway runs through the valley.

Directions: From south: M6 Junction 36. A590 to Greenodd. A5092 to A595 north until Broughton. A595 to Holmrook then road to Eskdale.
From north: M6 Junction 42 south on A595 to Gosforth. Turn into Gosforth and then to Eskdale.

Low season per week: £225.00–£325.00
High season per week: £350.00–£425.00
Short breaks: from £140.00–£165.00
1 cottage: Sleeps four people
Cards accepted: None

MW DW

50 : Ambleside, Cumbria

Pudding Cottage ★★★★★

Merewood Lodge, Ecclerigg,
Near Ambleside, Cumbria
Contact: Mrs J Morrison
Tel: 0151 342 1234
Web: www.pudding-cottage.com
E-mail: jacky.morrison@btinternet.com

Winner of the Cumbria Self-Catering Cottage of the Year Award 2004/5

Pudding Cottage is a magnificent lakeland stone cottage sleeping six in the heart of the Lake District, between Windermere and Ambleside. The cottage is superbly equipped and caters especially for children, with a huge variety of games, toys and videos. All baby equipment is also provided. There is an abundance of wildlife in this beautiful area with baby deer, rabbits and even woodpeckers almost knocking on the door. Brockhole Visitor Centre, with tea rooms, children's play area and ferries to Bowness and Ambleside is just across the road. Membership of a private local health club, with pool, jacuzzi, sauna, squash courts, gym and beauty salon is included in the rental of Pudding Cottage.

Directions: Come off junction 36 on M6. Pudding Cottage is just off A591 between Windermere and Ambleside.

Low season per week: £410.00
High season per week: £870.00
Short breaks: from £230.00
1 cottage: Sleeps six people

Cards accepted: None

MW DW membership

The Angel of the North

Drive along the A1 at the southern edge of Gateshead, and a remarkable winged figure will come into view. Its wings are outstretched as if welcoming you to Tyneside. Erected in February 1998, The Angel of the North, the creation of renowned sculptor Antony Gormley, has become as powerful a symbol of the North East as the Tyne Bridge. Towering 65ft (20m) over the landscape, it has a wingspan of 175 ft (54m), almost as wide as that of a jumbo jet.

The story of the Angel began in 1989 when a former bath block at the Team Colliery was reclaimed and Gateshead Council decided that it would be an ideal spot for a 'landmark sculpture'. The council asked a shortlist of international artists to pitch for the commission, a competition won in January 1994 by Gormley. The scale of the design called for considerable funding, but the expense – about £800,000 – was met without any contributions from the local council tax. Both the size and the exposed position meant that the 200-tonne angel would have to be enormously strong to cope with winds of up to 100mph (160kph). The engineering firm of Ove Arup was called in to advise and, after close consultation with the sculptor, fabrication began at nearby Hartlepool. By September 1997, vast sections of the sculpture, made from a weather-resistant steel designed to mellow to a rich red-brown, were arriving at Team Valley under police escort.

Thanks to its lofty position – it reminds the sculptor of a megalithic mound – more than one person every second will see the angel. This, in theory, works out at nearly 32 million a year. Given that its lifespan is thought to be 100 years or more, great numbers of people are going to witness this impressive and arresting structure.

The Angel of the North
www.gateshead.gov.uk/angel/

England's North Country — Self-Catering

51 : Bowness-on-Windermere, Cumbria

Lakelovers ★★★/★★★★★

Holiday Homes, Belmont House, Lake Road,
Bowness-on-Windermere, Cumbria LA23 3BJ
Tel: 015394 88855 • **Fax:** 0125394 88857
Web: : www.lakelovers.co.uk
E-mail: bookings@lakelovers.co.uk

Spoilt for choice – that's the obvious thing to say about the huge selection of sumptuous quality self-catering accommodation facing guests of Lakelovers Holiday Homes. There are more than 200 places to stay – from traditional Lakeland farmhouses set in the heart of the Langdale Valley and sleeping up to 14, to luxury modern apartments, sleeping two and complete with private tennis court and leisure complex. All holidays now include free Leisure Club membership with every booking. All our properties, throughout central and southern Lakeland are three to five star rated and inspected and graded by VisitBritain. Prices vary according to the kind of property and are available on request. The full range of accommodation appears in our brochure.

Low season per week: £195.00–£1000.00
High season per week: £300.00–£1800.00
Short breaks: from £150.00–£800.00
50 houses, 150 cottages, 20 bungalows. 3 lodges, 20 apartments
Cards accepted: Mastercard, Delta. Switch, Visa

52 : Sedbergh, Cumbria

The Mount ★★★★

Lock Bank Farm, Sedbergh,
Cumbria LA10 5HE
Contact: Mr R and Mrs S Sedgwick
Tel: 015396 20252
web: www.holidaysedbergh.co.uk
E-mail: lockbank@uk4free.net

Set in the midst of the Yorkshire Dales National Park with magnificent views of surrounding hills and dales, The Mount offers a comfortable, spacious and relaxing atmosphere for all guests. Enjoy the many original features which have been retained throughout the house. Relax by an open fire, or sit outside on the veranda and watch the world go by. The Mount has two reception rooms, a separate dining room, a fully-equipped kitchen, a utility room with all mod cons and a shower room and toilet on the ground floor. With four bedrooms, The Mount can easily accommodate eight people in tasteful comfort. Guests can enjoy the secluded area at the rear of the house, while planning their tours of the Dales and Lake District.

Low season per week: £280.00–£530.00
High season per week: £550.00–£1000.00
Short breaks: Please enquire
1 house
Cards accepted: None

Directions: Full directions sent out upon booking.

England's Heartland

Above: Tulip field, Spalding, Lincolnshire

Middle: Queen Elizabeth I hunting lodge, Essex

Left: Foxton Locks, Leicestershire

England's Heartland

Where the heart is

Want to get away from the crowds? Visit England's Heartland – stretching from the Fens of East Anglia to the rugged Welsh border country. With so many counties, it's not surprising there's such a rich mix of industry, history, culture and raw natural beauty.
Experience the buzz of Birmingham, one of the England's most happening cities.
Explore the magnificent castles and great houses that reflect a past prosperity.
Discover the home of Shakespeare, nestled on the banks of the River Avon, or the intriguing legend of Robin Hood. **Relax** on one of the east coast's deserted beaches.

Active pursuits, lazy days and great nights out – it's all on a plate in England's Heartland. Put on your walking boots ready to challenge the Pennines, peer through binoculars at the varied bird life of the Ouse Washes or paint the town red in Nottingham, the capital of the Midlands' club scene

Right: Flatford Mill in Suffolk gloriously immortalised by John Constable, England's finest landscape painter

Below: All the World's a Stage at the Royal Shakespeare Theatre in the Bard's home town of Stratford

Artistic roots

With landscape like this, it's easy to understand why England's Heartland inspired so much creative energy. Visit a solitary cottage near Flatford Mill in the Stour valley, and it immediately hits you. The Hay Wain – a masterpiece by local boy John Constable. On the streets of Stratford-upon-Avon, you just can't avoid references to the town's greatest son. William Shakespeare – England's greatest playwright. Book a seat at the Swan Theatre – home of the Royal Shakespeare Company. His words and ideas are just as relevant today. Find out what shaped DH Lawrence's early life at his birthplace in Eastwood, Nottingham. See at first hand the decadence of Lord Byron in the gothic Newstead Abbey.

Food-lovers feast

Has all this culture made you a bit peckish? There's a veritable cornucopia of traditional hearty foods to stop your tummy rumbling. Succulent Melton Mowbray pork pies – so naughty, but so nice. Red Leicester and Stilton – stinky or aromatic – it's up to you! Drop in to Bakewell for a slice of upside down

England's Heartland

pudding – often imitated, never matched. Is asparagus your favourite veg? Then don't miss the annual asparagus auction at the Fleece Inn in Bretforton in Worcestershire. Head for Britain's food capital, pretty Ludlow on the Welsh borders. Discover what lures so many top London chefs to the Ludlow Marches Food and Drink Festival. Lincolnshire plumbread, Malvern spring water, world-famous Worcestershire sauce – the list of epicurean delights continues. Wash it all down with some real ale at Derby's annual CAMRA festival. That'll do nicely.

City lights

Remember the Bull Ring in Birmingham? This is urban regeneration at its most stunning. A space the size of 26 football pitches – all dedicated to shopping and entertainment. Fifteen thousand spun aluminium discs later and you have Selfridges' shop front. See it to believe it. The upmarket Mailbox is yet another magnet for shoppers. Hit the town at the canalside Brindley Place. Birmingham is a must-visit weekend destination.

Coventry – like a phoenix, it has risen from the destruction of wartime bombing. Basil Spence's remarkable turn of the '60s modern cathedral vies for the city's skyline with timber-framed buildings and soaring church spires. Back to that phoenix. The Phoenix Initiative is breathing new life into the cathedral area. The impressive Whittle Arch makes its own mark on today's skyline. Follow the walkway that links Coventry Cathedral and Coventry Transport Museum. Visit some more exciting cities. Soak up the colourful atmosphere of multi-cultural Leicester or spend time in medieval Nottingham, now the pulsating clubbing capital of the Midlands.

England's Heartland

Life on the water

Need to relax? Choose from mile upon mile of sandy and shingle beaches running from Essex to Lincolnshire. Undeniably beautiful is the National Nature Reserve at Holkham, Norfolk. Here, see what is created when creeks, sand dunes, pinewood, pastures and marshes merge. For bustling seaside resorts, try Felixstowe, Southend-on-Sea and Great Yarmouth. For something a bit quieter, seek out the havens of Frinton, Covehithe and Anderby Creek and the coast's numerous quaint fishing villages. Find out what life was like aboard ship with the interactive 'below decks' experience at the Norfolk Nelson Museum in Great Yarmouth.

Moving inland, explore the rivers and dykes in the Fens – spread over the shires of Cambridge and Lincoln. Minsmere, Titchwell and Berney Marshes all make ideal spots for birdwatching. At the Fens Discovery Centre at Spalding, learn how man tamed the inhospitable marshland. For lazy days spent with friends and family, what could be more calming than the reed-fringed waterways of the Norfolk Broads? Reward yourself, having successfully negotiated the locks, with a quick pint. Sailing is child's play off the blustery Lincolnshire coast. Artificial, but no less exhilarating, there's whitewater rafting at Nene Whitewater Centre, or kayaking at the National Water Sports Centre in Nottingham.

Out and about

Want to experience the active life? Choose walking, cycling, climbing and potholing. Cross in and out of Wales on Offa's Dyke Path, tracing the route of the 8th century Mercian king's defensive ditch. Or follow the Heart of England Way. Challenge yourself to one of Britain's greatest long-distance walks. Beginning in Edale in the heart of the Peak District, the Pennine Way continues for 270 miles to the Scottish borders. Other long-distance paths explore East Anglia's numerous sandy beaches. The ancient Roman route of Peddars Way and the Norfolk Coast Path or the Suffolk Coast Path between Lowestoft and Felixstowe – but you'll need to take a ferry or two. Meander down a country lane on the northern reaches of the Cotswolds. Admire the vistas that stretch to the Malverns and Stratford-upon-Avon, or be inspired by the striking beauty of the Clee Hills.

Two wheels more your thing? You're in luck – the East of England is flat, ideal cycling terrain whatever your age. Discover a route for yourself, or follow one of the many cycle routes such as the Fens Cycle Way. Or zoom through the stunning Derwent Valley, a World Heritage Site. Take the Spring Blossom Trail in the Vale of Evesham. Explore the back roads from the comfort of your car.

Above: Centuries old entertainment, maybe, but Punch and Judy can still draw a seaside holiday audience

Above right: The hi-tech, high-speed thrills of the 21st century are more to the taste of visitors to Alton Towers

England's Heartland

Great days out

Stately homes. Picture postcard villages. Historic architecture. Living museums. White-knuckle rides. All the ingredients for a great day out. Spend time in the historic cities of Shrewsbury and Worcester – noted for uneven Tudor half-timbered architecture. A magnificent row of 15th century shops has withstood the onslaught of floodwaters in the medieval town of Tewkesbury. Reach for your camera as you pass through Much Wenlock, one of the beautiful black and white villages of Shropshire and Herefordshire. Castles and grand homes dot the landscape – Kenilworth Castle and Warwick Castle are favourites. For Elizabethan architecture at its most impressive, Hardwick Hall and Chatsworth House are hard to beat. Step back into the area's proud industrial past at the Ironbridge Gorge Museum. Have a chat with the working craftsmen at the Black Country Living Museum. Trace the history of fighter planes at the Imperial War Museum, Duxford in Cambridgeshire – the best collection of aviation in Europe. Feeling brave? Then hold on tight for high velocity rollercoaster thrills at Alton Towers in Staffordshire.

Contact

East Midlands Tourism
www.enjoyeastmidlands.com

East of England Tourist Board
tel: 0870 225 4800
www.visiteastofengland.com

Heart of England Tourism
tel: 01905 761100
www.visitheartofengland.com

England's Heartland   Hotels and Guest Accommodation

England's Heartland
Hotels and Guest Accommodation

53 : Hope Valley, Derbyshire

The Plough Inn ♦♦♦♦ Silver Award

Leadmill Bridge, Hathersage,
Hope Valley, Derbyshire S32 1BA
Contact: RW Emery
Tel: 01433 650319/650180 • **Fax:** 01433 651049
E-mail: sales@theploughinn-hathersage.com

Situated in nine acres of grounds, the 16th century Plough Inn has been restored to give visitors every modern facility and comfort. It is an idyllic location close to the meandering River Derwent and surrounded by magnificent countryside. Cosy and tastefully decorated the inn provides an ideal environment in which to unwind, or as a base to visit the many heritage sites of the Peak District National Park. Recommended by The Good Pub Guide as Derbyshire Dining Pub 2005, the Plough is within easy reach of major cities like Derby and Sheffield – though the quality of the food, which is a star attraction, is well worth coming home to.

Bed & Breakfast per night:
Single room from £55.00–£79.50
Double room from £69.50–£120.00

Bedrooms: 3 double/2 suites
Bathrooms: 5 en suite
Parking: Available
Cards accepted: Mastercard, Switch, Visa

Directions: From the south leave M1 junction 29. Take the A619 to Chatsworth, Baslow. Take the A623 to Calver, then B6001 through Grindleford, Hathersage. From the north, take M1 junction 33 through Sheffield via A625 to Hathersage.

54 : Buxton, Derbyshire

Cressbrook Hall ♦♦♦♦

Cressbrook, Buxton,
Derbyshire SK17 8SY
Contact: Mrs B Hull-Bailey
Tel: 01298 871289 • **Fax:** 01298 871845
Web: www.cressbrookhall.co.uk
E-mail: stay@cressbrookhall.co.uk

A period piece with pedigree! Cressbrook Hall is a fine William IV residence built in 1835 in a spectacular hillside location. The formal gardens by Edward Kemp are being restored. Self-catering cottages together with elegant serviced accommodation in the Hall are available for weekends or longer visits and ideal for reunions, wedding receptions, management training/team building and special family celebrations. Hall 'home catering' gives you more free time to enjoy this idyllic place. Accommodation which is decidedly, delightfully different!

Bed & Breakfast per night:
Single room from £55.00–£65.00
Double room from £75.00–£105.00

Bedrooms: 1 double/1 twin/1 family
Bathrooms: 3 en suite
Parking: Available
Cards accepted: Delta/Mastercard/Switch/Visa

Directions: From M1 take A619 to Baslow. A623 through Stoney Middleton for 3 miles. Turn left to Litton then left for Cressbrook. After 1¹/₂ miles fork right on a left hand bend down steep hill for 200 yards. Turn right down private drive.

55 : Buxton, Derbyshire

Buxton's Victorian Guest House

3a Broad Walk, Buxton,   ◆◆◆◆◆ Silver Award
Derbyshire SK17 6JE
Contact: Barbara and Alan Baxter
Tel: 01298 78759 • **Fax:** 01298 74732
Web: www.buxtonvictorian.co.uk
E-mail: buxtonvictorian@btconnect.com

Somewhere Special! Our beautifully refurbished Victorian home is on the Broad Walk promenade, overlooking the magnificent Pavilion Gardens and the Opera House Theatre. After leaving your car in our car park next to the house, you can relax in the tranquillity of the Guest Drawing room with a complimentary tray of tea or coffee, before settling into the luxury of your double/twin, individually styled bedroom. All rooms have en suite facilities, television, hospitality trays and hairdryers. Special rooms include the Four Poster Premier Room and the Family Suite, with en suite shower room and two bedrooms, sleeping up to three adults and two children. Breakfast in the Oriental Dining room includes cold buffet and full English breakfast.

Bed & Breakfast per night:
Single room from £43.00–£85.00
Double room from £61.00–£85.00

Bedrooms: 6 double/1 twin/1 family
Bathrooms: 8 en suite
Cards accepted: American Express, Delta, Mastercard, Switch, Visa

Directions: Please visit our website for access to map and further directions.

56 : Leek, Stafforshire

Peak Weavers   ◆◆◆◆

21 King Street, Leek,
Staffordshire ST13 5NW
Tel: 01538 383729 • **Fax:** 01538 387475
Web: www.peakweavershotel.com
E-mail: peak.weavers@virgin.net

Built in 1828 as a private home for a local mill owner the hotel is named from its proximity to the Peak District and from the textile industry that shaped the market town of Leek. A convent from the 1860s to 1978, it has been tastefully restored by the present owners and boasts an AA Rosette awarded restaurant. Through membership of the Peak District Cuisine initiative we try to ensure our produce is from North Staffordshire and the Peak District. Rooms are fully equipped to ensure your comfort and Peak Weavers is ideally-placed for you explore the antiques and amenities of Leek and the wider Peak District.

Bed & Breakfast per night:
single room from £30.00–£45.00
double room from £60.00–£70.00

Dinner, Bed & Breakfast per person, per night:
£40.00–£65.00

Bedrooms: 3 double/1 twin/3 single/1 family
Bathrooms: 5 en suite
Parking: Available
Cards accepted: Delta, Diners, Mastercard, Switch, Visa

Directions: From M6 south-bound exit junction 14 to Stone and Leek on the A520. From M6 north-bound exit junction 17 to Congleton, then enter town on A523.

England's Heartland | Hotels and Guest Accommodation

An atmosphere and hospitality unmatched in the picturesque Derbyshire Dales

57 : Ashbourne, Derbyshire

Omnia Somnia

♦♦♦♦♦ Gold Award

The Coach House, The Firs, Ashbourne, Derbyshire DE6 1HF
Contact: Alan Coker Mayes • **Tel:** 01335 300145 • **Fax:** 01335 300958
Web: www.omniasomnia.co.uk • **E-mail:** alan@omniasomnia.co.uk

Omnia Somnia – Everything is a Dream – and you may think you are dreaming when you come to stay at Ashbourne's award-winning guest accommodation. The house itself snuggles into a hillside and the three double en suite rooms have unique character, from a picture gallery and two-person bath in Oriens, to sumptuous panelling and a hand-crafted four-poster bed in Meridies, and the hideaway bedroom of Occidens. Fine detail is everywhere, with the highest quality furnishings and effects to delight the senses. There are pleasant surprises throughout Omnia Somnia – not least the fact that the bedrooms are on the ground floor, while the lounge and dining room are upstairs, as is access to the charming and unusual garden. Hospitality and food are second to none, making intimate celebrations the hallmark of Omnia Somnia.

Bed & Breakfast per night:
Single room £80.00–£85.00;
Double room £90.00–£95.00
Evening meal: £27.50 per person
Bedrooms: 2 double/1 suite
Bathrooms: 3 en suite
Parking: Available
Cards accepted: Mastercard, Visa, Switch/Delta

Directions: From A52 Derby Ashbourne Road, descend hill into Ashbourne. At the traffic lights turn very sharply left into Old Hill. Take first left into The Firs and follow the signs to Omnia Somnia.

Hotels and Guest Accommodation — England's Heartland

58 : Uttoxeter, Staffordshire

Manor House Farm

Quixhill Lane, Prestwood,   ★★★ Silver Award
Denstone, near Uttoxeter, Staffordshire ST14 5DD
Contact: Chris Basll
Tel: 01889 590415 • **Fax:** 01335 342198
Web: www.4posteraccom.com
E-mail: cm_ball@yahoo.co.uk

An enchanting, rambling Jacobean farmhouse – the kind of time capsule you can't reinvent – with oak timbers, tapestry drapes and an amazing collection of oak furniture. The bedrooms, all with four-poster beds and en suite bathrooms have beautiful views over the large and extensive terraced gardens or the dramatic Weaver Hills. Oak fires in the sitting and dining rooms add to the fabulous old world charm. But the new world is not far off – Alton Towers is just two miles away, while the charm of Chatsworth, Haddon and Sudbury are in easy reach. Our breakfasts are a real feast of quality home cooking to set you up for the day.

Bed & Breakfast per night:
Single room from £32.00–£40.00
Double room from £50.00–£60.00

Bedrooms: 2 double/1 family
Bathrooms: 3 en suite
Parking: Available
Cards accepted: Mastercard, Visa

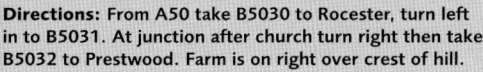

Directions: From A50 take B5030 to Rocester, turn left in to B5031. At junction after church turn right then take B5032 to Prestwood. Farm is on right over crest of hill.

Brewers of Burton-upon-Trent

Enter the Staffordshire town of Burton-upon-Trent and you'll soon notice the distinctive aroma of hops and malt. Acknowledged as the centre of British brewing, the town is home to three major breweries: Carlsberg Tetley, Marston's and Bass (now owned by Coors).

Burton initially attracted brewers for its abundance of mineral-rich water that was found to be particularly suitable for brewing beer. Indeed, the old wells – Nile and Cairo, The Hay, Andressey – are still tapped. Today, however, popular demand for lager means that the water must be completely purified, and, if needed for beer making, the necessary minerals such as calcium and magnesium salt, are now added afresh.

The industry dates back to medieval times when the monks of Burton Abbey first started brewing ales here. Even after the dissolution of the monastery in the 16th century, brewing continued and was a well-established industry when William Bass set up his brewery in 1777 and almost a century later the famous red triangle was registered as a trademark in 1875 – the first company mark to be so.

Discover more about Burton's brewing history at the former Bass Museum, now the Coors Visitor Centre & The Museum of Brewing. Visit the Dray Shed and Stables which house the magnificent Coors Shire Horses or learn more about the art of brewing process in the 19th century, which despite mechanisation has changed little over the years. The Coors Visitor Centre is also home to one of the oldest working micro-breweries in Britain. Marston's also offers tours of its traditional Victorian brewery for groups of up to 50.

www.coorsvisitorcenter.co.uk
0845 6000 598

Marston's Pedigree Brewery
Tel: 01283 507440, www.fullpint.co.uk

England's Heartland — Hotels and Guest Accommodation

59 : Much Wenlock, Shropshire

Old Quarry Cottage

Brockton, Much Wenlock,   ◆◆◆◆ **Silver Award**
Shropshire TF13 6JR
Contact: Jayne Lee
Tel: 01746 785596 • **Fax:** 01746 785596
Web: www.oldquarrycottage.co.uk
E-mail: triciawebb.oldquarrycottage@virgin.net

A warm welcome is assured at this lovely stone cottage and adjacent Coach House apartment suite. The odd beam, old pine doors, pretty window boxes, antiques, pictures, lovely linen, fluffy towels and comfy beds await you. So does the best local produce lovingly cooked on the AGA for our award-winning breakfasts, which are served in the delightful traditional conservatory overlooking the garden. This is 'the land of lost content' as the poet AE Housman put it. So much on the doorstep, like Much Wenlock, Ludlow, Bridgnorth, Ironbridge and Wenlock Edge itself. So beautiful – and a land you can return to, with Old Quarry Cottage as your wonderful base.

Bed & Breakfast per night:
Single room from £35.00 (single occupancy)
Double room from £48.00–£55.00
Bedrooms: 1 double/1 twin/1 suite/
Bathrooms: 3 en suite
Parking: Available
Cards accepted: None

Directions: From Much Wenlock take B4378 to Ludlow. Turn right at crossroads in Brockton towards Easthope. About 200 yards on right turn into small parish car park across a stone bridge. Driveway is up on the left.

60 : Ludlow, Shropshire

Ravenscourt Manor

Woofferton, Ludlow,   ◆◆◆◆◆ **Gold Award**
Shropshire SY8 4AL
Contact: Mrs E Purnell
Tel: 01584 711905 • **Fax:** 01584 711905
Web: www.smoothhound.co.uk
E-mail: ravenscourtmanor@amserve.com

Ravenscourt Manor is a delightful beamed Tudor manor house, set in two acres of garden surrounded by farmland. It is a listed building of architectural interest and just three miles from historic Ludlow, with its castle, three Michelin starred restaurants and well-preserved buildings. Accommodation at Ravenscourt is tastefully furnished and fully equipped. Home-cooked breakfasts are a special treat, with home made bread and jams. Ravenscourt also has two fully-fitted self-catering units – Ravenscourt 1 and Ravenscourt 2. Ravenscourt 1 has a double bed/sitting room and gallery bedroom, while Four-star rated Ravenscourt 2 is a superb two bedroom cottage, with its own enclosed garden.

Rates: Bed and Breakfast (Discount 3 nights or more)
Single: £45.00–£50.00
Double: £60.00–£70.00
Self-catering cottages from £140 per week
2 cottages for self-catering and 3 rooms for bed and breakfast
Cards accepted: None

Directions: Travel south from Ludlow on A49. Take Hereford direction over railway bridge, and Ravenscourt Manor is round bend on left.

Entries are cross-referenced by number to the maps on pages 62 and 63

61 : Malvern Wells, Worcestershire

Cottage in the Wood Hotel

Holywell Road, ★★★ Silver Award
Malvern Wells, Worcestershire WR14 4LG
Contact: John and Sue Pattin
Tel: 01684 575859 • **Fax:** 01684 560662
Web: www.cottageinthewood.co.uk
E-mail: reception@cottageinthewood.co.uk

Need to unwind? Thirty mile views across the Severn Valley from our award-winning two AA Rosette restaurant await you at this beautifully situated country house hotel. Privately owned by John and Sue Pattin supported by their family and extended family team of staff, Cottage in the Wood warmly welcomes you into a relaxing atmosphere. The cosy bedrooms are divided between the main house, Beech Cottage and The Pinnacles. They are all well-equipped, with thoughtful extras like binoculars in rooms with a view. The public areas are elegantly appointed and the lounge/bar area has a cosy log fire to greet you.

Directions: Malvern Wells is on the Ledbury side of Great Malvern on the A449 Worcester – Ledbury Road. We are easily reached from the M5. For full details visit our website.

Bed & Breakfast per night:
Single room from £79.00–£105.00
Double room from £99.00–£175.00

Bedrooms: 31
Bathrooms: All en suite
Parking: Available
Cards accepted: American Express, Mastercard, Switch, Visa

restaurant and some rooms

nearby

nearby

62 : Malvern, Worcestershire

Holdfast Cottage ★★ Silver Award

Marlbank Road, Little Malvern, Malvern,
Worcestershire WR13 6NA
Contact: Martyn Bishop
Tel: 01684 310288 • **Fax:** 01684 311117
Web: www.holdfast-cottage.co.uk
E-mail: enquiries@holdfast-cottage.co.uk

This pretty wisteria-covered country house hotel is set in two acres of gardens and private woodland, tucked into the foot of the Malvern Hills. It is highly recommended for its freshly-prepared menu which changes daily and uses the best local and seasonal produce. There is a delightful dining room and bar and a cosy lounge with log fire. Enchanting en suite bedrooms are individually furnished. Guests are assured of a personal welcome as they enter the handsome oak-beamed hallway and attentive service throughout their stay.

Directions: Leave the M50 junction, and take the A38 to Upton-on-Severn. Take the A4104 from Upton-on-Severn to Little Malvern.

Bed & Breakfast per night:
Single room from £50.00–£68.00
Double room from £84.00–£98.00

Dinner, Bed & Breakfast per person, per night:
£109.00–£127.00 (minimum 2 nights)

Bedrooms: 5 double/2 twin/1 single
Bathrooms: 8 en suite
Parking: Available
Cards accepted: Delta, Diners, Mastercard, Switch, Visa

England's Heartland | **Hotels and Guest Accommodation**

Warm and welcoming riverside home in beautiful Lincolnshire open countryside

63 : Woodhall Spa, Lincolnshire

Kirkstead Old Mill Cottage

Tattershall Road, Woodhall Spa, Lincolnshire LN10 6UQ
Contact: Mrs Barbara Hodgkinson • **Tel:** 01526 353637/07970 040401 • **Fax:** 01526 352 574
Web: www.woodhallspa.com • **E-mail:** barbara@woodhallspa.com

Our secluded cottage has no near neighbours, though it is just a seven minute drive from Woodhall Spa. We offer peace and tranquillity and splendid views across the flat countryside. Special attention has been paid to amenities for the elderly and people with mobility difficulties, with the ground floor bedroom attached to the sunroom, and having an en suite shower room with level access, non slip flooring and fully adjustable hand basin. Our sunny home has three double en suite bedrooms, all well furnished and equipped with TV, small fridge and beverage trolley. The main entrance opens onto the sun lounge which can comfortably seat six. This leads to the breakfast room. There is also a guests' lounge, with an open fire, TV and piano. In fine weather, our Gold Food and Health Award full English breakfasts, or a lighter option using much local produce, can be served on the decking overlooking the three-quarter acre gardens, which include a shady York stone courtyard. Walkers and cyclists are welcome.

Bed & Breakfast per night:
Single room £36.00–£40.00;
Double room £54.00–£60.00

Bedrooms: 1 double/2 twin
Bathrooms: 1 en suite, 2 en suite shower rooms
Parking: 5 spaces + 2 car ports
Cards accepted: None

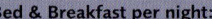

Directions: OS Map reference – 187602. Full directions with a map are sent to guests when they make a reservation.

Painswick Rococo Garden

A visit to Painswick Rococo Garden is a fascinating step back in time. Set in a hidden Cotswold valley with marvellous views of the surrounding countryside, the garden was created in the 1740s by Benjamin Hyett, following the death of his father George who had built the garden in its elevated position in the hope of easing a respiratory complaint.

Inspired by the latest fashion and in a departure from the formal gardens of the late 17th century, Benjamin chose rococo – a decorative style of the early 18th century, distinctive for its elaborate ornamentation and asymmetrical motifs. The designer of the garden is unknown although a 1748 painting by local artist Thomas Robins illustrates it in remarkable clarity – resulting in some claiming it to be the proposed design instead of a simple reproduction of the finished garden.

The six-acre garden was maintained by five gardeners until 1955. Ten years later, the then owner, unable to sustain the upkeep, planted a wood on the site. The garden lay neglected for 19 years until bulldozers arrived to clear the tangle of brambles and old man's beard. Since then, many elements of the splendid garden have been restored, using Robins's painting to create an exact match of what was there 250 years ago.

Features to look out for in this magical garden include the Red House, the Gothic Alcove, the Pigeon House, the Plunge Pool and the Eagle House – an ornate and partially subterranean building. But for a real treat, try to visit in February, when a thick carpet of snowdrops swathes the slopes.

Painswick Rococo Garden
Tel: 01452 813 204, www.rococogarden.co.uk

England's Heartland | Hotels and Guest Accommodation

64 : Old Hunstanton, Norfolk

The Neptune Inn ◆◆◆◆

85 Old Hunstanton Road,
Old Hunstanton, Norfolk PE36 6HZ
Contact: Paul Berriff
Tel: 01485 532122
Web: www.theneptune.co.uk
E-mail: pberriff@aol.com

The Neptune Inn and Restaurant's new owners, Paul and Hilary Berriff, have given this charming 19th century coastal coaching inn a new look. The Neptune, built in the 1830s, now resembles its counterparts on the New England coast of Maine – warm and friendly, with that extra touch of quality. The decor is mellow browns and white cladding, with Lloyd Loom sofas and chairs adding to the relaxed ambience in the bar. The bedrooms, with their stunning white furniture, create a stylish tranquillity. The food is lovingly created from fresh produce – worth a visit in itself.

Bed & Breakfast per night:
Single room from £50.00–£80.00;
Double room from £80.00–£110.00

Bedrooms: 6 double/1 twin
Bathrooms: 7 en suite
Cards accepted: Delta, Mastercard, Visa

Directions: From King's Lynn take the A149 to Hunstanton.

65 : Thursford Green, North Norfolk

Holly Lodge ◆◆◆◆◆ Gold Award

The Street, Thursford Green,
North Norfolk NR21 0AS
Contact: Robert Greenfield
Tel: 01328 878 465
Web: www.hollylodgeguesthouse.co.uk
E-mail: info@hollylodgeguesthouse.co.uk

Holly Lodge is the East of England Tourist Board's B&B/Guesthouse of the year for 2004 and AA Guest Accommodation of the Year 2004/2005. It's also Michelin recommended. Top quality wins top awards and Holly Lodge and its en suite guest cottages exude fully-equipped charm. Each cottage is luxuriously appointed. They lie just behind the orchard and give access to the landscaped gardens and sundeck overlooking the water gardens and open countryside. If you can bear to leave after a superb breakfast, Holly Lodge is in easy reach of Norfolk's great houses and the stunning north Norfolk coast.

Bed & Breakfast per night:
Single room from £70.00–£90.00
Double room from £80.00–£100.00

Bedrooms: 2 double/1 twin
Bathrooms: 3 en suite
Parking: Available
Cards accepted: None

Directions: Holly Lodge is located off the A148 Fakenham to Holt/ Cromer Road. Turn off at the Crawfish pub located about ten minutes/six miles from Fakenham. Please see our website for maps and further directions.

Hotels and Guest Accommodation — England's Heartland

66 : Mundesley, North Norfolk

The Durdans ◆◆◆◆

36 Trunch Road, Mundesley,
North Norfolk NR11 8JX
Contact: Caroline Griffin
Tel: 01263 722225 • **Fax:** 01263 722883
Web: www.thedurdans.co.uk
E-mail: info@thedurdans.co.uk

A warm welcome awaits you at The Durdans, an imposing Edwardian house sitting in two acres of grounds reached by a tree-lined drive and located on the edge of a the picturesque seaside village of Mundesley. Andrew and Caroline Griffin have refurbished the property, with all bedrooms en suite and newly furnished. The public rooms have been tastefully redecorated. The large entrance hall is light and airy with open, galleried landings above. The dining room and sitting room have views across the sunken lawns to the west. Breakfasts are a speciality, hearty in the Norfolk style with free-range eggs and local produce, or with croissants, fruit and yoghurt as an alternative.

Bed & Breakfast per night:
single room from £35.00–£40.00
double room from £50.00–£90.00

Bedrooms: 3 double/2 twin/1 single/1 family
Bathrooms: 6 en suite/one private
Cards accepted: Delta, Mastercard, Switch, Visa

Directions: From Norwich take the B1150 to North Walsham then the B1145 to Mundesley.

67 : Dersingham, Norfolk

Holkham Cottage ◆◆◆◆

34 Hunstanton Road,
Dersingham, Norfolk PE31 6HQ
Contact: Jane Curtis
Tel: 01485 544562
Web: www.holkhamcottage.co.uk
E-mail: accommodation@holkhamcottage.co.uk

Holkham Cottage is a large, detached Edwardian family house in its own large grounds. There are double, twin and single rooms, all en suite, and the house has been tastefully renovated and furnished to match the period. Dersingham is within reach of Norfolk's unspoilt coastline and nature reserves, Peddars Way and Royal Sandringham, Holkham Cottage, with its warm welcome, good food and large attractive garden will form an attractive backdrop to your holiday in this beautiful area of Eastern England, where fine scenery abounds and activities like riding, cycling and golf are readily available.

Bed & Breakfast per night:
Single room from £25.00–£28.00;
Double room from £50.00–£56.00
Dinner, Bed & Breakfast per person, per night:
£35.00–£38.00

Bedrooms: 1 double/1 twin/2 single
Bathrooms: 4 en suite
Parking: Available
Cards accepted: None

Directions: From King's Lynn take A149, at first roundabout take Dersingham turning. Through village past playing field on left. Cottage is on right in Hunstanton Road.

England's Heartland — Hotels and Guest Accommodation

68 : Corby, Northamptonshire

Spanhoe Lodge ♦♦♦♦ Gold Award

Harringworth Road, Laxton, Corby,
Northamptonshire NN17 3AT
Contact: Jennie Bell
Tel: 01780 450328 • **Fax:** 01780 450328
Web: www.spanhoelodge.co.uk
E-mail: jennie.spanhoe@virgin.net

Jennie and Steve assure you of a very warm welcome at their home in picturesque, rural East England. You can relax in the conservatory, overlooking beautiful open countryside, sit in comfort in our two acre gardens, or take a leisurely stroll along the many scenic walks from Spanhoe Lodge. We are the only Four Diamond Gold Award establishment in the area and we pride ourselves on personal service and five star quality. All our bedrooms are en suite and luxuriously appointed, with TV and video, a wide range of toiletries and full hospitality tray. Breakfasts at Spanhoe Lodge are a gourmet affair – a superb start to your day.

Bed & Breakfast per night:
Single room from £45.00–£65.00
Double room from £65.00–£75.00

Bedrooms: 3 double/2 twin
Bathrooms: 5 en suite
Parking: Available
Cards accepted: Mastercard/Switch/Visa

Directions: Between Stamford and Corby, Laxton Village will be well signposted from the A43. Travel through Laxton and after about half a mile you will find Spanhoe Lodge on the right hand side.

Cruck-framed buildings

Timber-framed or half-timbered buildings predominate in the Midlands. Half timbered takes its name from early medieval times when the timbers were formed by cutting logs in half.

These buildings are classified as either box-frame construction or cruck construction. The most common was box-frame, where jointed horizontal and vertical timbers formed a wall and either the panels were infilled or the whole wall was covered with a type of cladding. In cruck construction, the structure was supported by pairs of inclined, slightly curved timbers that normally met at the ridge of the roof and often of the walls too.

Wherever possible, crucks were cut from the trunk of one tree split along its length to get a symmetrical arch. Alternatively, they were taken from trees with a natural curve in the trunk and blades matched as closely as possible.

There are various forms of cruck construction. Full crucks extend from ground level to the apex, while base or truncated begin on the ground but stop below the apex and are joined by a tie-beam or collar that supports the roof. Raised crucks start a few feet off the ground in a solid wall, and in jointed cruck construction the curving blade is jointed to a vertical post that begins on the ground.

To discover the greatest concentration of cruck-framing, visit Hereford and Worcester, while Weobley is unmatched for its black-and-white buildings. Explore its streets and admire the skills of the 15th, 16th and 17th century craftsmen. Other towns in the county worth visiting for their half-timbering are Eardisley, Eardisland, Pembridge and Dilwyn, while the Avoncroft Museum of Historic Buildings in Bromsgrove has some reconstructions of excellent examples of cruck-framed buildings.

Avoncroft Museum of Historic Buildings, Bromsgrove
Tel: 01527 831363, www.avoncraft.org.uk

Hotels and Guest Accommodation — England's Heartland

69 : Huntingdon, Cambridgeshire

Old Bridge Hotel ★★★ Gold Award

1 High Street, Huntingdon,
Cambridgeshire PE29 3TQ
Contact: John Hoskins
Tel: 01480 424300 • **Fax:** 01480 411017
Web: www.huntsbridge.com
E-mail: oldbridge@huntsbridge.co.uk

This handsome 18th century building overlooks the River Ouse and yet is only 500 yards from the town centre. It has the atmosphere of a beautiful and luxurious hotel, yet is a busy meeting place for the local community. All rooms are individually decorated, with satellite television, CD stereos, power showers, and air conditioning. There is an eclectic modern menu (AA 2 Rosettes), and the hotel won the AA Wine Award in 1999 for the UK's best wine list. Its real ales are highly acclaimed by CAMRA. The Old Bridge is privately owned and run by Martin and Jayne Lee and John Hoskins.

Bed & Breakfast per night:
Single room from £95.00–£120.00
Double room from £125.00–£180.00

Bedrooms: 18 double/6 single
Bathrooms: 24 en suite
Parking: Available
Cards accepted: American Express, Delta, Diners, Mastercard, Switch, Visa

Directions: Huntingdon is clearly signposted from both the northbound A1 and the A14 from Cambridge.

70 : Bunwell, Cambridge

The Meadow House ♦♦♦♦

2a High Street, Bunwell,
Cambridge CB5 0HB
Contact: Hilary Marsh
Tel: 01638 741926 • **Fax:** 01638 741861
Web: www.themeadowhouse.co.uk
E-mail: hilary@themeadowhouse.co.uk

The Meadow House, Bunwell, is an outstanding modern house set in two acres of wooded grounds with lovely open outlooks all round. Set back from the B1102, we have a large car park and we are within walking distance of two pubs, both of which serve evening meals. We are known for our comfortable king-size beds and our generous breakfasts, which are a superb foundation for a day exploring the attractions and amenities of Cambridge itself or the mid-Anglia region at large.

Bed & Breakfast per night:
Single room from £25.00-£30.00
Double room from £50.00-£60.00

Bedrooms: 1 double/1 twin/3 family/1 suite
Bathrooms: 4 en suite
Parking: Available
Cards accepted: None

Directions: Take B1102 from A14 at Stow-Cum-Quy to Burwell via the Swaffhams. Look on the right as you come into the village for The Meadow House.

England's Heartland — **Hotels and Guest Accommodation**

The Swan is renowned for its historic significance and splendour

71 : Lavenham, Suffolk

The Swan Hotel

★★★★ Two AA rosettes

High Street, Lavenham, Suffolk CO10 9QA
Contact: John Hewitt, General Manager **Tel:** 01787 247477 • **Fax:** 01787 248286
Web: www.theswanatlavenham.co.uk • **E-mail:** info@theswanatlavenham.co.uk

The Swan Hotel is an enchanting 14th century hotel in the heart of historic Lavenham. Modern luxury sits alongside oak beams, panelled walls, flagged floors and huge inglenook fireplaces. The discovery of medieval wall paintings has influenced the style of the interior, which features mementoes of England's early history, including a copy of the oldest surviving map of England, dating from around 1250. Each of the 51 en suite bedrooms is decorated in calming colour schemes, with natural fabrics evoking the town's wool trade history, and equipped with CD player and mini-bar. The lounge areas are relaxing and soothing, while the Old Bar is full of the memorabilia of WWII airmen. The Swan prides itself on its imaginative cuisine created from fresh Suffolk and Norfolk produce, matched by a 150 bin wine cellar.

Bed & Breakfast per night:
Single room from £80
Double room from £145.00–£220.00

Dinner, Bed & Breakfast per person, per night: £80.00–£260.00 (minimum two nights)

Bedrooms: 37 double/4 twin/7 single/3 suites

Bathrooms: 51 en suite

Parking: Available

Cards accepted: American Express, Delta, Mastercard, Switch, Visa, Euros

Directions: Lavenham is situated close to the market town of Sudbury, half an hour from Newmarket.

Hotels and Guest Accommodation — England's Heartland

72 : Woodbridge, Suffolk

Seckford Hall ★★★ Silver Award

Woodbridge, Suffolk IP13 6NU
Contact: Sonia Colchester
Tel: 01394 385678 • **Fax:** 01934 380610
Web: www.seckford.co.uk
E-mail: reception@seckford.co.uk

A romantic Elizabethan mansion set in 32 acres of landscaped gardens and woodlands. Personally supervised by the owners, Seckford Hall is a haven of seclusion and tranquillity. Oak panelling, beamed ceilings, antique furniture, four-poster beds, suites, a leisure club with indoor pool, beauty salon, gym and spa bath and adjacent 18-hole golf course all create a feeling of relaxation for our guests. There are two restaurants featuring fresh lobster and game from local farms, together with an extensive wine cellar. Picturesque Woodbridge, with its tide mill, antique shops and yacht harbour is a stroll away, with Constable Country also nearby.

Bed & Breakfast per night:
Single room from £85.00–£130.00
Double room from £130.00–£200.00

Dinner, Bed & Breakfast per person, per night:
£170.00–£240.00 (minimum 2 nights)

Bedrooms: 14 double/10 twin/3 single/4 family

Bathrooms: 32 en suite

Parking: Available

Cards accepted: American Express, Delta, Diners, Mastercard, Switch, Visa

Directions: Join the A12 Woodbridge bypass and look for the distinctive blue and white hotel sign.

73 : Dunmow, Essex

Canfield Moat ◆◆◆◆◆ Gold Award

Canfield Moat, Little Canfield, Dunmow,
Essex CM6 1TD.
Contact: Vivian Falk
Tel: 01371 872565 • **Fax:** 01371 876264
Web: www.canfieldmoat.co.uk
E-mail: falk@canfieldmoat.co.uk

Set in eight acres of grounds, this peaceful Georgian rectory enjoys the calm of the Essex countryside and yet is only 10 minutes from the M11 and Stansted Airport. It is within easy reach of London, Cambridge and the marvellous Constable Country of Suffolk. Canfield Moat's large and elegant bedrooms are supplied with almost every conceivable luxury. Breakfasts are a special pleasure, with our own eggs and produce from our vegetable garden. Guests are welcome to use the tennis court and the outdoor heated swimming pool. Pubs and restaurants nearby offer fine food and relaxation after a day exploring this lovely corner of England.

Bed & Breakfast per night:
Single room from £45.00–£50.00;
Double room from £70.00–£75.00

Bedrooms: 1 double/1 twin

Bathrooms: 2 en suite

Parking: Available

Cards accepted: None

Directions: From junction 8 of the M11 take B1256 to Takeley. After 5 miles, turn right into High Cross Lane West (signposted Langthorns). Entrance to our drive is on the left, after 300 yards.

England's Heartland | **Hotels and Guest Accommodation**

Perfect stunning countryside location with superb cuisine and service

74 : Hertford, Hertfordshire

Ponsbourne Park Hotel

★★★★ Silver Award

Newgate Street Village, near Hertford, Hertfordshire SG13 8QZ
Contact: Lynn Marsh-Jones • **Tel:** 01707 876191 • **Fax:** 01707 875190
Web: www.ponsbournepark.co.uk • **E-mail:** reservations@ponsbournepark.co.uk

Located within easy reach of London and the M25, Ponsbourne Park Hotel is a peaceful oasis set in 200 acres of Hertfordshire countryside. The hotel is an ideal venue for weekend breaks; boasting a renowned restaurant, nine-hole golf course, outdoor heated swimming pool and five all-weather tennis courts. The hotel is within easy reach of the major Hertfordshire towns and places of natural beauty and historical interest. Horse riding and sailing facilities are nearby. With quality decor and furnishings throughout and high levels of service, Ponsbourne House Hotel offers a truly unique and relaxing environment.

Bed & Breakfast per night:
Double room from £88.00–£128.00

Dinner: Extra at £28.00 approximately per person

Bedrooms: 11 de luxe, 24 superior, 16 standard

Bathrooms: 51 en suite

Parking: Available

Cards accepted: American Express, Mastercard, Diners, Visa, Euros

Directions: Exit M25 Junction 25 on to A10 northbound. Take B198 towards Cheshunt, take first left at next roundabout. At Goff's Oak mini-roundabout turn right into Newgatestreet Road, left to Darnicle Hill (signposted Newgate Street). Hotel is down a drive on the right two miles along the road.

Blue John

The Derbyshire town of Castleton lies in the White Peak, a rolling limestone plateau carved into steep gorges and valleys by the last ice age. As glaciers melted, huge volumes of water were forced downwards through joints in the limestone to form turbulent underground rivers, gouging out from the rock a network of caverns, four of which are in the immediate vicinity of Castleton.

Two of these, Treak Cliff Cavern and Blue John Cavern, contain the world's only deposit of a beautifully veined fluorspar mineral known as Blue John. The origin of its name is uncertain, but it may derive from the French bleu-jaune (blue-yellow), two of the mineral's predominant colours.

The mineral's use dates back to Roman times – vases found at Pompeii were believed to have been made with Blue John. However, it was at its height of popularity in the 18th century when it was commercially mined. The architect Robert Adam used the mineral to decorate fireplaces in the music room at Kedleston Hall in 1762, and also created the famous Chatworth Tazza, the largest bowl ever constructed from a single piece of Blue John.

At their peak, the mines yielded more than 20 tons annually, although extracting the prized mineral was far from easy. Blue John occurs in two distinct formations – either as cylindrical nodules of up to 30cm in diameter, completely buried by clay, or as flat veins sandwiched between hard layers of limestone. Today, only a quarter of a ton is produced each year, which is mainly to be found on jewellery, cutlery handles and small bowls, sold in Castleton's souvenir shops.

For a fascinating insight into a unique Peak District industry, take a guided tour of Blue John Cavern and Treak Cliff Cavern, and prepare to be amazed by the sheer scale of the caves and the impressive rock formations that are found there.

Tel: 01433 620 571, www.bluejohnstone.com

England's Heartland — Self-Catering

England's Heartland — Self-Catering

75 : Ashbourne, Derbyshire

Throwley Moor Farmhouse

Throwley Cottage and Lathem Hall Farmhouse, Ashbourne, Derbyshire ★★★★

Contact: Muriel Richardson
Tel: 01538 308202 • **Fax:** 01538 308243
Web: www.throwleyhallfarm.co.uk
E-mail: throwley@btinternet.com

Our self-catering accommodation is set in the heart of rural England in the beautiful undulating limestone landscape of the Peak District National Park. Lambs and calves gamboling in the fields in spring and the singing of skylarks in the summer add to the charm of this unspoilt countryside. All properties are traditional farmhouses, which have been converted into comfortable, well-equipped and spacious holiday houses. All have cosy lounges with open fires. Kitchens are very well-appointed, while outside there are large private gardens with furniture and barbecues. The properties are within a few miles of the beautiful Manifold Valley and Dovedale.

Low season per week: £320.00–£600.00
High season per week: £450.00–£1000.00
Short breaks: from £200.00–£400.00
2 farmhouses plus 1 cottage
Cards accepted: None

Directions: Take A52 from Derby or Stoke. Take A523 from Leek. Follow signs for Calton then Throwley and Ilam.

76 : Parwich, Ashbourne, Derbyshire

Tom's Barn ★★★★★

Orchard Farm, Parwich, Ashbourne, Derbyshire DE6 1QB
Contact: Marion Fuller-Sessions
Tel: 01335 390519
Web: tomsbarn.co.uk
E-mail: tom@orchardfarm.demon.co.uk

Tom's Barn blends every modern comfort with the charm of a traditional 18th century farm building. From the woodburner, to the two-seater whirlpool bath, tasteful decor and furnishings, and fully-equipped kitchen, this is a quality base from which to explore the many delights of the Peak District. There is a welcoming loaf of fresh bread, butter, milk and free-range eggs to greet guests on their arrival. The area is rich in outdoor activities, walks on the High Peak or Tissington Trails, cycling, water sports, fishing, golf. We can even arrange stabling and grazing for your horse. Historic attractions abound, as do good restaurants and pubs.

Low season per week: £250.00–£400.00
High season per week: £375.00–£450.00
Short breaks: from £125.00–£315.00
1 cottage: Sleeping 2 people, or one
Cards accepted: None

Directions: Parwich is seven miles north of Ashbourne (A515, B5056). We always send a map and detailed directions to guests.

Self-Catering | **England's Heartland**

The Shropshire Hills

Nestled between the Welsh border and the River Severn, the Shropshire Hills are often referred to as the 'Shropshire Alps' or 'Little Switzerland'. Here, ancient earth movements have tilted great layers of different rock strata, each now forming its own ridge of hills stretching in a roughly south-westerly to north-easterly direction.

The most easterly of the ridges, the Clee Hills, are formed of rich red sandstone, topped with basalt, and consist of two separate ridges, the highest, Brown Clee Hill at 1,792ft (546m) and Titterstone Clee Hill. To their west, the River Corve flows through a wooded valley, before the land rises again to Wenlock Edge, a steep-sided ridge of limestone flanked with trees. Continuing west, the hump of Caer Caradoc dominates the Caradoc Hills around the town of Church Stretton – use this as a base for getting details of walks or fixing up guided hikes – before meeting the forbidding plateau of the Long Mynd. A favourite launch point for gliders, this 10-mile (16km) stretch of moorland offers some of the best walking in Shropshire. An ancient path, the Port Way, runs the entire length of the crest, and offers the best views of the Wrekin (1,335ft, 407m), which rises dramatically from the Shropshire Plain, its volcanic rocks the oldest in England. Along the eastern flank of the Long Mynd, find a number of deep ravines, of which the popular Carding Mill Valley is considered the most beautiful. Move westward and encounter the Stiperstones, a rocky outcrop where, according to folklore, devils gather on Midwinter Night – and at 1,731ft (528m), a wonderful vantage point.

Take a break from bracing walks, with visits to Shrewsbury, Bridgnorth, Bewdley and Ludlow – all within easy reach. Other attractions include a string of impressive castles and fortified manors (Ludlow and Clun), fine ecclesiastical ruins (Buildwas and Wenlock) and an insight into the area's industrial heritage (Ironbridge).

Church Stretton Tourist Information Centre
Tel: 01694 723133 (April to October only)
Ludlow Castle
Tel: 01584 87355, www.ludlowcastle.com
Ironbridge Museum
Tel: 01952 884391, www.ironbridge.org.uk

At-a-glance symbols are explained on the flap inside the back cover

England's Heartland — Self-Catering

77 : Owthorpe, Nottingham

Woodview Cottages ★★★★

Woodview Cottages, Newfields Farm,
Owthorpe, Nottingham NG12 3GF
Contact: Jane Morley
Tel: 01949 81279 • **Fax:** 01949 81279
Web: www.woodviewcottages.co.uk
E-mail: enquiries@woodviewcottages.co.uk

A warm welcome awaits you at our idyllic cottages located in a beautiful rural setting just 20 minutes from Nottingham/Leicester. Both cottages have been tastefully converted from a traditional barn to provide cosy accommodation with log-burning stoves, beamed ceilings and character furniture. Nestling on the edge of the Vale of Belvoir, surrounded by picturesque gardens and beautiful woodland views. Ideal for nature lovers and wildlife enthusiasts. Providing high standards, each self-catering cottage comprises living/dining room and well-equipped kitchen. One double, one twin bedroom with linen and towels included. Bathroom and separate shower. Cot/high chair available.

Low season per week: £350.00–£400.00
High season per week: £400.00–£550.00
Short breaks: From £200.00–£350.00
2 cottages
Cards accepted: None

Directions: From Nottingham take the A606 through Tollerton to intersection with A46. Take first left towards Newark. After 2 miles, look out for sign to Newfields Farm.

78 : Ashby-de-la-Zouch, Leicestershire

Norman's Barn ♦♦♦♦

Ingles Hill Farm, Burton Road,
Ashby-de-la-Zouch, Leicestershire LE65 2TE
Contact: I C Stanley
Tel: 01530 412224
Web: www.normansbarn.co.uk
E-mail: isabel_stanley@hotmail.com

Norman's Barn has been converted from farm sheds and granaries into a luxurious residence and, since 2000, 130 acres of woodland and parkland have been planted, returning the old Prestop Park to its historical roots, as one of the three great parks of Ashby. To the north, views extend over Ivanhoe's valley and there are beautiful walks to enjoy. The accommodation includes a spacious fitted kitchen, two en suite bedrooms and a flagged living room with oak-galleried landing. Norman's Barn is part of a working farm, but is in easy reach of major places of interest, including Chatsworth, Kedleston Hall, and Haddon Hall, with Birmingham, Leicester, Derby and Nottingham within striking distance.

Low season per week: £250.00–£390.00
High season per week: £270.00–£410.00
Short breaks: £210.00–£300.00
1 barn conversion
Cards accepted: None

Directions: Exit A42 at junction 13. Take A511 towards Burton-upon-Trent. At third roundabout turn left to Ashby.

Self-Catering   **England's Heartland**

79 : Much Wenlock, Shropshire

Set in the heart of the medieval market town of Much Wenlock

Moreton Cottage

2 St Mary's Lane, Much Wenlock, Shropshire TF13 6NS
Contact: Samantha Gray • **Tel:** 01952 728169
Web: moretoncottage.co.uk • **E-mail:** dgray@dgray96.fsnet.co.uk

History and modern good taste combine in this recently renovated 300-year-old cottage, set in the heart of the medieval market town of Much Wenlock. The Five star accommodation is beautifully furnished, with two bedrooms comfortably sleeping three. The kitchen and outhouse are fully-equipped, and there is a pretty cottage garden for relaxation. As well as the beauty of the countryside the area is full of history, with Telford and Ludlow within easy reach.

Low season per week: £250.00–£300.00
High season per week: £400.00–£400.00
Short breaks: from £60.00 per night
1 cottage: Sleeps 3 people
Cards accepted: None

Directions: Leave M54 at Junction 6 (A5223 to Much Wenlock and Ironbridge). At fourth roundabout take third exit. At the bottom of steep hill turn left towards Much Wenlock. Follow road for approx 5 miles and at T junction turn left onto A458 towards Bridgnorth. Left after BP garage onto St Mary's Road which leads onto St Mary's Lane. Continue until you reach a white cottage with a red door on right. Parking is adjacent.

Packwood Yew Garden

Take a first glimpse of immaculately clipped yew bushes standing to attention on the carefully manicured lawn at Packwood House. You would be forgiven for thinking that you are witnessing a gathering of silent hooded figures. Indeed, the arrangement of 100 trees, surrounding a single large yew, the Master, standing atop a mount, is said to represent the Sermon on the Mount. Meanwhile, a row of 12 on a raised terrace is called the Apostles.

It is not known if the garden's original designer, John Fetherston, intended to convey this symbolism, when he planted the scheme between 1650 and 1670. It is possible that many of the trees were planted some time later – indeed, references to the Sermon of the Mount are not mentioned in documents until the late 19th century.

The fine timber-framed mansion, probably built by John Fetherston's father, is also of considerable interest. Under the Fetherston family's ownership, the original Tudor building underwent considerable alterations, in particular the addition of fine stables and outbuildings in the 1670s. When Packwood House was bought by the Ash family in 1905, its restoration became Graham Baron Ash's passion and he eventually donated it to the National Trust, hoping it would continue to be kept as the perfect monument to the Tudor age – and so it has.

Packwood House
Tel: 01564 783294, www.nationaltrust.org.uk

Self-Catering | **England's Heartland**

80 : Hingham, Norfolk

River Lodge ★★★★

River Lodge, River House,
Southburgh, Norfolk IP25 7TQ
Contact: Mrs Susan Burton
Tel: 01362 821570 • **Fax:** 01362 820639
Web: aburtonassociates.com
E-mail: andy@abaltd.demon.co.uk

A log cabin oasis set in its own quiet grounds, two-bedroomed River Lodge is in easy reach of Norwich and just three miles from the historic town of Hingham. The cosy accommodation is well-equipped and an ideal base for a relaxing break, pursuits, or a business trip. Sandringham, the north Norfolk coast and the Broads are comfortable journeys away. The area is ideal for walking and cycling, and there is a golf and leisure centre with dining and bar facilities just three miles away. There is also the opportunity for local fishing. We can even provide accommodation for your horse. There is wheelchair access to the lodge entrance.

Low season per week: £190.00–£300.00
High season per week: £350.00–£400.00
Short breaks: from £120.00–£150.00
1 log cabin: Sleeping 4 people
Cards accepted: None

Directions: River Lodge is located three miles north-west of the historic town of Hingham. It is well-positioned for access to Norwich (14 miles) and the B1108 Watton Road.

81 : Stilton, Peterborough

Orchard Cottage ★★★★

17 Denton Village, near Stilton,
Peterborough PE7 3SD
Contact: JJW Higgo
Tel: 01572 737420
Web: www.higgo.com/orchard
E-mail: orchard@higgo.co

The owner stays here regularly – which says just about all you need to know about the standards of this delightful cottage in the heart of 'The Shires'. The furnishings are antique – even in the Victorian bathroom – and the cottage, with its three double bedrooms is fully-equipped to ensure you enjoy your stay. Extensive gardens surround your haven and there is a fully-equipped croquet lawn for those relaxing times when you are not out exploring some of the most historic country in England. This is the land where Mary Queen of Scots was beheaded, where Oliver Cromwell lived. Splendour at Orchard Cottage, wonderment all round.

Low season per week: £500.00–£600.00
High season per week: £650.00–£900.00
Short breaks: from £350.00–£675.00
1 cottage
Cards accepted: None

Directions: About three miles from Stilton which is just off the A1M (exit 16) between Peterborough and London.

England's Heartland | **Self-Catering**

82 : Diss, Norfolk

Ivy House Farm ★★★★

Wortham, Diss,
Norfolk IP22 1RD
Contact: Paul Bradley
Tel: 01379 898395 • **Fax:** 01379 898395
Web: www.ivyhousefarmcottages.co.uk
E-mail: prjsbrad@aol.com

This peaceful complex consists of a 17th century Suffolk longhouse and four purpose-built cottages set in spacious grounds in the heart of East Anglia, on the Norfolk/Suffolk border. Ivy House Farm stands in the middle of a medieval sheep and goose station. The house and cottages are all comfortable and fully-equipped and they form an ideal base for excursions in any direction. North lie Norwich, Sandringham and the Broads, east is the coast for birdwatching and walking, at Walberswick and Dunwich, for example, or the fun and amenities of Great Yarmouth, while south lies Constable Country and Lavenham, and to the west are Cambridge, Newmarket and the Brecklands nature reserve.

Low season per week: £238.00–£665.00
High season per week: £492.00–£1465.00
Short breaks: From £155.00–£933.00
1 house 4 cottages
Cards accepted: None

Directions: From Bury St Edmunds take A143. Turn left at village sign then left again towards Long Green and Redgrave.

83 : Saxmundham, Suffolk

Bluebell, Bonny, Buttercup and Bertie ★★★★

Park Farm, Sibton, Saxmundham,
Suffolk IP17 2LZ
Tel: 01728 668 324
Web: www.farmstayanglia.co.uk/parkfarm
E-mail: margaret.gray@btinternet.com

Don't the names say it all? These are four charming cottages creating their own atoll of tranquillity away from the madding crowd. All of them are fully-equipped, with Bluebell, Bonny and Buttercup grouped round their own flower bedecked courtyard, while Bertie sits in splendid isolation with its own garden and view across the fields beyond. This is unspoilt Suffolk, with the Heritage Coast not far away, and there are shops in nearby Peasenhall and Yoxford villages. If you can't live without bustle, thriving Ipswich is no distance, while the beauty of Aldeburgh and its seafood restaurants is tantalisingly close.

Low season per week: £225.00–£290.00
High season per week: £300.00–£440.00
Short breaks: from £135.00–£170.00
4 cottages
Cards accepted: None

Directions: From London take A12, then A1120 at Yoxford. From west leave A14 at Stowmarket on A1120.

Self-Catering | **England's Heartland**

Norfolk Lavender

Throughout the ages, lavender has endured as one of the most popular herbs. The Romans used it as a healing agent and as an insect repellent, in massage oils and to scent their bath water. Whether or not it was already growing here, Roman soldiers would have certainly planted lavender as part of their herbal first-aid kit and later it was grown for medicinal uses in medieval monastic gardens. The Tudors used a dried lavender to scent closets and repel bed bugs, its cleansing properties were valued during the plague of 1665, and Victorian women used it to scent themselves, their linen and their clothes.

In Victorian times, there were a number of prized lavender fields in southern England. At the beginning of the 20th century, however, the bushes were devastated by a deadly disease, shab, which all but halted the commercial growing of lavender. Today, Norfolk Lavender founded in 1932 at Heacham, Norfolk, still grows seven varieties of lavender – five for distilling and two for drying. Breathe in the delicate aromas as you take a tour of the grounds, the distillery and the fields. Harvest starts in mid July – with one third of the crop destined for pot-pourris and sachets. The flowers are packed loosely into sacks through which warm air is blown for several days, before the heads are removed and sifted.

The other two thirds of the crop is distilled using an ancient process. Steam distillation is used to extract the lavender oil stored in the glands of each floret.

About 500lb (230kg) of flowers are loaded into each still that is trodden down by foot. Steam is then passed through the still which collects with the oil vapour in the condenser, leaving the pure essential oil ready to be drawn off at about half a litre per still-load. The process ends with the oil being matured for a year and then blended with other oils and fixatives.

Norfolk Lavender, Heacham, Norfolk
Tel: 01485 570384, www.norfolk-lavender.co.uk

England's Heartland — Self-Catering

84 : Great Eversden, Cambridge

Red House Farm ★★★★

Great Eversden, Cambridge CB3 7HW
Contact: Margaret Tebbit
Tel: 01223 262154 • **Fax:** 01223 264875
Web: redhousefarm.uk.com
E-mail: info@redhousefarmuk.com

Red House Farm stands in its own acreage of working arable farmland and garden, with holiday cottages created from the converted Rose Barn. The cottages have been tastefully decorated and furnished and are fully equipped. Each cottage has two bedrooms and sleeps up to four people. The cottages lie to the north of the unspoilt village of Eversden and an easy walk to the shop and pub. Just seven miles away is Cambridge, and Rose Cottages are an ideal base to explore farther afield, with the Norfolk Broads, Duxford Air Museum and picturesque Ely all within easy reach.

Low season per week: £200.00–£300.00
High season per week: £250.00–£450.00
2 cottages
Cards accepted: None

Directions: Junction 12 M11. Take A603 west for 4 miles. Turn north opposite Wheatsheaf pub. Go through Little and Great Eversden, carry on for 1/4 mile and Red House Farm is on the right.

85 : Hardwick, Cambridgeshire

Glebe Cottage ★★★★

44 Main Street, Hardwick, Cambridgeshire CB3 7QS
Contact: Mrs FM Key
Tel: 01954 212895 • **Fax:** (01234) 789012
Web: www.camcottage.co.uk
E-mail: key_fiona@hotmail.com

The historic 14th century St Mary's Church stands next to peaceful, secluded and well-equipped Glebe Cottage in the Domesday village of Hardwick, with its highly-rated Blue Lion pub, village green and parish pump. The cottage, which sleeps four is in a conservation area, but within easy distance of the local shops, while the bustle of Cambridge is only six miles away. The cottage is set in spacious gardens bordered with trees and up a private drive. Just 15 minutes away is Wimpole stately home and Duxford, home of the Imperial War Museum's world-famous collection of historic aircraft. We pride ourselves on the warm welcome we offer guests.

Low season per week: £225.00–£250.00
High season per week: £300.00–£450.00
Short breaks: from £150.00–£225.00
1 cottage: Sleeping 2 people
Cards accepted: Mastercard, Visa, Switch/Delta

Directions: Exit Junction 13 of the M11.

Self-Catering — England's Heartland

86 : Bury St Edmunds, Suffolk

Francis Farm Cottages ★★★★

Francis Farm, Upper Somerton,
near Bury St Edmunds, Suffolk IP29 4NE
Contact: Sarah Worboys
Tel: 01284 789241
Web: www.francisfarmcottages.co.uk
E-mail: enquiries@francisfarmcottages.co.uk

The Granary and Cartlodge are original farm buildings that have been sympathetically restored and offer accommodation full of charm and character on this working farm producing cereals and free-range eggs. The Granary features a super king-sized four-poster bed, with en suite bathroom, a conservatory, and many other lovely features. The Cartlodge, with its original flint walls, is on one floor and has a king-sized bed. The properties have an interconnecting door and can be joined into one cottage, if needed. Both cottages are fully-equipped to ensure your stay is comfortable and relaxing in a peaceful retreat set amidst rolling countryside.

Low season per week: £182.00–£373.00
High season per week: £300.00–£426.00
Short breaks: from £128.00–£359.00
2 cottages
Cards accepted: Mastercard, Delta, Switch, Visa

Directions: Situated 2 miles from the village of Hartest, which is on the B1066 from Bury St Edmunds, 10 miles North East.

87 : Lavenham, Suffolk

Blaize Cottages ★★★★★

Blaize House, Church Street,
Lavenham, Suffolk CO10 9QT
Contact: Jim and Carol Keohane
Tel: 01787 247402 • **Fax:** 01787 247402
Web: www.blaizecottages.com
E-mail: info@blaizecottages.com

Winner: "Self-Catering Holiday of the Year 2004" awarded by the East of England Tourist Board.

Blaize Barn (sleeps 4) and Lady Cottage (sleeps 2) are luxury 5 star cottages in the heart of Lavenham, Suffolk. Lavenham is a stunning medieval village in the heart of the Suffolk countryside. Both cottages are within a two-minute walk of excellent pubs, restaurants and village shops. Both cottages feature original medieval oak vaulted ceilings, Sky TV and DVD player/library, private gardens, large beds and bath, power shower, highest quality furnishings and fittings and new kitchens. Blaize Barn has a log fire and private parking. Lady Cottage has a gas effect log fire.

Low season per week: £310.00–£410.00
High season per week: £400.00–£620.00
Short breaks: From £210.00–£350.00
2 cottages
Cards accepted: Mastercard, Delta, Switch, Visa

Directions: Please see our website for full directions.

Brasses of East Anglia

Connoisseurs of monumental brass will find much to interest them in the churches of East Anglia. Created to mark a grave and glorify the departed, a veritable wealth of brasses is to be found in the region's churches. They offer significant clues into daily medieval life, in terms of information on local families, details of coats of arms and an illustration of costumes of the day.

The earliest brasses date from the late 13th and early 14th centuries. A brass in Isleham church in Cambridgeshire, features Sir Geoffrey Bernard and is dated to 1275 by the type of tailed surcoat he wears over his armour. Crusaders such as Sir Roger de Trumpington, a brass of whom is found in the village church of St Mary and St Michael in the village of Trumpington, are denoted, many believe, by their crossed legs. While the most famous military brass in England, found in Acton, Suffolk, features another crusader, Sir Robert de Bures, and shows his military garb in some detail. Other brasses depict family life, such as the commemoration of John Day, of Little Bradley, Suffolk, who is shown surrounded by his wife and 13 children. Weston Colville in Cambridgeshire has a brass of Sir Robert Leverer, dated 1427, showing him in armour and surrounded by flowers, next to his wife who is dressed in a flowing headdress.

As floor monuments, brasses have been subject to heavy wear and their conservation is now of great concern. Three of the best brass-rubbing centres are St Mary's Church, Bury St Edmunds, the Cambridge Brass Rubbing Centre and Ely Cathedral (pictured) which has replicas from all over Britain.

Cambridge Brass Rubbing Centre
Tel: 01223 871 621

88 : Aldeburgh, Suffolk

Cragside   ★★★★

9 Hertford Place, Aldeburgh, Suffolk
Contact: Lesley Valentine, Rookery Farm, Cratfield, Halesworth, Suffolk IP19 0QE
Tel: 01986 798609 • **Fax:** 01986 798609
Web: www.aldeburgh-cragside.co.uk
E-mail: j.r.valentine@btinternet.com

This is a characterful and deceptively spacious self-contained ground floor flat in a large Victorian House on Crag Path, just 20 yards from the sea. Comfortably furnished, with central heating and inglenook fireplaces, the apartment is very well equipped, even including good lighting for reading in bed. There is a twin and a single bedroom, with very comfortable beds with good quality duvets and electric blankets. The kitchen has every appliance to make life easy, including microwave, dishwasher, washer/dryer and fridge/freezer. Comfortable and cosy in an unrivalled position on Crag Path, the apartment is delightful in summer or winter.

Low season per week: £200.00–£280.00
High season per week: £280.00–£390.00
Short breaks: from £100.00–£180.00
1 ground floor flat
Cards accepted: None

Directions: Take the A1094 off the A11. At Aldeburgh head towards Slaughden Quay. Hertford Place is the second turn left after the White Hart pub.

89 : Colchester, Essex

Castle Road Cottages

6, 17, 64 Castle Road,   ★★★★/★★★★★
Colchester, Essex C02 7AA
Contact: Castle Road Cottages, 19 High Street, Nayland, near Colchester, Essex CO6 4JG
Tel: 01206 262210 • **Fax:** 01206 262210
E-mail: tim.shackleton@virgin.net

These three cosy and characterful Victorian cottages have been painstakingly restored and renovated using authentic period features, from cast iron fireplaces and traditional bed linen to Victorian furnishings and antique panelling. There is underfloor heating and the kitchens are fully-equipped. The cottages have pretty gardens and secluded courtyard areas. These town centre cottages are in a quiet, leafy cul-de-sac in a conservation area beside Colchester Castle and the spacious Victorian park. They form an ideal base in Colchester from which to explore major cities like Norwich and Ipswich and the East Anglian coast.

Low season per week: £385.00
High season per week: £420.00
3 cottages
Cards accepted: None

Directions: Ten minutes from A12 and five minutes from railway and bus station.

England's Heartland — Self-Catering

90 : Halstead, Essex

Froyz Hall Barn

★★★★

Halstead, Essex CO9 1RS
Contact: Judi Butler
Tel: 01787 476684 • **Fax:** 01787 474647
Web: www.froyzhall.co.uk
E-mail: judibutler@dsl.pipex.com

Froyz Hall Barn welcomes everybody, from family groups to hen parties and disabled guests, including wheelchair users, who will find this 200-year-old converted granary a splendid base from which to explore historic cities and towns like Cambridge and Colchester and the beauties of Constable Country. The barn, which can accommodate nine guests, includes a tastefully-furnished 40ft sitting room and dining area with an open fire, a fully-equipped kitchen, heated pool, tennis court, private fishing lake and woodlands for walking and cycling. Children are welcome. Beauty treatments, therapies and fitness training are available. You will be made welcome by the Butler family who live at the hall.

Low season per week: £450.00–£600.00
High season per week: £600.00–£900.00
Short breaks: from £200.00–£350.00
1 barn: Sleeping 9 people
Cards accepted: None

Directions: Froyz Hall Barn is situated close to the Essex/Suffolk border between Halstead and Braintree on the A131. Accessible from M11 or Stansted Airport.

Greensted's Log Church

Looking every bit the quintessentially pretty English parish church, St Andrew's in Greensted, near Chipping Ongar in Essex, is actually the oldest wooden building in Europe. Previously thought to date back to Saxon times, around 845AD, St Andrew's Church was said to have been the resting place for the body of the martyred King Edmund – a stained glass window even depicts the story of his martyrdom. Scientific analysis of the wood by examining the spacing of its tree rings undertaken in 1995, however, revealed that the church could not have been built earlier than 1066, the date of the Norman conquest. Edmund's body was transported in 1013, half a century before the present church was built. There may have been earlier buildings on the site, but the structure we find today clearly never housed the saint.

Despite this discovery, the church is still one of the most visited in the country, attracting some 100,000 visitors every year. Now the nave of the present building, the primitive wooden church is constructed from huge logs, felled in nearby Epping Forest (pictured), which were split in half and joined with wooden wedges. The rounded sides of the logs form the exterior wall, while the smooth sides face the interior.

Lacking windows, the original church was lit by oil lamps. Dark patches in the wood are thought to be scorch marks. Transformed gradually over time, the church was substantially added to in Tudor and Victorian times.

England's West Country

Above: Horse riding along the beach, St Michael's Mount

Right: Swimming at night, Cornwall

England's West Country

The wonders of the West

Experience the glorious gardens, brooding moorland, ancient monuments and sandy shores of the West Country. There's certainly a gentler pace of life and a warmer climate. **Discover** the picture postcard villages of the Cotswolds and the Georgian elegance of Bath, the prehistoric aura of Stonehenge and the Jurassic Coast. **Explore** the fishing villages of Devon and Cornwall where it seems that life has almost stood still. Visit the weird and wonderful rock formations of Wookey Hole and enjoy the art at Tate St Ives. **Relax** in a hip boutique hotel, enjoying the best in cuisine and hospitality.

Right: Surfers' delight – the beach at Woolacombe
Far right: The Eden Project at St Austell, Cornwall

Chill out in hidden bays and sandy coves. Indulge your love of cream teas and clotted cream fudge. Stroll along part of the South West Coast Path. Brave the waves at Newquay's surfing festival. Wonder at the Cerne Abbas Giant and the Lost Gardens of Heligan There's so much to experience in the wonderful West Country.

A walk on the wild side

The South West is truly a walker's paradise. The South West Coast Path runs for 630 miles from Minehead to Poole and offers dramatic views of the coastline. For a shorter stroll, or perhaps an exhilarating horse ride, head to one of the three moors, Exmoor, Dartmoor and Bodmin. Take a walk through time on the Jurassic Coast, a UNESCO World Heritage Site. You'll see 185 million years of earth history along 95 miles of spectacular coastline. Discover the quaint villages in its path, cycle along miles and miles of quiet lanes, soar above in a hot air balloon, or, for something completely different, why not try llama trekking?

Down by the sea

How's this for the perfect antidote to modern life? Sandy bays, sheltered coves and wilder stretches – perfect for taking it easy or hitting the waves. The town of Newquay buzzes in the summer as surfers and fun seekers converge for

England's West Country

some serious partying. Bude, Croyde and Woolacombe are also great places to learn to surf or even kitesurf – while you can try sailing and windsurfing in Poole. Shipwreck-rich waters mean a feast for divers. Or you can explore the artificial reef off Cornwall's Whitsand Bay near Plymouth. Discover Devon's English Riviera, between the River Dart and the Exe. Here the bustling seaside towns of Torquay, Paignton and Brixham throng with a mix of families, and yachties going ashore for supplies. Get to know some friendly coastal creatures from penguins and puffins to playful fur seals at Living Coasts. Away from the beach, lose yourself in one of the West Country's charming fishing villages. Places like Clovelly, Port Isaac and Beer are a picturesque maze of narrow streets and unbelievably steep roads.

Secret gardens

The South West boasts three of the most extraordinary gardens in Britain, if not beyond. Its balmy sub-tropical climate a perfect breeding ground for more exotic flora. Delight in the romantic sounding Lost Gardens of Heligan at Mevagissey – an 80-acre garden neglected for 70 years until 1991. The highlight is the Jungle, a 22-acre steep-sided valley home to some of the lushest vegetation in the country, including a banana plantation and palms. Be amazed by the remarkable Eden Project, near St Austell. It is home to thousands of plants, from Britain's temperate zone and other climatic zones. Wander around the enormous glass biomes – where nature and technology meet. More exotic gardens await visitors to the Isles of Scilly – the Abbey Gardens at Tresco. Windbreaks shield the garden from the Atlantic gales, leaving plants to grow that you wouldn't expect to see in our northern climes. Home to species from 80 countries, discover cacti, date palms, giant lipstick-red flame trees and rarities like Lobster Claw.

Feast for the senses

Go on – indulge yourself in the South West's delicious specialities. The Cornish pasty tastes

England's West Country

especially good washed down with a pint of sweet cider. A bewildering range of fudge and the equally calorific cream teas await those with a sweet tooth. Enjoy mouth-watering scones straight from the oven and topped with indulgent clotted cream.

Cheese is synonymous with the region. Think Cheddar, Double Gloucester and Somerset Brie, while Cornish Yarg, a unique, nettle-wrapped cheese graces the best cheeseboards. Get the best catch of the day at a harbourside eatery such as Olga Polizzi's ultra-chic Hotel Tresanton, or at TV chef Rick Stein's Seafood Restaurant. Or improve your own skills in the kitchen and learn from the man himself at his cookery school in Padstow. End your culinary quest with Julian Temperley's award-winning Somerset apple brandy. Truly scrumptious!

Magic and mystery

Quirky customs and mysterious places abound in the South West. Strange rock formations, mystical festivals, outrageous fertility symbols – even cheese rolling! Overlooked by the majestic Tor, Glastonbury is unlike anywhere else. Today, thousands of people arrive, attracted to its mystical charms as well as the world-famous music festival it hosts. Ponder the mysteries of the ancient stone circle of Stonehenge – erected between 2800BC and 1800BC. How were such enormous stones transported and arranged? Be amused or outraged by the fantastic chalk drawing of the Cerne Abbas Giant, striding across the hill outside Cerne Abbas.

Chipping Campden in Gloucestershire is the location of the Cotswolds' unique version of the Olympick Games, first held in 17th century. Gloucester is also the home of the annual Cheese Rolling Festival at Cooper's Hill. Competitors from all over the world gather to chase a 9lb Double Gloucester cheese down the hill. What's the reward for their efforts? Yes, you've guessed it – more cheese! Hear the sound of trampling feet at the Annual Worm Charming Competition in Blackawton, Devon. The team that persuades the most worms to rise to the surface, wins. It's simple, really.

City splendours

The buzzing university cities of Bristol and Bath are filled with attractions. Revel in the Georgian beauty of Bath – its townhouses shaped in elegant crescents. Visit Number 1 Royal Crescent for perhaps the finest example of Palladian architecture. Be impressed by the best-preserved Roman religious spa from the ancient world, which lies under the watchful gaze of Bath Abbey. Enjoy Bristol's infectious vitality. Down by the rejuvenated harbour front discover vibrant bars and restaurants, and the magical At-Bristol – bringing science, nature and art to life. Stroll along the pleasant shopping streets of Clifton and be awestruck by the feat of engineering that is the Clifton Suspension

Right: The Roman spa at Bath

Below: Stonehenge in Wiltshire

England's West Country

Bridge, built by Isambard Kingdom Brunel to span the Avon Gorge. Continue your journey with a trip to some of the West's other great cathedral cities. Discover Exeter, Wells and Gloucester and marvel at Salisbury Cathedral with the tallest spire in England.

the honey-coloured limestone villages of the Cotswolds. Happy days will be spent exploring the beautiful towns of Cheltenham and Cirencester, and the lovely villages of Bourton-on-the-Water and Castle Combe.

Great days out

If you're looking for even more inspiration on great days out, try these for starters. Learn about the history of the railway at Swindon's interactive attraction STEAM – the Museum of the Great Western Railway and meet the animals at Longleat's famous Safari Park. Relive the seafaring history of the South West at the National Maritime Museum in Falmouth, or catch a performance of a Greek tragedy in the stunning cliffside setting of the Minack Theatre at Porthcurno. Finally, take a driving tour around

Contact

South West Tourism
tel: 0870 442 0800
www.visitsouthwest.co.uk

England's West Country — Hotels and Guest Accommodation

England's West Country — **Hotels and Guest Accommodation**

91 : Barnstaple, Devon

The Spinney ♦♦♦♦ Silver Award

Country Guest House, Shirwell,
Barnstaple, Devon EX31 4JR
Contact: Mrs J Pelling
Tel: 01271 850282
Web: thespinney@shirwell.co.uk
E-mail: thespinny@shirwell.fsnet.co.uk

Set in over an acre of grounds, with views towards Exmoor, this spacious former rectory offers well-equipped and furnished accommodation within easy reach of Exmoor National Park, Arlington Court stately home and the beautiful gardens of Marwood Hill. Sandy beaches, too, are a short distance away. The chef/proprietor has a deserved reputation for delicious meals which, in the summer, are served in the Victorian conservatory beneath an ancient vine. Restored and decorated to a high order, The Spinney offers a warm welcome to guests throughout the year.

Bed & Breakfast per night:
Single room from £22.00–£25.00
Double room from £44.00–£50.00

Dinner, Bed & Breakfast per person, per night:
£38.00–£39.00

Bedrooms: 1 double/1 twin/1 single/2 family
Bathrooms: 3 en suite, two private
Parking: Private, in own grounds
Cards accepted: Most debit and credit cards accepted

Directions: Take A39 Lynton Road out of Barnstaple, pass hospital on right and travel another three miles. We are on the left, on main road opposite layby.

92 : Lifton, Devon

Tor Cottage ♦♦♦♦♦ Gold Award

Chillaton, Lifton, Devon PL16 0JE
Tel: 01822 860248 • **Fax:** 01822 860126
Web: www.torcottage.co.uk
E-mail: info@torcottage.co.uk

If the romantic setting of a tranquil, private valley, with beautiful en suite garden rooms, log fires and moonlight swims in the heated outdoor pool sets your pulse racing then Tor Cottage is for you. Judging from the comments of previous guests and four National Excellence Awards, you will enjoy this superb retreat from the hurly-burly. The bedrooms are elegant and spacious and fully-equipped and the garden rooms have their own private terrace and garden for your privacy. The cuisine is expertly prepared and as well as the traditional menu we cater for vegetarians and vegans. 'A perfect escape from the real world,' as one guest put it.

Bed & Breakfast per night:
Single room from £89.00
Double room from £130.00–£140.00

Bedrooms: 3 double/1 twin/1 suite
Bathrooms: 5 en suite
Parking: Available
Cards accepted: Mastercard, Switch, Visa, Delta

Directions: From M5 at Exeter take A30 (Okehampton direction). At Sourton Cross leave A30, signposted A386 Tavistock. At bottom of slip road, turn right and then left. Remain on that road, following Lewdown signs for 6 miles. When you reach crossroads signposted Chillaton 4 miles turn left.

Hotels and Guest Accommodation | **England's West Country**

93 : Camelford, Cornwall

Higher Trezion ◆◆◆◆

Tresinney, Advent, Camelford, Cornwall PL32 9QW
Contact: Janet Wood
Tel: 01840 213761 • **Fax:** 01840 212509
Web: www.highertrezion.co.uk
E-mail: higher.trezion@virgin.net

Do peace and relaxation beckon? Then Higher Trezion is for you. Ideal as a base for touring Cornwall, our sheep farm is in a unique setting off the beaten track. Start the day with our real farmhouse breakfast before you taste the delights of Bodmin Moor, the Eden Project, a cycle on the Camel Trail to Bodmin and Padstow, maybe surf at Polzeath, Bude and Newquay, all within easy reach, as are the many golf clubs in the area. Our family – including the dog and cats – offer a warm welcome. There are many good local pubs and restaurants for evening meals.

Bed & Breakfast per night:
Single room from £25.00–£28.00
Double room from £50.00–£56.00

Bedrooms: 3 double/2 twin/1 family
Bathrooms: 3 en suite
Parking: Available
Cards accepted: None

Directions: From Camelford: A39 then left onto B3266 towards Bodmin, after one mile left to Advent Church. We are opposite Advent Church Driveway. From Bodmin: B3266 to Camelford, look for Advent Church sign on right hand side.

94 : Bodmin, Cornwall

Glenview ◆◆◆◆

Ruthernbridge, Bodmin,
Cornwall PL30 5NP
Contact: MJ Till
Tel: 01208 831585
Web: www.glenviewb-b.co.uk
E-mail: enquiries@glenviewb-b.co.uk

This well-appointed Victorian house is set in the picturesque Ruthern Valley, near Bodmin and Wadebridge. The rooms are well-equipped to offer comfortable accommodation, and Mike and Norma Till offer a warm welcome to guests. Although it is set in a tranquil spot, Glenview is within easy reach of much of Cornwall's most beautiful scenery and many major attractions, including the Eden Project and Lanhydrock Gardens. It is also close to the main trunk routes, making it an ideal place from which to explore this fascinating part of the country.

Bed & Breakfast per night:
Double room from £56.00–£60.00

Bedrooms: 2 double
Bathrooms: 2 en suite
Parking: Available
Cards accepted: None

Directions: The main Cornwall trunk routes of the A30, A38 and A39 are all within easy reach of Glenview Bed & Breakfast.

England's West Country — **Hotels and Guest Accommodation**

95 : Liskeard, Cornwall

Lampen Farm ♦♦♦♦

St Neot, Liskeard, Cornwall PL14 6PB
Contact: Joan Bunt
Tel: 01579 320284 • **Fax:** 01579 320284
Web: www.lampen-farm.co.uk
E-mail: joan@lampenfarm.fsnet.co.uk

Situated in beautiful and peaceful surroundings on the edge of Bodmin Moor, Lampen is a delightful 16th century farmhouse offering spacious accommodation, including lounge and garden for guest use. The bedrooms are elegantly furnished, have en suite shower rooms, colour TV, hairdryer, and tea/coffee making facilities. All rooms have lovely views across the garden and the surrounding countryside, Our traditional and tempting English breakfast is served in the dining room, together with a selection of cereals and fruits. Lampen is ideally placed for visiting the Eden Project and the Lost Gardens of Heligan, and nearby St Neot has a store, post office and pub restaurant.

Bed & Breakfast per night:
Single room from £30.00–£35.00
Double room from £50.00–£60.00
Bedrooms: 2 double/1 twin
Bathrooms: 3 en suite
Parking: Available
Cards accepted: None

Directions: From either A30 or A38, follow signs to St Neot. At village car park, opposite village hall, turn into Lampen Road. Lampen Farm is 350m from car park.

96 : Bude, Cornwall

Harefield Cottage ♦♦♦♦ Silver Award

Upton, Bude, Cornwall EX23 0LY
Contact: Sally-Ann Trewin
Tel: 01288 352350 • **Fax:** 01288 352712
Web: www.coast-countryside.co.uk
E-mail: sally@coast-countryside.co.uk

Welcomed with a cup of tea and home-made shortbread, guests of Harefield Cottage are assured that everything here is aimed at their enjoyment and comfort. The en suite rooms are individually decorated and furnished with four-poster and king-sized beds for restful nights, and hospitality trays and sweets to entice you. The garden is a wonderful place to enjoy the quiet countryside, while a short walk away is the coastal edge. After a strenuous walk or ride there is our welcoming hot tub to relax those muscles. And in the morning our breakfasts are guaranteed to fortify you for the day.

Bed & Breakfast per night:
Double room from £50.00
Dinner, Bed & Breakfast per person, per night: £40.00
Bedrooms: double/twin
Bathrooms: 3 en suite
Parking: Available
Cards accepted: American Express, Mastercard, Switch, Visa

Directions: From A39, Follow signs to Bude town centre. Left at roundabout, over canal bridge. Travelling for 1 mile you will see a red phone box on the right hand side. Past this, there is a left hand turning. Harefield Cottage is on your left.

Hotels and Guest Accommodation — England's West Country

97 : Liskeard, Cornwall

Tregondale Farm ♦♦♦♦ Silver Award

Menheniot, Liskeard,
Cornwall PL14 3RG
Contact: Stephanie Rowe
Tel: 01579 342407 • **Fax:** 01579 342407
Web: www.tregondalefarm.co.uk
E-mail: tregondale@connectfree.co.uk

Come and join us at our fully-restored, stylish farmhouse, full of natural character on the site of an old manor. Lovely en suite bedrooms, fully co-ordinated furnishing, local quality produce, personal service, log fires and a conservatory all add up to a relaxing and cosy ambience. Tregondale Farm is a 200-acre traditional mixed farm with a prize winning herd of South Devon cattle and long-wool sheep. There is a farm trail through a beautiful wooded valley with delightful wild flowers and bird song. We offer high-class accommodation at a sensible price. We also have a self-catering character cottage, where guests can expect something special – Cornish excellence culminating in a memorable holiday.

Bed & Breakfast per night:
Single room from £35.00–£40.00
Double room from £52.00–£60.00

Dinner, Bed & Breakfast per person, per night: £47.50

Bedrooms: 1 quin sized/1 double/1 twin
Bathrooms: 3 en suite
Parking: Available
Cards accepted: Delta, Mastercard, Switch, Visa

Directions: From A390 head to Menheniot, follow signs to farm. From A38 exit at Hayloft restaurant, through village, left at t-junction after 1 mile, turn right at entrance sign.

98 : St Austell, Cornwall

Wisteria Lodge Country House

Boscundle, Tregrehan,   ♦♦♦♦♦ Silver Award
St Austell, Cornwall PL25 3RJ
Contact: Sally Wilkins
Tel: 01726 810800
Web: www.wisterialodge.co.uk
E-mail: info@wisterialodgehotel.co.uk

Your very special place to stay, just one mile from the Eden Project, Wisteria Lodge offers a truly unique experience. Timeless elegance, gourmet cooking, and beautiful, luxurious bedrooms and suites with the highest levels of personal service. The Lost Gardens of Heligan are a five-minute drive away and there are a number of delightful beaches within 15 minutes' walk. There are two spacious en suite bedrooms and two executive suites with luxury lounge areas and jacuzzi baths. There is complimentary cream tea on arrival, and all rooms have a mini bar, satellite television and video.

Bed & Breakfast per night:
Double room from £125.00–£190.00

Dinner, Bed & Breakfast per person, per night:
£92.50–£125.00

Bedrooms: 3 double/1 twin/2 suites
Bathrooms: 4 en suite
Parking: Available
Cards accepted: Mastercard, Switch, Visa, Delta

Directions: Coming up the A3(M), Junction 2. End of the slip road, turn right to Horndean. At roundabout turn left to Horndean. Next roundabout, take second turning into the A3. Additional directions are available on our website.

The Lizard

Not to be confused with its more famous most westerly counterpart, Land's End, the Lizard is Britain's most southerly point. Opinions vary as to how it got its name: some claim it means high place, others say it derives from the Celtic for outcast.

Both theories are plausible, for the Lizard is a level moorland plateau about 200ft (61m) above sea level, almost cut off from the rest of Cornwall. Much of the peninsula is formed of serpentine stone, a soft, easily-worked material used in local churches. A farmer reputedly chanced upon its ornamental qualities when he erected some large rocks in his field as rubbing posts for his cows. He soon noticed that the 'polished' areas showed patterns resembling snakeskin, and colours ranging from grey-green to pink. Once Queen Victoria had chosen it for Osborne House its popularity was assured.

Kynance Cove (pictured), owned by the National Trust, is typical of the majestic coastline of the Lizard. Its rocky outcrops enjoy some exotic names, including Lion Rock, the Devil's Postbox, the Devil's Bellows and Asparagus Island (where the plant grows wild).

The flora of the Lizard is a botanist's delight. Discover plants too tender to grow outdoors elsewhere in the country (such as tamarisks and the Hottentot fig) and others unique to this corner of England, such as Cornish Heath.

The Lizard is particularly hazardous for sailors – more shipwrecks have occurred here than almost anywhere else in the country. Off the eastern coast are the Manacles, a group of ferocious rocks extending over a couple of square miles. In 1770, parishioners of the nearby church of St Keverne in the village of the same name redesigned the steeple as a landmark to warn passing ships. They may have been successful, but there are still over 400 victims of shipwrecks buried in the churchyard.

Kynance Cove (Lizard countryside office)
Tel: 01326 561407, www.nationaltrust.org.uk

Hotels and Guest Accommodation | **England's West Country**

99 : Looe, Cornwall

Cardwen Farm ♦♦♦♦

Pelynt, Near Looe, Cornwall PL13 2LU
Contact: David Keilthy
Tel: 01503 220213 • **Fax:** 01503 220213
E-mail: Cardwenfarm@freenet.co.uk

Cardwen Farm is a Grade II listed building dating to the 17th century and located in three acres of landscaped gardens surrounded by farmland. The River Pol runs through the garden to the nearby picturesque fishing village of Polperro. The en suite accommodation at Cardwen is spacious and well-equipped, with views over the surrounding farmland. You are likely to be greeted by the delicious aroma of home-baked bread and home-made preserves and marmalade, with Cardwen's own free-range eggs and local bacon and sausages on the breakfast menu. Just the thing to set you up for a day exploring the delights of Looe and Polperro and this beautiful part of Cornwall.

Bed & Breakfast per night:
Single room from £30.00–£35.00
Double room from £45.00–£50.00

Bedrooms: 2 double/1 twin
Bathrooms: 3 en suite
Parking: Available
Cards accepted: American Express, Delta, Diners, Mastercard, Switch, Visa, Euros

Directions: From Plymouth go through Looe on the Polperro Road. After 2 miles take B3359 and head for Pelynt, once in the village, turn left by the church. Cardwen is 600 yards along this road.

100 : West Looe, Cornwall

Fieldhead Hotel ★★ Silver Award

Portuan Road, Hannafore,
West Looe, Cornwall PL13 2DR
Contact: Barrie and Gill Pipkin
Tel: 01503 262689 • **Fax:** 01503 264114
Web: www.fieldheadhotel.co.uk
E-mail: enquiries@fieldheadhotel.co.uk

Originally built as a grand private residence in a prime position on West Looe, the Fieldhead is now a country house-style hotel by the sea. Set in one and a half acres of award-winning landscaped gardens, the elevated position of the Fieldhead provides quite stunning views across Looe Bay from virtually every room. All rooms are stylish, well-equipped and en suite. The Fieldhead's restaurant, with its daily changing menu, specialises in fresh, locally-caught seafood. With its prime position the hotel is well placed as a base to explore local beauty spots and sites of interest – for example, the Eden Project, which is just half an hour away.

Bed & Breakfast per night:
Single room from £30.00–£50.00
Double room from £60.00–£110.00

Dinner, Bed & Breakfast per person, per night:
£50.00–£75.00

Bedrooms: 10 double/3 twin/2 single/1 family
Bathrooms: 16 en suite
Parking: Available
Cards accepted: Mastercard, Switch, Visa

Directions: Take A387 to Looe, cross seven-arch bridge and turn left along the quay and on to seafront at Hannafore. Then take first right and right again.

England's West Country — **Hotels and Guest Accommodation**

101 : Plymouth, Devon

Bowling Green Hotel

9-10 Osbourne Place, ♦♦♦♦♦ Silver Award
The Hoe, Plymouth, Devon PL1 2PU
Contact: Tom Roberts
Tel: 01752 209090 • **Fax:** 01752 209092
Web: www.bowlinggreenhotel.com
E-mail: info@bowlinggreenhotel.com

This elegant Georgian hotel is situated in the heart of the historic naval city of Plymouth opposite the world famous Drake's Bowling Green. All bedrooms are fully en suite, with either bathroom or shower and are fully equipped with every amenity. The hotel is within five minutes' walk of the Elizabethan quarter of the famous Barbican and five minutes from the ultra modern shopping centre of the city. An appetising English breakfast in the bright and cheerful dining room will be the ideal start to a day exploring this historic city or, farther afield, the sights and attractions of this beautiful region.

Bed & Breakfast per night:
Single room from £42.00–£45.00
Double room from £54.00–£58.00
Bedrooms: 9 double/2 twin/2 family/1 single
Bathrooms: 12 en suite
Parking: Available
Cards accepted: Mastercard, Euros

Directions: Off A38 head to city centre, follow signs to The Hoe. Take this road turn left in to Hoe Approach, turn right into Citadel road. Hotel is on left at crossroads.

102 : St Ives, Cornwall

Blue Hayes ♦♦♦♦♦ Gold Award

Blue Hayes Private Hotel,
Trelyon Avenue, St Ives, Cornwall TR26 2AD
Contact: Malcolm Herring
Tel: 01736 797129 • **Fax:** 01736 799098
Web: www.bluehayes.co.uk
E-mail: bluehayes@btconnect.com

Blue Hayes is a small, private hotel set in its own grounds above Porthminster beach, overlooking St Ives Bay and harbour, with its own car park in front of the hotel. You can walk directly from our garden gate to the beach below in about five minutes and on to the harbour in about ten minutes. We have five luxurious rooms, all of them with en suite bathrooms with baths and state-of-the-art showers with body jets. The Master Suite has its own balcony, the Godrevy and Bay Suites each have stunning sea views, the Garden Suite has direct access to the gardens and the Trelyon Suite enjoys its own private roof terrace. Our breakfasts are prepared with the finest local produce, while supper on the terrace is a guest favourite.

Bed & Breakfast per night:
Single room from £115.00–£145.00
Double room from £130.00–£190.00
Dinner, Bed & Breakfast Per Night: Supper available 7pm – 8.30pm for an additional £12 – £25 per person
Bedrooms: 5 double/4 twin/1 single/1 family
Bathrooms: 6 en suite
Parking: Available
Cards accepted: American Express, Mastercard, Switch, Delta.

Directions: Leave A30 at St Erth and take A3074 to St Ives. Pass through Lelant and Carbis Bay. We are down the hill just past the garage on the right.

Hotels and Guest Accommodation — England's West Country

103 : Marazion, Cornwall

Mounts Bay House ♦♦♦♦

Turnpike Hill, Marazion,
Cornwall TR17 0AY
Contact: Heather and Paul Kamara
Tel: 01736 711040
Web: www.mountsbayhouse.com
E-mail: relax@mountsbayhouse.com

"An Oasis in the Heart of Marazion"

Mounts Bay House is a high quality bed & breakfast in a unique coastal location, with panoramic sea views overlooking St Michael's Mount and Mounts Bay. This spacious house with a contemporary ambience is surrounded by a private garden. Our en suite rooms are individually designed to complement our peaceful, tranquil atmosphere. They are non-smoking and fully-equipped with everything you will need for a comfortable stay. We offer a comprehensive breakfast menu using Cornish produce. St Michael's Mount, Coastal Path and sandy beaches are all a short walk away. Disabled access and facilities.
For Short Break Offers see our website!

Directions: Travelling West on A30, 1.5 miles after Crowlas take 2nd exit at roundabout, follow signs to Marazion. In town, turn right at slow sign on the road.

Bed & Breakfast per night:
Single room from £29.00–£56.00
Double room from £58.00–£84.00
Autumn/Spring breaks: Stay 4 nights, pay for 3.
Holistic breaks: Free Reiki treatment in our new therapy room with a 3 night stay
Bedrooms: 3 double/2 twin/1 family
Bathrooms: All en suite
Parking: Private secure guest parking
Cards accepted: Most cards accepted

104 : Falmouth, Cornwall

Budock Vean ★★★★ Silver Award

Helford Passage, Mawnan Smith,
near Falmouth, Cornwall TR11 5LG
Tel: 01326 252100 • **Fax:** 01326 250892
Web: www.budockvean.co.uk
E-mail: relax@budockvean.co.uk

This family-run, four-star hotel, nestles in 65 acres of gardens and parklands on the banks of the River Helford. Our award-winning restaurant uses the finest local produce, with fresh seafood very much the speciality. The hotel has its own golf course, private foreshore with sunseeker motorboat, large indoor pool, snooker room, all-weather tennis courts and natural health spa. Many of the great gardens of Cornwall are close by and this is an ideal place from which to explore Britain's most dramatic coastline. Budock Vean has been awarded Cornwall Tourist Board Hotel of the Year in 2002, 2003 and 2004, and was South West Tourism's Large Hotel winner in 2003.

Directions: At Exeter take the A30 west through Devon and into Cornwall. From Truro, take the A39 towards Falmouth and follow the brown tourist Information signs to Trebah Garden. Budock Vean is half mile past Trebah.

Bed & Breakfast per night:
Single room from £56.00–£87.00
Double room from £112.00–£174.00
Dinner, Bed & Breakfast per person, per night:
£68.00–£112.00
Bedrooms: 24 double/23 twin/7 single/2 family/1 suite
Bathrooms: 57 en suite
Parking: Available
Cards accepted: Mastercard, Switch, Visa, Delta, Diners

England's West Country — **Hotels and Guest Accommodation**

Special location, special views and special care for our guests

105 : Salcombe, Devon

Tides Reach Hotel

★★★ Gold Award

South Sands, Salcombe, Devon TQ8 8LJ
Contact: John Edwards • **Tel:** 01548 843466 • **Fax:** 01548 843954
Web: www.tidesreach.com • **E-mail:** enquire@tidesreach.co.uk

Tides Reach Hotel is located on a tree-lined sandy cove, right on the sands in an area of outstanding natural beauty, with superb views of the Salcombe estuary. With 35 rooms, the hotel is large enough to provide the best facilities, but small enough to retain a personal touch — with a carefully recruited staff team which excels in giving friendly, caring service to enable guests to relax and have a totally enjoyable experience. That's made easier by the overall quality of the bedrooms and the wealth of things to enjoy at Tides Reach, from gym and games room to the indoor swimming pool and sauna and, nearby, golf and pony trekking facilities. This is a glorious part of Glorious Devon and Tides Reach Hotel is the ideal place to recuperate from the hurly-burly or as a base to explore this beautiful area.

Bed & Breakfast per night:
Single room from £60.00–£115.00
Double room from £120.00–£270.00

Dinner, Bed & Breakfast per person, per night: £75.00–£155.00

Bedrooms: 18 double/10 twin/2 single/3 family/2 suites
Bathrooms: 35 en suite
Parking: Available
Cards accepted: Mastercard, Switch, Visa, American Express, Delta, Diners

Directions: On the A38 (Devon Expressway) travel to Totnes and on to Salcombe using the A381. On entering Salcombe follow the brown tourist signs to South Sands.

Hotels and Guest Accommodation — England's West Country

106 : Chipping Campden, Gloucestershire

The Bantam Tea Rooms ♦♦♦♦

High Street, Chipping Campden,
Gloucestershire GL55 6HB
Contact: Jonathan Roberts
Tel: 01386 840386
Web: www.thebantam.co.uk
E-mail: thebantam@hotmail.com

This quaint, historic High Street tea room has luxurious and well-equipped guest accommodation. You will find us right opposite the historic town hall on the most beautiful High Street in England. All our rooms have been tastefully restored to create comfort for our guests, yet retain all their old world charm and character. They are furnished with antiques as well as offering the usual modern facilities, such as tea and coffee making trays and colour TV. There is also a private guest lounge for you to enjoy. The Bantam also offers a quintessential English Tea Room, with roaring log fire and a selection of delicious home-made cakes and pastries.

Bed & Breakfast per night:
Single room from £45.00–£49.50
Double room from £65.00–£75.00

Bedrooms: 2 double/1 twin/1 single
Bathrooms: 4 en suite
Parking: Available
Cards accepted: American Express, Delta, Mastercard, Switch, Visa

Directions: Take the A44 Oxford-Evesham road and then the B4081 to Chipping Campden.

107 : Moreton-in-Marsh, Gloucestershire

Neighbrook Manor ♦♦♦♦♦

Near Aston Magna, Moreton-in-Marsh,
Gloucestershire GL5 9QP
Contact: John and Camilla Playfair
Tel: 01386 593232 • **Fax:** 01386 593500
Web: www.neighbrookmanor.com
E-mail: info@neighbrookmanor.com

A Cotswold dream, Neighbrook Manor was first mentioned in the Domesday Book commissioned by William the Conqueror in Gloucester Cathedral. It was a church. Now, set in 37 acres with its own trout lake and half a mile of river frontage, it offers a rare opportunity to stay in stylish and tasteful accommodation in a real Cotswold manor house. The building was converted in 1610 and has later Georgian additions. Neighbrook is at the heart of things, with Stratford, Blenheim Palace, Warwick Castle, Chipping Campden and Stow-on-the-Wold all in comfortable reach, as are many of the country's finest gardens.

Bed & Breakfast per night:
Single room from £48.00–£52.00
Double room £85.00 maximum

Bedrooms: 1 double/1 twin/1 single
Bathrooms: 2 en suite
Parking: Available
Cards accepted: Mastercard, Visa, Switch, Euros

Directions: Three and a half miles north of Moreton-in-Marsh on A429. Turn left to Aston Magna, at first building turn right to Paxford and Neighbrook Manor is three quarters of mile on right down a half-mile drive.

England's West Country — Hotels and Guest Accommodation

108 : Painswick, Gloucestershire

Cardynham House ◆◆◆◆

The Cross, Painswick,
Gloucestershire GL6 6XX
Tel: 01452 814006 • **Fax:** 01452 8123212
Web: www.cardynham.co.uk
E-mail: info@cardynham.co.uk

Painswick is the Queen of the Cotswolds and Cardynham House is a beguiling gateway to the delightful villages and centres of interest in this beautiful part of the country. The hotel – a 15th century wool merchant's house – has nine themed rooms, all equipped to offer the highest standards of comfortable accommodation. Nearby are regency Cheltenham and the cathedral city of Gloucester, while Painswick itself is one the most picturesque villages in the region. And, after a day of exploring, Cardynham House offers guest residents of the exclusive Pool Room the chance to unwind in the splendid heated pool with its own wave machine and private patio.

Bed & Breakfast per night:
Single room from £50.00–£85.00
Double room from £69.00–£175.00

Bedrooms: 6 double/3 family
Bathrooms: 9 en suite
Parking: Available nearby
Cards accepted: Mastercard, Visa, Switch, Delta, American Express, Euros

Directions: On A46 between Stroud and Cheltenham. Turn into Victoria Square by church, follow 100 yards as road turns left, Cardynham House is on next intersection.

109 : Fairford, Gloucestershire

Milton Farm ◆◆◆◆

Fairford, Gloucestershire GL7 4HZ
Contact: Suzie Paton
Tel: 01285 712205 • **Fax:** 01285 711349
Web: www.milton-farm.co.uk
E-mail: stay@milton-farm.co.uk

This working farm is set in spectacular Cotswold countryside. Milton Farm is an impressive Georgian farmhouse with luxuriously spacious and distinctive en suite bedrooms and a comfortable guest lounge with a large open fireplace. Warm hospitality and real farmhouse, Aga-cooked breakfasts with locally-sourced quality produce ensure a memorable stay. Milton Farm has a quiet, pleasant outlook on the edge of this most attractive Cotswold market town, with numerous beautiful walks across meadowland beside the River Coln. We are exceptionally welcoming, with facilities for families, business guests, walkers, cyclists and visitors to the Cotswold Water Park. We can also stable horses for equestrian guests.

Bed & Breakfast per night:
Single room from £28.00–£35.00
Double room from £45.00–£55.00

Bedrooms: 1 double/1 twin/1 family
Bathrooms: 3 en suite
Parking: Available
Cards accepted: Please enquire

Directions: Take A417 to Fairford. At the crossroads on Cirencester side of the town turn up beside the Marlborough Arms. Milton Farm is 300 yards on left.

Hotels and Guest Accommodation — **England's West Country**

110 : Chippenham, Wiltshire

Lucknam Park

Colerne, Chippenham, Wiltshire SN14 8AZ
Contact: Carol Wilson • **Tel:** 01225 742777 • **Fax:** 01225 743536
Web: www.lucknampark.co.uk • **E-mail:** reservations@lucknampark.co.uk

> Tranquil setting and award-winning cuisine combine to make a memorable experience

A magnificent Palladian mansion, dating from 1720, Lucknam Park is set in extensive parkland of 500 acres six miles from the historic city of Bath. It was maintained as a family home until 1987 when it opened its doors as a hotel. Lucknam Park has been lovingly restored to the elegance and style of its past glory. Each of our 13 suites and 28 bedrooms is individually designed, with fabrics, antiques and ornaments specially chosen to reflect the character of the rooms. They all have marble bathrooms and splendid views across the park or the lovely courtyard. In addition to round the clock attention and service, Lucknam Park offers a whole range of services to ensure each of our guests has a memorable stay.

Per night: Double, room only, from £225.00–£770.00 (minimum 2 nights at weekends)

Dinner, Bed & Breakfast per person, per night: £142.50–£407.50 (minimum 2 nights at weekends)

Bedrooms: 13 double/15 twin/13 suites
Bathrooms: 41 en suite
Parking: Available
Cards accepted: American Express, Delta, Diners, Mastercard, Visa, Switch

Directions: Take M4 and exit at junction 17, head towards Chippenham via A350. At Bumpers Farm roundabout take A420 towards Bristol. After four miles, turn left for Colerne and Lucknam Park.

England's West Country — Hotels and Guest Accommodation

111 : Corsham, Wiltshire

Heatherly Cottage

Ladbrook Lane, Gastard,   ◆◆◆◆ **Gold Award**
Nr Corsham, Wiltshire SN13 9PE
Contact: Mrs Daniel
Tel: 01249 701402 • **Fax:** 01249 701412
Web: www.smoothhound.co.uk/hotels/heather3.html
E-mail: ladbrook1@aol.com

Heatherly Cottage is in a quiet lane approximately nine miles from Bath and close to the National Trust village of Lacock, the site of several films, including Harry Potter. The 17th century cottage has a large garden to relax in, with beautiful views across open countryside. There is plenty of off-road parking. Accommodation for guests is in a separate wing with its own entrance. All bedrooms have colour TV, clock radio, hairdryer, tea and coffee trays and ironing facilities. Full English breakfasts are served with our own free-range eggs, or there is continental breakfast with croissants.

Bed & Breakfast per night:
Single room from £38.00–£42.00
Double room from £54.00–£60.00
Bedrooms: 2 double/1 twin
Bathrooms: 3 en suite
Parking: Available
Cards accepted: None

Directions: M4 Junction 17. Take A350 towards Chippenham. A4 towards Bath, left at traffic lights to Corsham. At third roundabout turn left, then travel 100 yards before turning right towards Gastard B3353. Travel 1 mile before turning left into Ladbrook Lane.

112 : Bath, Somerset

Corston Fields Farm

Corston, Bath, BA2 9EZ   ◆◆◆◆ **Silver Award**
Tel: 01225 873305 • **Fax:** 01225 874421
Web: www.corstonfields.com
E-mail: corston.fields@btinternet.com

Corston Fields is an arable farm placed conveniently between Bath and Bristol, where guests can enjoy the serenity of beautiful countryside near these two great cities with all their attractions and amenities. The house is a listed 17th century farmhouse, featuring mullion windows, hearth fires, dressers with old china, and Chinese rugs. The bedrooms are beautifully furnished, large and well-equipped, with lovely views. The farm holds a prestigious conservation Gold Award under the Duke of Cornwall's Habitat Scheme – even the central heating is powered by renewable energy.

Bed & Breakfast per night:
Single room from £45.00–£45.00
Double room from £70.00–£80.00
Bedrooms: 3 double/1 twin
Bathrooms: 3 en suite
Parking: Free parking on site
Cards accepted: Mastercard, Switch, Visa

Directions: On the A39 between Corston and Marksbury take the turning that runs beside the Wheatsheaf pub. You will find us 300 yards on the right.

113 : Bath, Somerset

The Firs ★★★★

2 Newbridge Hill, Bath,
Somerset BA1 3PO
Contact: Dawn Osborne
Tel: 01225 334575 • **Mob:** 07970 602769

This beautifully renovated Victorian house offers cosy and tasteful accommodation in one of the most interesting cities in the country. The en suite rooms are spacious and tastefully decorated and fully-equipped. Because this is a small business the focus is on ensuring our guests enjoy their stay, from the excellent breakfasts to the relaxing gardens and guests' lounge. The Firs is within easy reach of the city centre with all its wonderful Regency and Georgian architecture. It is also an ideal base from which to explore the beautiful countryside and places of interest that are the essence of this part of the West Country.

Bed & Breakfast per night:
Double en suite for one person £40
Double room for two people £55.00–£60.00
Bedrooms: 2 double/1 family
Bathrooms: 3 en suite
Parking: Off-street parking available
Cards accepted: None

Directions: From the city centre, follow the upper Bristol Road to Newbridge Hill.

The Tarka Trail

The writer Henry Williamson (1895–1977) is perhaps best known for his book, *Tarka the Otter*, a work that displays his fascination for these shy and beautiful creatures as well as his deep love for the wildlife and landscapes of Devon. The book was inspired by an orphaned otter cub which Williamson reared and cared for, while living in the Devonshire village of Georgeham, near Barnstaple.

Tarka Country is an area roughly corresponding to that featured in the book – along Devon's north coast from Bideford to Lynton, and southwards to the northern fringes of Dartmoor. The Tarka Country Tourism Association has set up a long-distance route – the Tarka Trail – designed to encourage visitors to discover the beautiful countryside without the use of the car. Describing an irregular figure of eight, the trail loops between Exmoor and Dartmoor, with Barnstaple at its centre, covering 180 miles (290km) of varied and often stunning scenery. Walking the entire length of the Tarka Trail (except the section between Eggesford and Barnstaple which is a train journey) is a challenge, so shorter walks and cycle routes have also been devised.

The Tarka Trail passes many places mentioned in Williamson's famous book. Tarka's fictional birthplace, for example, is on the Torridge, just upstream from Bideford, while remote Cranmere Pool on Dartmoor was visited by Tarka after the death of his mate, Greymuzzle. But don't expect to see any otters on your travels. Due to river pollution and loss of habitat, otters are one of Europe's most endangered mammals. The best place to see them is at the Tamar Otter Sanctuary, near Launceston, Cornwall (about 25 miles – 40km – from Barnstaple) where otters are bred and reintroduced to the wild in a bid to save them from extinction.

Tamar Otter Sanctuary, Launceston,
tel: 01566 785646
Tarka Country Tourism Association,
www.tarka-country.co.uk
The Tarka Trail, www.visitsouthwest.co.uk

England's West Country | **Hotels and Guest Accommodation**

114 : Bath, Somerset

Marlborough House ♦♦♦♦

1 Marlborough Lane, Bath, BA1 2NQ
Contact: Laura Dunlap
Tel: 01225 318175 • **Fax:** 01225 466127
Web: www.marlborough-house.net
E-mail: mars@manque.dircon.co.uk

Marlborough House is an enchanting and unusual B&B in the heart of Georgian Bath. It is exquisitely furnished with elegant antiques, but run in a friendly and informal style, and we offer our guests a relaxed and intimate retreat in beautiful surroundings close to all the heritage sites of Bath. We serve only vegetarian organic food, with breakfast choices including San Francisco-style pancakes, fluffy French toast with maple syrup, as well as delicate omelettes with savoury mushrooms and breakfast potatoes. All our rooms have en suite bathrooms and feature four-poster, Victorian brass or iron beds – and each room has a welcoming complimentary sherry and a hostess tray.

Bed & Breakfast per night:
Single room from £55.00–£85.00
Double room from £65.00–£95.00

Bedrooms: 3 double/1 twin/2 family/1 single
Bathrooms: 7 en suite
Parking: Available
Cards accepted: American Express, Delta, Diners, Mastercard, Switch, Visa, Euros

Directions: Take M4 to exit 18 for Bath, head for city centre and follow road through Queen Square and on to Marlborough Lane. Full directions sent on booking.

115 : Bath, Somerset

Ayrlington Hotel

24/25 Pulteney Road,
Bath BA2 4EZ   ♦♦♦♦♦ Gold Award
Contact: Simon Roper
Tel: 01225 425495 • **Fax:** 01225 469029
Web: www.ayrlington.com
E-mail: mail@ayrlington.com

Located within an easy five-minute level walk of Bath city centre, The Ayrlington is a small, tranquil, non-smoking luxury hotel. Its 14 elegantly appointed rooms boast every modern amenity, and some feature four-poster beds and spa baths. Each of its rooms is individually and tastefully themed using period furniture, fine fabrics and thought-provoking artwork, ensuring that a stay at the hotel will be as memorable as it is comfortable and relaxing. The hotel offers secure private parking and is also within easy reach of the railway and bus stations. The Ayrlington won the Southwest Tourism Chairman's Award for Excellence in 2004 and was shortlisted again for 2005.

Bed & Breakfast per night:
Single room from £80.00–£160.00
Double/family room from £80.00–£180.00

Bedrooms: 10 double/1 twin/3 family
Bathrooms: 14 en suite
Parking: Available
Cards accepted: American Express, Mastercard, Switch, Delta, Visa

Directions: Please see website for map and full directions.

Hotels and Guest Accommodation — England's West Country

116 : Chippenham, Wiltshire

Glebe House ♦♦♦♦

Chittoe, Chippenham,
Wiltshire SN15 2EL
Contact: Ginny Scrope
Tel: 01380 850864
Web: www.glebehouse–chittoe.co.uk
E-mail: gscrope@aol.com

Glebe House has been extensively renovated to a high standard of interior decoration to give the accommodation a feel of luxury and comfort. Both Bill and Ginny Scrope have had many years of experience of hosting guests and providing delicious food for special occasions. A warm welcome is assured in a truly unusual and tranquil setting. Within easy distance are the World Heritage Sites of Stonehenge and Avebury, the market towns of Devizes and Marlborough. Salisbury, Wells, Bath and Glastonbury are nearby national centres of culture, while Bowood and Badminton, Corsham and Castle Combe along with the Harry Potter village of Lacock offer a spectacular range of interesting visitor centres.

Bed & Breakfast per night:
Single room from £30.00–£35.00
Double room from £55.00–£65.00

Dinner, Bed & Breakfast per person, per night:
£48.00–£50.00

Bedrooms: 1 double/2 twin
Bathrooms: Private facilities
Parking: Off-street parking
Cards accepted: None

Directions: From A342 take turning to Chittoe and Spye Park. Continue over a small crossroad and on to a narrow lane. Glebe House is the second turning on the left.

117 : Wells, Somerset

Glencot House ♦♦♦♦♦

Glencot Lane, Wookey Hole,
Wells, Somerset BA5 1BH
Contact: Mrs MJ Attia
Tel: 01749 677160 • **Fax:** 01749 670210
Web: www.glencothouse.co.uk
E-mail: relax@glencothouse.co.uk

Glencot House, privately owned and operated, offers high-class accommodation, fine cuisine and friendly service, in a relaxed country house atmosphere. It offers peace and tranquillity, where guests can relax and unwind, walking in the beautiful gardens, catching trout in the river, playing snooker, table tennis or croquet, or enjoying a sauna or swim in the indoor pool. Each of the 13 guest rooms enjoys excellent views of the gardens or surrounding countryside. Many have four-poster beds, and all double rooms are en suite with bath and shower, while single rooms have an en suite shower. In the evenings log fires beckon in the drawing room or library while delicious food is prepared to order by the chef.

Bed & Breakfast per night:
Single room from £74.00–£86.00
Double room from £96.00–£128.00

Dinner, Bed & Breakfast per person, per night:
£74.50–£92.50

Bedrooms: 6 double/3 twin/3 single/1 family
Bathrooms: 13 en suite
Parking: Available
Cards accepted: American Express, Delta, Mastercard, Switch, Visa

Directions: Leave M5 at Junction 22, follow signs for Cheddar and Wookey hole. Go through Easton on to Haybridge and take left at road signed to Wookey Hole. Follow road over bridge turn left in to Glencot Lane.

At-a-glance symbols are explained on the flap inside the back cover

England's West Country — Hotels and Guest Accommodation

118 : Wells, Somerset

Beryl ♦♦♦♦♦

Top of Hawkers Lane, Wells,
Somerset BA5 3 JP
Contact: Holly or Mary-Ellen Nowell
Tel: 01749 678738 • **Fax:** 01749 670508
Web: www.beryl-wells.co.uk
E-mail: stay@beryl-wells.co.uk

Beryl is a precious gem in a perfect setting. This small 19th century Gothic mansion with its own peaceful gardens, is just a mile from the centre of historic Wells. Beryl has comfortable and well-equipped bedrooms and beautifully-furnished reception rooms. Children and pets are welcome and there is an outdoor heated pool in use from June to September. There is also a chairlift to the first floor bedrooms. And, before you set off in the evenings to sample the excellent restaurants and pubs in Wells, there is an honesty bar for an aperitif to begin your enjoyment.

Bed & Breakfast per night:
Single room from £55.00–£75.00
double room from £44.00–£50.00

Dinner, Bed & Breakfast per person, per night:
£75.00–£110.00

Bedrooms: 5 double/3 twin
Bathrooms: 8 en suite
Parking: Available
Cards accepted: Mastercard, Switch, Visa

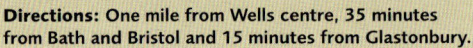

Directions: One mile from Wells centre, 35 minutes from Bath and Bristol and 15 minutes from Glastonbury.

Cerne Abbas Giant

Even without its most famous landmark, Cerne Abbas in Dorset has many attractions. The town grew up around a Benedictine abbey founded in 987, and although only a few ancient remains of the abbey still stand, many of the houses date from the abbey's 500-year domination of the community. Today it ranks as one of the loveliest villages in Dorset, complete with duckpond, village stocks, a holy well in the churchyard and a superb 14th-century tithe barn.

But the real treat for visitors to Cerne Abbas is the extraordinary figure cut into the chalky hillside near by. Brandishing a knobbly club, the Cerne Abbas giant strides across the turf, arms outstretched, his naked form leaving little to the imagination. His origins and identity are obscure, although many think he is a representation of the Roman god Hercules, carved during the first few centuries AD.

Only two other similarly ancient hill-carvings now exist in Britain – the White Horse of Uffington, Oxfordshire (see page 157), and the Long Man of Wilmington, East Sussex. The giant has survived regular and rigorous 'scourings', usually at seven-year intervals, a practice that was presumably, and rather surprisingly, condoned by the Benedictines despite the giant's obviously pagan nature. Today the National Trust is responsible for maintenance.

For obvious reasons, the Cerne Abbas giant has always been regarded as something of a fertility symbol. It is thought that the village's annual spring revelries were held on a site nearby, while some still claim a cure for infertility by sitting on the giant's impressive 30ft (9m) member. This is not to be encouraged, however, because of the risk of eroding the carving's most prominent feature. For the best view of the Cerne Abbas giant, go to the junction where Duck Street meets the A352 Sherborne–Dorchester road.

Hotels and Guest Accommodation — England's West Country

119 : Bridgwater, Somerset

Castle of Comfort ♦♦♦♦♦ Silver Award

Dodington, Nether Stowey,
Bridgwater, Somerset TA5 1LE
Contact: Nigel Venner
Tel: 01278 741264 • **Fax:** 01278 741144
Web: www.castle-of-comfort.co.uk
E-mail: reception@castle-of-comfort.co.uk

The Castle of Comfort offers luxurious accommodation of the highest standard for families, business people and honeymoon couples on the glorious northern slopes of the Quantocks, overlooking the Bristol Channel. All rooms are en suite with TV, radio, alarm clock, direct dial telephones and tea and coffee-making facilities. This historic 16th century country house hotel, set in four acres of parkland has even played host to Wordsworth and Coleridge in its time. Once a haven for copper miners, now it is a superbly appointed island of tranquillity, but close to the amenities of the north Somerset coast and the splendour of Exmoor.

Bed & Breakfast per night:
Single room from £38.00–£84.00
Double room from £95.00–£129.00

Dinner, Bed & Breakfast per person, per night:
£65.00–£111.00

Bedrooms: 3 double/1 twin/1 single/1 family
Bathrooms: 6 en suite
Parking: Available
Cards accepted: Delta, Mastercard, Switch, Visa

Directions: From M5 junction 23 or 24 then proceed through Bridgwater to A39. Continue for 8 miles bypassing Nether Stowey. Hotel further along on left.

120 : Taunton, West Somerset

Northam Mill ♦♦♦♦♦ Silver Award

Water Lane, Stogumber, Taunton TA4 3TT
Tel: 01984 656916 • **Fax:** 01984 656144
Web: www.northam-mill.co.uk
E-mail: bmsspicer@aol.com

Hidden for 300 years, Northam Mill which lies in a remote valley between the Quantock and Brendon Hills is a place to refresh the spirit. The finely furnished rooms are all en suite and all have bubbly toiletries and towelling bathrobes. In the summer the little bridge over the stream is a splendid place to enjoy a glass of wine. In the winter crackling log fires add to the feeling of well-being, a feeling generated by the fine cooking of Kate and the hospitable approach of Richard who are there to make your stay something to remember for a very long time.

Bed & Breakfast per night:
Single room from £40.00–£70.00
Double room from £70.00–£100.00

Dinner, Bed & Breakfast per person, per night:
£68.00–£98.00

Bedrooms: 2 double/2 twin/1 single/1 suite
Bathrooms: 5 en suite
Parking: Available
Cards accepted: Mastercard, Visa, Switch, Delta, American Express

Directions: Junction 25 of the M5 to Northam Mill is 14.6 miles. Follow Minehead signs from Taunton. Approximately 12 miles past Taunton turn left off the A358 towards Stogumber. Take second left then first right into Water Lane. Northam Mill is at the bottom of the hill under the West Somerset Steam Railway bridge.

England's West Country — **Hotels and Guest Accommodation**

121 : Honiton, Devon

Combe House Hotel

Gittisham, Honiton, ★★ **Gold Award**
Near Exeter, Devon EX14 3AD
Contact: Ruth Hunt
Tel: 01404 540400 • **Fax:** 01404 46004
Web: www.thishotel.com
E-mail: stay@thishotel.com

The alluring combination of heritage and the welcoming live-in feel, make Combe House a special place to stay. This Grade I Elizabethan Country Manor – winner of *The Sunday Times* Travel Award for Best Country House Hotel 2004 – welcomes guests with an understated elegance, style and warmth. Each of the 16 en suite bedrooms is different, some with sweeping views of the Devon countryside, others with distinctive murals and mullioned ivy clad windows. All greet the visitor with crisp cotton bed linen, rich fabrics, patchwork quilts and fresh flowers. Exceptional food, using local produce, and well-chosen wines add to the sheer enjoyment of Combe House.

Bed & Breakfast per night:
Single room from £128.00–£140.00
Double room from £148.00–£298.00

Dinner, Bed & Breakfast per person, per night:
£210.00–£348.00

Bedrooms: 16
Bathrooms: 16 en suite
Parking: Available
Cards accepted: Visa, Mastercard

Directions: Heading south take exit 28 of M5, take A373 to Honiton. Follow signs to Sidmouth then brown signs to Combe. Northbound on M5 exit at junction 29 take A30 to Honiton exit at Patteson's Cross and head for Combe.

122 : Christchurch, Dorset

Druid House   ♦♦♦♦♦ **Gold Award**

16 Sopers Lane, Christchurch,
Dorset BH23 1JE
Contact: Angela Barnicoat
Tel: 01202 485615 • **Fax:** 01202 473484
Web: www.druid-house.co.uk
E-mail: reservations@druid-house.co.uk

Everything you could need you can find at the delightful, family-run Druid House in the heart of Christchurch. All rooms are fully-equipped and tastefully furnished and there are excellent areas for relaxation, from the residents' bar and lounge to the sun lounge and the patioed garden. There is lots to see in Christchurch, including the 11th century priory and the town quay. The town is also rich in fine restaurants. And if you're planning a day out in the surrounding countryside, Druid House can send you on your excursion well-fortified by one of their superb breakfasts, even served in bed for that extra bit of pampering.

Bed & Breakfast per night:
Single room from £30.00–£60.00
Double room from £60.00–£80.00

Dinner, Bed & Breakfast per person, per night:
£30.00–£40.00

Bedrooms: 4 double/3 twin/1 single/3 family
Bathrooms: 8 en suite
Parking: Available
Cards accepted: Mastercard, Visa, Switch, Delta, American Express

Directions: Take M3/M27 from London, or M40/M34 from the Midlands. Take A35 to Christchurch main roundabout, and Sopers Lane. Druid House is on the left.

Hotels and Guest Accommodation — England's West Country

123 : Corfe Castle, Dorset

Townsend House ♦♦♦♦

Corfe Castle,
Dorset BH20 5EG
Contact: Sally-Anne Parsons
Tel: 01929 480265

The magnificence of the Purbeck Hills and the magic of the Swanage steam railway combine their attractions in Townsend House, where top quality comfort is provided in peaceful and beautiful surroundings. Just five-minutes stroll away from this well-equipped Purbeck stone house is Corfe Castle, while in easy reach are the coastlines of Swanage, Studland and Kimmeridge. The two en suite double and one en suite twin rooms are well-equipped and there is a beautiful south-facing garden with wonderful views of the Purbeck Hills, perhaps while enjoying local produce and a glass of wine.

Bed & Breakfast per night:
Single room from £40.00–£45.00
Double room from £60.00–£65.00

Bedrooms: 2 double/1 twin
Bathrooms: 3 en suite
Parking: Available
Cards accepted: None

Directions: Take A351 through Wareham. At Corfe Castle travel through village. Townsend House is at the far end of the village.

124 : Bournemouth, Hampshire

Cransley Hotel ♦♦♦♦ Silver Award

11 Knyveton Road,
Bournemouth BH1 3QG
Tel: 01202 290067 • **Fax:** 0709 2381721
Web: www.cransley.com
E-mail: info@cransley.com

The East Cliff area of Bournemouth was once the haunt of King Edward VII and his mistress, the actress Lillie Langtry. It still has that elegance and the Cransley Hotel is one of its gems. Committed to guest comfort, the hotel offers comfortable accommodation, good food and value for money – all within easy distance of the beach and major road and rail links. The Cransley has been tastefully refurbished and is ideally situated for the New Forest, Hardy Country, Poole Harbour and Brownsea Island. The private hotel garden is a Bournemouth in Bloom award-winner and a great place to relax and unwind.

Bed & Breakfast per night:
Single room from £30.00–£35.00
Double room from £60.00–£70.00
Optional dinner at £12

Bedrooms: 6 double/3 twin/2 single
Bathrooms: 10 en suite
Parking: Available
Cards accepted: Visa, Mastercard, Delta and Maestro

Directions: Turn off A338 at St Paul's roundabout by ASDA store. Continue over next roundabout keeping Unisys building on right. Knyveton Road is first left.

England's West Country — Hotels and Guest Accommodation

125 : Sidmouth, Devon

Hotel Riviera ★★★★ Gold Award

The Esplanade, Sidmouth,
Devon EX10 8AY
Contact: Peter Wharton
Tel: 01395 515201 • **Fax:** 01395 577775
Web: www.hotelriviera.co.uk
E-mail: enquiries@hotelriviera.co.uk

Hotel Riviera is splendidly positioned at the centre of Sidmouth's esplanade, overlooking Lyme Bay. With its mild climate and the beach just on the doorstep, the setting echoes the south of France and is the choice for the discerning visitor. Behind the hotel's fine Regency facade lies an alluring blend of old-fashioned service and present-day comforts. Glorious sea views can be enjoyed from the recently redesigned en suite bedrooms, which are fully appointed and have many thoughtful extras. In the elegant bay-view dining room guests are offered a fine choice of dishes from extensive menus prepared by French and Swiss-trained chefs, with local seafood a particular speciality.

Bed & Breakfast per night:
Single room from £97.00–£130.00
Double room from £172.00–£238.00

Dinner, Bed & Breakfast per person, per night:
£98.00–£143.00

Bedrooms: 11 double/7 twin/7single/2 suites
Bathrooms: 27 en suite
Parking: Available
Cards accepted: Mastercard, Switch, Visa, American Express, Diners

Directions: From London, take M5 junction 30, then A3052.

126 : Teignmouth, Devon

Britannia House ♦♦♦♦♦ Silver Award

26 Teign Street, Teignmouth,
Devon TQ14 8EG
Tel: 01626 776051 • **Fax:** 01626 776302
Web: www.britanniahouse.org
E-mail: gillettbritannia@aol.com

A luxurious home from home in a 17th century Grade 11-listed town house – that's Britannia House set in a charming conservation area of Old Teignmouth. From the welcoming cup of tea on arrival to the superb breakfasts and locally-sourced produce, this guest house prides itself on putting visitors first. The bedrooms are all tastefully furnished and well-equipped with very comfortable beds to ensure a stressbusting sleep. You can relax in our walled garden or head for water sports, golf and pony trekking which are all nearby. Museums, wildlife centres and historic buildings abound and the major centres of Exeter, Torquay and Teignmouth are in easy reach.

Bed & Breakfast per night:
Double room from £50.00–£70.00

Bedrooms: 2 double/1 twin
Bathrooms: 3 en suite
Cards accepted: Mastercard, Visa, Maestro, Electron and Euros

Directions: From M5 junction 31, take A38 taking left fork on to A380. Turn left on to B3192. After 4 miles turn left at lights. Turn right at next lights, Teign Street is first left by Blue Anchor pub.

Hotels and Guest Accommodation **England's West Country**

127 : Collaton St Mary, Devon

The Old School House ♦♦♦♦♦

Blagdon Road, Collaton St Mary,
Devon TQ3 3YA
Contact: Sarah Abdy
Tel: 01803 523011
Web: www.theoldschoolhousedevon.co.uk
E-mail: abdy13@tiscali.co.uk

Your stay at The Old School House will be comfortable, unhurried and calm, so you really unwind and relax. Your hosts, Ann and Sarah Abdy have turned this old Victorian school house into a wonderful retreat to base your holiday. We offer a hearty breakfast and a real feeling of home from home. Attention to detail is the key to your stay with us. Exceptionally comfortable accommodation, combined with relaxing holistic therapies like Reflexology and Reiki, add to the feeling of calm enjoyment in this beautiful part of South Devon. There are excellent local restaurants and countless activities including golf and falconry to experience during your stay with us.

Bed & Breakfast per night:
single room from £50.00
double room from £65.00
Bedrooms: 1 double/1 twin
Bathrooms: 2 – 1 en suite, 1 private
Parking: Available
Cards accepted: None

Directions: M5 to end, then A38 and A380 to Torbay. Turn right at large set of lights to Totnes on A385. Turn right after Ocean BMW into Blagdon Road.

Arthurian Legends of the South West

No one knows if Arthur really lived. When the Romans left Britain in the early 5th century AD, recorded history went with them, at least for several hundred years. However, historians think Arthur did exist, probably a 5th- or 6th-century British chieftain who fought the invading Saxons. Meanwhile, Camelot may have been at South Cadbury, near Sherborne, as excavations have revealed that this Iron Age hill fort was reoccupied and refortified in the late 5th or early 6th century.

The complex web of Arthurian myth, however, claims earlier beginnings. One story has Joseph of Arimathea sailing to Cornwall, perhaps to trade in tin. With him on one trip to the West Country is the young Christ who walks on the Mendips at Priddy. Another version has Joseph hiding the Holy Grail, the cup Christ used at the Last Supper, on Glastonbury Tor, his staff, stuck firmly into the ground miraculously growing shoots and known as the Glastonbury Thorn.

The British king is said to have visited Glastonbury (pictured) at least twice, once to rescue his wife Guinevere from the clutches of Melwas, and again when he went to Avalon (often equated with Glastonbury) to die. In 1191, the monks of Glastonbury Abbey found a tomb, apparently inscribed with the words 'Here lies the famous King Arthur in the Isle of Avalon'. Only the cynical would see this as a clever (and successful) ploy to attract pilgrims to an abbey recently devastated by fire.

Other West Country Arthurian sites can be found at Amesbury (where Guinevere became abbess after Arthur's death), Dozmary Pool on Bodmin Moor (where Excalibur was caught by a mysterious hand), Tintagel (Arthur's birthplace) and Badbury Rings in Dorset (one of a number of possible locations for the site of the Battle of Mount Badon, one of Arthur's greatest victories when 960 men died in one attack).

England's West Country — **Hotels and Guest Accommodation**

128 : Torquay, South Devon

Haldon Priors

Meadfoot Sea Road, Torquay TQ1 2LQ
Contact: RG Taylor • **Tel:** 01803 213365 • **Fax:** 01803 215577
Web: www.haldonpriors.co.uk • **E-mail:** travelstyle.ltd@talk21.co.uk

A touch of luxury greets you at this Victorian villa overlooking Meadfoot Bay and 200 yards from the beach. The hotel itself has recently been refurbished and is elegantly furnished. All rooms are en suite with colour TV, radio, CD player and complimentary tea and coffee. The hotel has extensive sub-tropical gardens, a delightful conservatory, sun terrace, games room, exercise room, sauna and a superb heated swimming pool with an original Roman end. Haldon Priors is within easy reach of all the attractions of Torquay, including its bars and restaurant, and is a relaxing centre from which to explore the coastline and countryside of Devon. The proprietors have a well-earned reputation for the quality of food and service provided at this six-bedroom hotel.

Bed & Breakfast per night:
single room from £47.00–£67.00
double room from £64.00–£104.00

Bedrooms: 4 double/1 twin, 1 family
Bathrooms: 6 en suite
Parking: Available
Cards accepted: Mastercard, Visa, Switch

Directions: Pass Torquay harbour on your right. Turn left at the clock tower and first right at the traffic lights. Haldon Priors is on the left just before the beach.

129 : Torquay, Devon

Cary Court Hotel

Cary Court Hotel, Hunsdon Road,
Torquay, South Devon TQ1 1QB
Contact: Paul and Linda Garwood
Tel: 01803 209205 • **Fax:** 01803 201003
Web: www.carycourthotel.co.uk
E-mail: carycourt@aol.com

This plantation-style house in the leafy conservation area of Torquay offers tastefully decorated and furnished accommodation a few minutes away from the main hub of Torquay, with its shops, theatre, restaurants and pubs. All rooms are en suite and fully equipped – including one with an antique four-poster. Premiere rooms have king-sized beds. There is a garden room and a beautiful veranda. In summer, ceiling fans cool the air, while in winter log fires offer a cosy welcome – and all-year-round our splendid breakfasts are a great start to a day of sightseeing or relaxing on the beach.

Bed & Breakfast per night:
Single room from £40.00–£50.00
Double room from £50.00–£75.00

Bedrooms: 10 double/2 twin
Bathrooms: 12 en suite
Parking: Available
Cards accepted: None

Directions: Follow signs to seafront and harbour. At clock tower roundabout turn left on to Babbacombe Road. Pass museum on left, take left turn into Braddon Hill Road East. At the top of the hill turn right into Hunsdon Road. Cary Court Hotel is the second drive on the left.

---

130 : Torquay, Devon

The Hillcroft

9 Matlock Terrace, St Lukes Road,
Torquay TQ2 5NY
Contact: Dick Rogers
Tel: 01803 297247
Web: www.thehillcroft.co.uk
E-mail: info@thehillcroft.co.uk

The Hillcroft opened in 2003 and is a small, luxurious boutique hotel situated in a quiet position just minutes away from the beaches, shops, restaurants and nightlife. We offer a range of rooms, including a one bedroom suite, and a two bedroom penthouse, with widescreen TVs, video or DVD players, supported by our own private library of titles. The suites also have freeview satellite TV, and there is free WiFi connectivity for guests with AirPort cards. Our restaurant serves varied breakfast and evening menus with special vegetarian options, and there is a fully-stocked bar for your convenience. As well as attentive service throughout your stay, we also offer visiting therapeutic massage services with a range of treatments.

Bed & Breakfast per night:
Single room from £35.00–£65.00
Double room from £70.00–£90.00

Dinner, Bed & Breakfast per person, per night:
£47.50–£77.50

Bedrooms: 4 double/1 single/2 suites
Bathrooms: 6 en suite
Parking: Available
Cards accepted: American Express, Delta, Mastercard, Switch, Visa

Directions: On Torbay seafront turn sharp right at lights just after Palm Court Hotel, take second right into St Lukes Road. Hillcroft is 50 yards on the left.

England's West Country — Self-Catering

Self-Catering — England's West Country

England's West Country — SELF-CATERING

131 : Barnstaple, Devon

Martinhoe Cleave ★★★★

Martinhoe Cleave Cottages, Martinhoe, Parracombe, Barnstaple, Devon EX31 4PZ
Contact: Heather Deville
Tel: : 01598 763313
Web: www.hgate.co.uk
E-mail: info@hgate.co.uk

These three lovely cottages just below the hamlet of Martinhoe each accommodate two people, secluded from the hassles of the 21st century, but with all the comforts necessary for an ideal break. They are in easy reach of some of the most dramatic and beautiful coastline in the country, yet nestle in the Exmoor National Park. Bedrooms are double or twin and each cottage has a comfortable sitting room and well-equipped kitchen. In easy reach of amenities, including the attractions of Barnstaple.

Directions: Exit M5 at Junction 27. Take A361 to South Molton. At roundabout 3rd exit to Combe Martin, Lynton, and Blackmoor Gate. At Blackmore Gate road junction, turn right onto A39 for Lynton. At Martinhoe Cross, turn left for Martinhoe and Woody Bay. At next crossroads turn left, signposted Hunters Inn and straight across at the next junction. Follow road down into the valley, our drive is on right about quarter way down hill.

Low season per week: £280.00–£350.00
High season per week: £350.00–£420.00
Short breaks: from £180.00–£210.00
3 cottages
Cards accepted: None

The Camel Trail

The Camel Trail forms part of the growing national cycle network which is being developed by the charity SUSTRANS for the use of cyclists, walkers and horse-riders.

Its 17-mile (27km) route clings, more or less, to the banks of the River Camel. Between Padstow and Wadebridge, it runs for 5½ miles (9km) along the trackbed of the former London and South Western Railway line and then from Wadebridge it follows part of the old Bodmin and Wadebridge Railway, one of Britain's earliest locomotive-hauled railways, to Boscarne Junction on the western outskirts of Bodmin (5½ miles – 9km) and then, turning north, to Poley's Bridge (6 miles – 9.5km).

From Padstow the trail hugs the southern edge of the estuary, crossing Little Petherick Creek on a magnificent triple-span girder bridge.

Built in 1898, this is a rare survivor, most girder bridges having been demolished for scrap. East of Old Town Cove are relics of Penquean slate quarry. In Wadebridge the trail passes through the remains of the station and then a mile or so east of the town crosses over Pendavey bridge on to the north bank of the river and along a steep, wooded stretch that offers good views across the Camel.

North of Bodmin the trail follows the river's eastern bank through quiet woodland between Dunmere and the hamlet of Hellandbridge.

From here there follows a particularly pretty stretch, before the trail ends in a car park at Poley's Bridge, near the buildings of the Wenfordbridge clayworks that were the raison d'être of what was always a mineral line.

This section of the Bodmin and Wadebridge was used solely for the carrying of china clay right up to its closure in 1983.

National Cycle Network/Sustrans
Tel: 0845 113 0065,
www.nationalcyclenetwork.org.uk

Self-Catering **England's West Country**

132 : Barnstaple, Devon

> Situated in an unspoilt area of natural beauty within easy reach of the best attractions

Hartpiece

★★★★

Shirwell, near Barnstaple, Devon EX31 4LG
Contact: Chris Baker or Heather Lindsey • **Tel:** 01628 637111 • **Fax:** 01628 773030
Web: www.hartpiece.co.uk • **E-mail:** chris@hartpiece.co.uk

Deer can be seen as the early mists rise on the valley and wooded hills at Hartpiece. An updated 17th century longhouse and stone barn set in 90 acres, Hartpiece offers casually elegant accommodation, ideal for groups of friends, colleagues or families visiting North Devon. French doors give onto decking and patios equipped with barbecues. Indoors is a hot tub, original art, oak beams and fireplaces. The spacious accommodation – nine rooms in all – can be let as one, or separately. Walks and fishing are on the doorstep, with golf, riding, cycling, surfing and climbing in easy reach. Barnstaple's theatres, nightlife and markets are two miles away. Flowers welcome you on arrival.

Low season per week:
£247.50–£646.25
High season per week:
£495.00–£1292.50
Short breaks: from £173.00–£905.00
1 house, 2 cottages
Cards accepted: Mastercard, Switch, Visa

Directions: 2 miles north of Barnstaple, on the Muddiford Road, around 6 miles from the coast.

England's West Country / Self-Catering

133 : Abbotsham, North Devon

Bowood Farm ★★★★

Abbotsham, North Devon EX39 5AX
Contact: Toad Hall Cottages, 73 Church Street, Kingsbridge, South Devon TQ7 1BY
Tel: 08700 777345 • **Fax:** 01548 853087
Web: www.toadhallcottages.com

A holiday at Bowood Farm cottages begins with a scrumptious home-made tea. The three cottages have all been renovated and are full-equipped bases from which to explore the North Devon and Cornish coastline. Within easy reach are Bideford, Westward Ho! and Rosemoor RHS. Exmoor, too, is just a short drive away. Just a half-mile stroll brings you to Abbotsham, with its church, post office and thatched pub. Each cottage has a small garden enclosed from the surrounding farm, and there is a Dutch barn games area with table tennis and badminton. Dogs are welcome as long as they are sheep-friendly.

Low season per week: £201.00–£288.00
High season per week: £565.00–£747.00
Short breaks: from £180.00–£288.00
1 house Sleeping 5/6 people
2 cottages: Sleeping 6/8 people
Cards accepted: American Express, Mastercard, Switch, Visa, Euros

Directions: Leave M5 at Junction 27 on to A39. Cross Torridge bridge and first roundabout. Turn right at next roundabout to Abbotsham Cross, at next roundabout, turn right, down narrow lane 50 yards, turn left into courtyard.

134 : Launceston, Cornwall

Bamham Farm Cottages ★★★★

Higher Bamham, Launceston, Cornwall PL15 9LD
Contact: J A Chapman
Tel: 01566 772141 • **Fax:** 01566 775466
Web: www.bamhamfarm.co.uk
E-mail: jackie@bamhamfarm.co.uk

Bamham Farm Cottages sleep two to eight people. Full size electric cookers, microwaves, colour TV, video recorders, DVD and CD players are standard equipment, and some cottages have open fires and dishwashers. The cottages, open all year, share facilities of a heated indoor swimming pool (36' x 16'), sauna, games room, children's play area, laundry room, trout fishing and a large garden. The cottages are situated in beautiful countryside on the Cornwall/Devon border near Launceston, ancient capital town of Cornwall, dominated by its Norman castle. The North and South Cornish coast, Bodmin Moor and Dartmoor National Park are within easy reach.

Low season per week: £210.00–£320.00
High season per week: £535.00–£1185.00
Short breaks: from £120.00–£275.00
8 cottages
Cards accepted: Mastercard, Delta, Switch, Visa

Directions: 2 miles from the A30 trunk road and half a mile from Launceston.

Self-Catering | **England's West Country**

135 : Wadebridge, North Cornwall

Great Bodieve Farm Barns ★★★★★

Bodieve, Wadebridge,
North Cornwall PL27 6EG
Contact: Mrs T Riddle
Tel: 01208 814916 • **Fax:** 01208 812713
Web: www.great-bodieve.co.uk
E-mail: info@great-bodieve.co.uk

These four spacious and luxuriously appointed barns offer top quality accommodation on a working farm. The barns are five-star rated and fully equipped to ensure our guests have everything they need during their stay with us. The en suite conversions are: Mill House, which has four bedrooms (two king size, two twin) sleeping eight, plus cot; Orchard Cottage, with one king size and one twin bedroom, sleeping four, plus cot; The Granary, which sleeps four plus cot in one king size and one twin bedroom and The Goose House, with one king size bed, sleeping two plus cot. Guests receive a welcome pack when they arrive at Great Bodieve, in this beautiful part of Cornwall.

Directions: Either follow the A30 to Bodmin, or turn off the A30 at Kennards House just west of Launceston and take the A395 to Davidstow and then A39 to Wadebridge.

Low season per week: £250.00–£500.00
High season per week: £450.00–£1200.00
Short breaks: from £175.00
4 barn conversions
Cards accepted: None

136 : Wadebridge, North Cornwall

Swallow Court Cottage ♦♦♦♦

Molesworth Manor, Little Petherick,
near Wadebridge, North Cornwall PL27 7QT
Contact: Geoffrey French
Tel: 01841 540292
Web: molesworthmanor@aol.com
E-mail: steve@wreahead.co.uk

Swallow Court Cottage is a beautifully furnished converted barn which sleeps six, in the courtyard of Molesworth Manor (pictured). Elegantly decorated it retains many original features, including wooden beams and a slate floor. There are three twin or double rooms, all en suite. The solid beech kitchen is fully-equipped and the large lounge/diner has a four-seater sofa and two-seater sofa bed. The cottage, near Padstow, is in an area of outstanding natural beauty and there is plenty of storage for equipment like bikes and surfboards for guests who enjoy sporting activities as well as the less physical beauties of the area.

Directions: Off the A389 between Wadebridge and Padstow in the village of Little Petherick halfway up/down the hill.

Low season per week: £400.00–£500.00
High season per week: £600.00–£810.00
1 cottage
Cards accepted: None

At-a-glance symbols are explained on the flap inside the back cover

England's West Country — Self-Catering

137 : Wadebridge, North Cornwall

April Cottage ★★★★★

Roserrow Golf and Country Club, St Minver, Wadebridge, North Cornwall PL27 6SB
Contact: Rock Holidays, Trebetherick House, Trebetherick, Wadebridge, Cornwall PL27 6SB
Tel: 01208 863399 • **Fax:** 01208 622218
Web: www.rockholidays.co.uk
E-mail: rockhols@aol.com

This is an outstanding property nestling at Roserrow and a glorious 20 minute walk away from Polzeath beach. The cottage is fully and luxuriously equipped, with superb views across an outstanding area of Cornwall. April Cottage sits in its own garden with a patio and barbecue to enjoy on balmy summer evenings. Close by are Newquay, Wadebridge and Bodmin with their restaurants, pubs and amenities, while all around there is marvellous wildlife attracted to the area by the nearby lake. Rock Holidays have 80 properties available. Please check their web site.

Low season per week: £500.00–£700.00
High season per week: £1300.00–£1600.00
Short breaks: From £300.00–£500.00
60 houses, 20 cottages
Cards accepted: Mastercard, Switch, Visa

Directions: Supplied on application.

138 : Delabole, Cornwall

The Mill House — Gold Award

Helland Barton,
Delabole, Cornwall PL33 9EP
Contact: Rebecca Daglish
Tel: 01840 212526
Web: www.themill-house.co.uk

The Mill House has been beautifully converted from a former mill, built in 1840, to provide very comfortable accommodation. There are three double bedrooms on the ground floor, sleeping six people. One bedroom is en suite and there is a separate shower room. Both have power showers. The focal point of the Mill House is the outstanding open plan living area upstairs. It is comfortably furnished and spacious — 28 feet by 21 feet — with magnificent views of the surrounding, beautiful countryside. There is a fully-equipped kitchen, and a games room. The Mill House is an ideal base from which to explore the attractions of this delightful part of Cornwall. The nearest beach is two miles away.

Low season per week: £375.00–£500.00
High season per week: £475.00–£800.00
Short breaks: From £200.00–£450.00
5 cottages
Cards accepted: None

Directions: Go through Delabole village, heading westwards. At the end of the village turn left, straight after the Atlantic Garage. Follow the road to the bottom.

Self-Catering — England's West Country

139 : Tavistock, Devon

Edgemoor Cottage ★★★★

Middlemoor, Tavistock, Devon PL19 9D.
Tel: 01822 612259
E-mail: fox@dartmoorcottages.info

An attractive, fully furnished and equipped country cottage in a peaceful hamlet 100 metres from open moorland. Ideally situated to enjoy walking, cycling, golfing or riding. over breathtakingly scenic Dartmoor. A perfect base to explore Dartmoor, Devon and Cornwall, with the Eden Project and the north and south coasts in easy reach. The cottage has two en suite bedrooms (one twin and one double) and well-equipped kitchen and a comfortable lounge with sun lounge/diner and patio overlooking fields. Nearby are many historic attractions.

Low season per week: £200.00–£300.00
High season per week: £300.00–£400.00
1 cottage
Cards accepted: None

Directions: At Tavistock follow signboards to Whitechurch. Turn up hill at crossroads past church. At cattle grid turn right into Middlemoor and then right again. Edgemoor is on the right.

140 : Yelverton, Devon

Harrabeer Country House Hotel ♦♦♦♦

Harrowbeer Lane, Yelverton,
Devon PL20 6EA
Contact: Amanda Willats
Tel: 01822 853302 • **Fax:** by request
Web: www.harrabeer.co.uk
E-mail: reception@harrabeer.co.uk

Next to the Hotel, we have converted our old stone barn into two beautiful, self-contained units which are tastefully decorated, comfortably furnished and well-equipped. We have preserved a wealth of the old timbers and exposed stonework to recapture the ambience of the past and combined these with up to-the-minute facilities including colour TV with DVD or video, and microwave. Each self-catering suite has an en suite double bedroom, a living room with put-u-up settee and a well-equipped kitchen. Guests can also enjoy breakfasts and evening meals in the Hotel restaurant by prior arrangement, perhaps while planning their next trip to the local places of interest.

Low season per week: £250.00
High season per week: £350.00
2 suites in barn conversion: Each suite sleeps 2 to 5 people
Cards accepted: American Express, Mastercard, Switch, Delta, Visa

Directions: From Plymouth take the B386 to Tavistock, at Yelverton roundabout take first exit to Tavistock. Sign for hotel is 200 yds on left. At the bottom of Grange Road turn right. Hotel is on the left hand side after road narrows.

England's West Country — Self-Catering

141 : Liskeard, Cornwall

Treworgey Cottages ★★★★★

Duloe, Liskeard, Cornwall PL14 4PP
Tel: 01503 262730 • **Fax:** 01503 269380
Web: www.cornishdreamcottages.co.uk
E-mail: treworgey@enterprise.net

These are enchanting 18th century cottages set near the sea in the beautiful Looe river valley. You have your own private garden with roses round the door and breathtaking views to the river itself. Exclusively furnished with antiques and fully equipped to modern standards, the cottages offer old oak beams, inglenook fireplaces, log fires, even a four-poster bed and fresh flowers to greet you – and, if you don't want to cook, delicious home-prepared candlelit meals can be delivered to your door. Of course, if romantic relaxation isn't your thing we have horse riding on site, all-weather tennis, a heated pool and indoor and outdoor play areas. Goodby stress, hello happiness.

Low season per week: £250.00–£400.00
High season per week: £745.00–£1850.00
12 cottages
Cards accepted: Delta, Mastercard, Switch, Visa

MW DW

Directions: M5 or A303 to Exeter, then A38 to Plymouth and Liskeard.

The Leach Pottery

St Ives had already been a flourishing artists' colony for several decades when Bernard Leach set up a pottery here in 1920 with his lifelong Japanese friend, Shoji Hamada. Born in Hong Kong of English parents, Leach studied pottery in Japan, one of the first Westerners to learn the techniques of Oriental pottery.

Leach and Hamada set up shop just outside the town, by the Stennack stream. They wanted to produce 'genuine handicrafts of quality rather than machine craft in quantity', the aim being to combine the traditions of craftsmanship that were still alive in the East with pre-Industrial Revolution English handcrafted pottery.

Leach also proved to be an inspirational teacher, passing on not only practical skills, but also his philosophy of what it meant to be an artist potter, and attracted visitors and students from all over the world, the first being Michael Cardew, who later built Wenford Bridge Pottery, near Bodmin.

In 1923 Hamada went back to Japan, but remained in close touch with Leach. The skill was carried on by Leach's sons, David and Michael, who set up in Bovey Tracey, Devon, and Yelland, North Devon, respectively. Bernard Leach's grandson, John maintains the family tradition at Muchelney Pottery in Somerset.

In 1956 Bernard married an American potter, Janet Darnell, and she took over the management of the pottery, showroom and students, while continuing to pot in her own right. Bernard was therefore free to concentrate on more writing and travel, only giving up potting when his sight began to fail in the mid-1970s.

After his death in 1979, Janet Leach kept the pottery going, a Mecca for collectors and admirers of the art, until her death in 1997. In 1999 locals Alan and Sally Gillam bought the Leach Pottery and have worked to bring a new lease of life to this important heritage site.

The Leach Pottery, St Ives
Tel: 01736 796398, www.leachpottery.com

Self-Catering   England's West Country

142 : St Austell, Cornwall

Central for both coasts and close to Heligan Gardens and the Eden Project

Tregongeeves Farm   ★★★★

Polgooth, St Austell, Cornwall PL26 7DS
Contact: Mrs J Clemo • **Tel:** 01726 68202 • **Fax:** 01726 68202
Web: www.cornwall-holidays.co.uk

Set around a gravelled courtyard surrounded by 22 acres of green fields and rolling countryside in the heart of Cornwall, Tregongeeves Holiday Cottages provide the perfect location from which to enjoy the sights and sounds of Cornwall. All seven cottages exude warmth and comfort, with exposed beams and natural colours. They are decorated and equipped to an extremely high standard – even down to toy boxes and the daily delivery of your favourite newspaper. Each cottage has its own patio with furniture, barbecue and heater, and Tregongeeves also has an indoor swimming pool, spa bath, recreation room, gym and all-weather tennis court. Within easy reach are soft golden beaches, small fishing harbours and the Eden Project, to name just a few attractions.

Low season per week:
£250.00–£325.00

High season per week:
£325.00–£995.00

7 cottages

Cards accepted: Mastercard, Switch, Visa, Delta, Euros

Directions: Take A390 from St Austell to Truro. After one and a half miles turn left into Tregongeeves Lane and cottages are 200 yards on the right.

England's West Country — Self-Catering

143 : Redruth, Cornwall

Higher Laity Farm ★★★★★

Portreath Road, Redruth,
Cornwall TR16 4HY
Contact: R and ML Drew
Tel: 01209 842317
Web: www.higherlaityfarm.co.uk
E-mail: info@higherlaityfarm.co.uk

Situated on the picturesque, rugged coastline of Portreath, set amidst the Cornish countryside, with superb views over rolling farmland. The original barns have been transformed to provide exceptional five star accommodation. Tastefully converted they provide fully-equipped traditional kitchens, tranquil en suite bedrooms, sumptuous sofas and cottage stoves, all combining to create a restful and relaxing atmosphere. There is a Pets' Corner for our younger visitors. Wonderful sandy beaches and the fishing village of St Ives are nearby. Portreath beach is only a five-minute drive away. Falmouth, home of the National Maritime Museum, and Newquay, Cornwall's surfing capital are in easy reach. There is so much to see and do, and Higher Laity Farm is an ideal base.

Low season per week: £220.00–£300.00
High season per week: £240.00–£640.00
Short breaks: From £125.00–£240.00
Barn conversions: 3, sleeping from 2 to 6 people
Cards accepted: None

Directions: From M5 take A30 to Redruth/Porthtowan slip road towards Redruth. Full details on website.

144 : Newent, Gloucestershire

Highleadon ★★★★

Holiday Cottages, New House Farm,
Highleadon, Newent, Gloucestershire
Tel: 01452 790209 • **Fax:** 01452 790209
E-mail: cjojan@aol.com

The three cottages on this working organic farm have been tastefully converted from an old stables and cart shed. They are all comfortable and well-equipped. One cottage is suitable for guests who are disabled. There is a large patio with barbecue and furniture for those relaxing summer evenings. Relaxing it is, too – there is an abundance of wildlife, from badgers to buzzards, kestrels, owls, pheasants, partridges and woodpeckers. Yet, not far from this haven, are the major centres of Gloucester, Cheltenham and Hereford. Close, too are vineyards and the National Birds of Prey Centre and The Shambles Victorian Village. Perfect peace, but plenty to do.

Low season per week: £175.00–£200.00
High season per week: £350.00–£450.00
Short breaks: From £105.00–£120.00
3 cottages
Cards accepted: None

Directions: From Gloucester A40 take B4125 signposted Newent and Ross-on-Wye. Turn right opposite nurseries at Highleadon.

SELF-CATERING | **England's West Country**

145 : Cheltenham, Gloucestershire

Hotels-apart   ★★★★★ Gold Award

4,5,6 Imperial Court, Imperial Lane,
Cheltenham, Gloucestershire GL50 1PQ
Contact: Stephen Morgan
Tel: 01242 510523 • **Fax:** 01242 523163
Web: www.hotels-apart.com
E-mail: mail@hotels-apart.com

Hotels-apart is situated just off the Promenade in Cheltenham, the heart of The Cotswolds. The company offers ten five star, serviced two bedroom apartments with a twist of urban chic. We provide spacious comfort for that weekend away or a corporate stay. And our service is flexible, providing as much or as little as you like, depending on your requirements. Hotels-apart has developed from our desire to enable you to stay in an apartment that can provide a near perfect living space, leave you in peace, but also take care of you. All this, in the thriving town of Cheltenham with its tremendous shopping centre, theatre and world-famous racecourse.

Low season per week: £450.00–£650.00
High season per week: £650.00–£850.00
10 apartments
Cards accepted: American Express, Mastercard, Switch, Delta, Diners, Visa

Directions: The apartments are based on Imperial Lane, a one-way street connecting to the Promenade. There is no parking on the lane, secure care parking is available in the basement of Hotels-apart.

146 : Stow-on-the-Wold, Gloucestershire

Lilac Cottage   ★★★★★

The Counting House, Stow-on-the-Wold,
Gloucestershire GL54 1AL
Contact: Mary Wilson
Tel: 01451 830794 • **Fax:** 01451 830794
Web: broadoakcottages.fsnet.co.uk
E-mail: mary@broadoakcottages.fsnet.co.uk

Newly-restored and extended, early 19th century Lilac Cottage combines the peace of being set back from the road in this delightful part of The Cotswolds, with easy access to antique and gift shops, characterful pubs and first-class restaurants. Beamed ceilings, an open log fire, and Persian rugs add to the charm of this Cotswold stone dwelling. This is echoed by window seats in the double and twin bedrooms. Double-glazing adds to the tranquillity, while outside there is a delightful Costwold garden with large south-facing patio, BBQ and furniture.

Low season per week: £250.00–£285.00
High season per week: £400.00–£540.00
Short breaks: from £160.00–£190.00
4 cottages: 3 sleeping 4 people, and 1 sleeping 2 people
Cards accepted: None

Directions: From traffic lights on A429 main north/south Fosse Way (near BP Garage/Little Chef) take the A436 to Chipping Norton. Follow road until you see the Bell Inn on the right. Next left into Union Street. After 20 metres turn right into Mount Pleasant Close. After 80 metres you come to what appears to be a T-Junction. Turn right and Lilac Cottage is immediately in front of you.

England's West Country | **Self-Catering**

Lakeside location in the Cotswold Water Park. What House? award winner

147 : South Cerney, Gloucestershire

The Watermark Club

★★★★★

Isis Lakes, Spine Road, South Cerney, Gloucestershire GL7 5TL
Contact: Robert Cowley • **Tel:** 01285 869181 • **Fax:** 01285 862488
Web: www.watermarkclub.co.uk • **E-mail:** enquiries@watermarkclub.co.uk

These luxurious lakeside lodges in the heart of The Cotswolds sleep six to eight people and are equipped and furnished to an exceptional standard. The Watermark Club is open for self-catering holidays and short breaks all year round. The lodges have open plan lounge/dining rooms, with French windows leading to the deck overlooking the lakes. Most lodges have en suite facilities and contain everything to make your holiday perfect, from video/dvd to barbecues for those balmy Gloucestershire evenings. There are lots of activities on site or nearby, including golf, fishing and pony trekking as well as a gym and sauna. And Watermark is ideally placed to explore The Cotswolds and the surrounding towns and cities.

Low season per week:
£515.00–£730.00

High season per week:
£860.00–£1070.00

60 cottages

Cards accepted: Mastercard, Switch, Visa

Directions: The Watermark Club is situated just off the A419, only 4 miles from Cirencester – follow the B4696 and The Watermark Club is a few hundred yards along the Spine Road on your right hand side. For Spring Lakes, carry on past Isis and Windrush Lakes and take the next right into Station Road and Spring Lakes is found on the left hand side.

SELF-CATERING — England's West Country

148 : Devizes, Wiltshire

The Old Stables ★★★★

Tichborne's Farm, Etchilhampton,
Devizes, Wiltshire SN10 3JL
Contact: Jon and Judy Nash
Tel: 01380 862971 • **Fax:** 01380 862971
Web: www.tichbornes.co.uk
E-mail: info@tichbornes.co.uk

Tichborne's is a working farm and the three Old Stables luxury cottages are close to the farmhouse. All three sleep four people and one has wheelchair access. Each cottage is distinctively and tastefully decorated and furnished, and fully-equipped. The cottages are well away from the road, safe from traffic for children and ideal for birdwatchers. There is a patio and garden for barbecues or summer breakfast. Horses can be stabled and there is a pedigree herd of Aberdeen Angus cattle in the fields. The nearest pub is just a mile away and Devizes two and a half miles. In a five mile radius there are several excellent pubs and restaurants.

Low season per week: £224
High season per week: £448
Short breaks: from £112.00–£224.00
3 cottages: Each sleeping 4 people
Cards accepted: Mastercard, Switch, Visa, Delta, Diners, Euros

Directions: Devizes to Andover A342. Turn left at Lyon Monument over the hill. At bottom turn right and then first left to The Old Stables at Tichborne's Farm.

149 : Falmouth, Cornwall

The Foredeck ★★★★★

Apartment A, Maritime House,
Discovery Quay, Falmouth, Cornwall
Tel: 01749 870230 • **Fax:** 01749 870230
E-mail: derekpagets@aol.com

The property is brand new, built in the style and finish of the Maritime Museum and fitted to the highest standard. The Foredeck is the end apartment of six, occupying the first and second floor, with a very large roof garden/balcony extending to approximately 50 square metres. The apartment, which sleeps four to five people, is tastefully furnished throughout, with an ultra-modern, fully-equipped kitchen, oak floors and underfloor heating. Pubs, shops and restaurants are all just minutes away, and the Foredeck, which is next to Falmouth waterfront, enjoys superb views of the harbour.

Low season per week: £475.00–£650.00
High season per week: £750.00–£975.00
Short breaks: By negotiation
1 apartment
Cards accepted: Delta, Diners, mastercard, Switch, Visa, Euros

Directions: Follow signs for the Maritime Museum, The Foredeck is adjacent to the museum entrance.

England's West Country — Self-Catering

150 : Warminster, Wiltshire

Eastleigh Farm ★★★★

Eastleigh Farm Holiday Cottages, Bishopstrow, Warminster, Wiltshire BA12 7BE
Contact: Roz Walker
Tel: 01985 212325 • **Fax:** 01985 219191
Web: www.eastleighfarm-holidaycottages
E-mail: roz@chalkstream.co.uk

This former cow byre has been sympathetically converted into three cottages, each individual and completed to an exceptionally high standard, providing well-equipped comfortable, stylish and spacious accommodation. Each cottage has its own enclosed garden and ample undercover parking. Eastleigh is a working farm growing mainly crops. There are free-range ducks and chickens, as well as horses and sheep on the farm. We welcome 'well-behaved' dogs and are well-placed for the perfect walk in the woods and countryside. Eastleigh Farm is in an Area of Outstanding Natural Beauty, and in easy reach of Bath, Salisbury, Longleat, Stonehenge, Glastonbury and Cheddar Gorge.

Low season per week: £225.00–£300.00
High season per week: £280.00–£600.00
3 cottages
Cards accepted: None

Directions: Please see website for full details.

151 : Tiverton, Devon

Three Gates Farm ★★★★

Huntsham, near Tiverton, Devon EX16 7QH
Contact: Mrs Alison Spencer
Tel: 01398 331280 • **Fax:** 01398 332476
Web: www.threegatesfarm.co.uk
E-mail: alispencer34@hotmail.com

Three Gates is a converted 17th century farm, close to Exmoor and deep in the heart of the Devon countryside. Our barns have been renovated in keeping with their original style and provide high quality holiday accommodation. The barns sleep from two to six people in double and twin rooms. Each has a fully fitted kitchen with dishwasher and microwave, and open plan sitting areas with TV and video. Three barns have log burners for extra cosiness on winter breaks, and the largest barn boasts a spacious conservatory in which to dine. This is a great place for children, with the bonus of tranquillity and beautiful views for parents.

Low season per week: £150.00–£285.00
High season per week: £355.00–£910.00
5 cottages
Cards accepted: None

Directions: Take A361 from M5 Jct 27, signed Tiverton for 7 miles to roundabout (not first Tiverton sign). Turn left and at next roundabout, left again. After half mile, take left turn signed Chettiscombe. Cross dual carriageway and turn immediately right. Stay on road for 3.5 miles turning right at Van Post crossroads signed Huntsham. After mile, sharp left hand bend. Three Gates is 300 yards on the right.

Self-Catering — England's West Country

152 : Tiverton, Devon

Tiverton Castle

★★★★

Park Hill, Tiverton, Devon EX16 6RP
Tel: 01884 253200 • **Fax:** 01884 254200
Web: www.tivertoncastle.com • **E-mail:** tiverton.castle@ukf.net

This was the home of Princess Katherine in 1495 – and even she didn't find the comfort that now exists in the elegant and spacious apartments that have been created in Tiverton Castle. There are four apartments, three sleeping four people and the fourth sleeping two people. They are fully-equipped and welcoming, contrasting modern style with medieval magic. The castle itself is fascinating, and the holiday apartments are an ideal centre for visiting the superb countryside and coast of North and South Devon. In easy reach are Exeter, Exmoor and Dartmoor. Locally, the shops of Tiverton are a stroll away and at the castle there are the delights of croquet, regular barbecues and fresh seasonal produce from the kitchen garden.

Low season per week:
£246.00–£495.00

High season per week:
£345.00–£654.00

4 apartments

Cards accepted: None

Directions: From Junction 27 of the M5, take the A361 towards Tiverton. Follow signs to castle.

England's West Country — Self-Catering

153 : Cullompton, Devon

Glen Cottage

★★★★

Gaddon Down, Ashill,
Cullompton, Devon EX15 3NR
Tel: 01884 840331 • **Fax:** 01749 870230
Web: www.glencott.co.uk
E-mail: enqs@glencott.co.uk

The fully self-contained annex to our lovely country cottage offers charming and tastefully decorated accommodation in beautiful countryside. There is a good-sized cosy lounge with a woodburner, TV with full Sky package, and a music centre with CD player. The bedroom is light and airy with views of the garden and paddock beyond. It has a king-sized bed and ample storage space. The shower room and kitchen are both bright and fully-equipped with everything you need. The colourful and sunny garden, with its furniture and barbecue is a delightful place for al fresco dining. Glen Cottage is an ideal base to explore Dartmoor, Exmoor or the Quantocks and the tourist attractions that abound in this part of Devon.

Low season per week: £150.00–£220.00
High season per week: £260.00–£350.00
Short breaks: From £90.00–£150.00
1 cottage
Cards accepted: Delta, mastercard, Switch, Visa

Directions: Leave the M5 at junction 27. Drive through Uffculme towards Ashill. Glen Cottage is approximately 1 mile from village. Full directions on booking.

Clapper bridges

Explore the countryside that runs along the River Barle Ashway, near Ashway, Exmoor, and you'll come across a magnificent walkway of vast stone slabs, known as the Tarr Steps (pictured).

A type of ancient bridge known as a clapper bridge, the Tarr Steps is the longest and most elaborate of its type in England at 177ft (54m) in length. Possibly derived from the Angle Saxon 'cleaca' meaning 'stepping stone, a clapper bridge describes any bridge constructed from large, flat slabs of stone forming a level pathway over a river or stream. Indeed, many may well have begun as simple stepping stones, which later formed the piers upon which linking slabs of stone were balanced. While some clapper bridges consist simply of a single slab thrown across the stream, multi-span bridges have typically between two and five spans – Tarr Steps with its magnificent 17 spans, is an anomaly.

Most clapper bridges were built in the 14th century on packhorse routes, but a few appeared as late as the 18th and 19th centuries. They were simple and functional and, when routes changed or more superior structures superseded them, they were very often allowed to disappear. Today, only about 40 remain in England.

Clapper bridges are found in parts of the country where the local rock yields large slabs of strong stone. The greatest number are in Dartmoor: Postbridge, a lonely village in the heart of the Moor, has one of the finest of its type. It consists of three vast slabs of granite, some 17ft (5m) by 7ft (2m) in size, supported by four piers of granite blocks. Also on Dartmoor are Teignhead's bridge, built in 1790, and one over the Cowsic River at Two Bridges, built in 1837. At Wallabrook is a single-span clapper bridge, while the bridge at Yar Tor Down, Hexworthy, has three spans.

154 : Dorchester, Dorset

Stable Cottage ★★★★

School House, Rampisham,
Dorchester, Dorset DT2 0PR
Contact: Diane Read
Tel: 01933 83555
E-mail: usatschoolhouse@aol.com

Converted from a stable, this luxury detached cottage is set in the grounds of an old school built more than 150 years ago. Located in deepest West Dorset, it is surrounded by fields where birds and wildlife abound. It is a delightful and peaceful place for two, with a king-sized bedroom with en suite shower room. The maple-furnished kitchen is fully equipped and the sitting/dining room is tastefully decorated. Stable Cottage has villages nearby offering all facilities, including post offices, pubs and restaurants. There are numerous walks to choose in this beautiful countryside and the World Heritage coastline and historic sites are close by.

Low season per week: £250.00
High season per week: £295.00
1 cottage: Sleeping 2 people
Cards accepted: none

Directions: A37 from Dorchester or Yeovil. At Holywell crossroads take turning to Beaminster. Go through Evershot, after 1 mile turn left to Rampisham. School is next door to village hall.

155 : Dorchester, Dorset

Domineys Cottages ★★★★

Domineys, Buckland Newton,
near Dorchester, Dorset DT2 7BS
Contact: Mrs JD Gueterbock
Tel: 01300 345295 • **Fax:** 01300 345596
Web: www.domineys.com
E-mail: cottages@domineys.com

These three delightful, comfortable, early 19th century two bedroom cottages are situated peacefully on the edge of Buckland village, between the Dorset Downs and Blackmore Vale. They are furnished, equipped and maintained to a high standard, combining the cosy comfort of wood or coal burning fires with modern facilities throughout. Each cottage has its own furnished patio leading to a large garden. Heated swimming pool in owner's adjacent sheltered garden. Tucked away, off a no-through-road, Domineys Cottages make an ideal tranquil base to relax in, or from which to discover the beautiful South West.

Low season per week: £200.00–£360.00
High season per week: £360.00–£480.00
Short breaks: From £130.00–£230.00
3 cottages
Cards accepted: None

Directions: Buckland Newton is just over ten miles from Dorchester and Sherborne. Signposted via the A352 and the B3143.

England's West Country — Self-Catering

156 : Dorchester, Dorset

River Cottage ★★★★

Athelhampton, Dorchester,
Dorset DT2 7LG
Contact: Tracy Winder
Tel: 01305 848363 • **Fax:** 01305 848135
Web: www.athelhampton.co.uk
E-mail: enquiry@athelhampton.co.uk

River Cottage is located in the Grade 1 listed gardens of Athelhampton House on the banks of the River Piddle, just off the A35 and only five miles from the county town of Dorchester. Recently restored and refurbished to a high order, the one double, one king-size and one twin bedrooms have en suite facilities with both bath and shower. There is a beautifully furnished lounge and well-equipped modern kitchen. A decked patio area with seating and barbecue is ideal for those balmy evenings and there is a three-hole pitch and putt course. Guests of River Cottage enjoy complimentary admission to Athelhampton House and gardens and access to the bar and restaurant during normal opening hours.

Low season per week: £533.00–£797.00
High season per week: £811.00–£1153.00
Short breaks: From £408.00–£506
1 cottage
Cards accepted: American Express, Mastercard, Switch, Delta, Diners, Visa

Directions: Take the Northbrook junction off the A35 and follow the brown tourist signs to Athelhampton House.

157 : Lyme Regis, Dorset

Sea Tree House ★★★★

18 Broad Street,
Lyme Regis, Dorset DT7 3QE
Contact: David Parker
Tel: 01297 442244
Web: www.lymeregis.com/seatreehouse
E-mail: seatree.house@ukonline.co.uk

Experience Georgian elegance with a touch of romance in the heart of Lyme Regis. These spacious, completely private, one-bedroom apartments have large bright sitting rooms and each has south-facing bay windows with magnificent sea views. They are ideal for couples wanting to celebrate an anniversary or special occasion in style. Your kitchen is fully-equipped, with extras such as washer/dryer and dishwasher. Sea Tree House is just minutes from the beach, shops, restaurants and heritage coastal walks. And the immediate area is full of historic houses and places of interest.

Low season per week: £215.00–£365.00
High season per week: £415.00–£595.00
Short breaks: from £195.00–£375.00
2 apartments: Sleeping 2-3 people
Cards accepted: None

Directions: Take B3052 or B3165 into Lyme Regis. Sea Tree House is in the heart of the town, near the seafront with steps leading off Broad Street to the entrance.

Self-Catering | **England's West Country**

158 : Dartmouth, Devon

Sarah Elliot's Cottage ★★★★

Dittisham, near Dartmouth
Contact: Mrs C Clark c/o Dart Valley Cottages,
Parklands, Dartmouth Road,
Stoke Fleming, Devon TQ6 0GY
Tel: 01803 771127
Web: www.dartvalleycottages.co.uk
E-mail: enquiries@dartvalleycottages.co.uk

A cosy haven from the daily bustle, Sarah Elliot's Cottage is a dear little detached cottage just a few yards from the River Dart and the quay in Dittisham. Refurbished to a very high standard, it is full of beautiful furnishings, furniture and artefacts. It is fully-equipped throughout. The double bedroom has superb views of the River Dart and Dittisham. The small private patio garden offers peaceful relaxation after a day exploring the area, perhaps, or travelling slightly farther afield to Dartmouth, Torquay or Brixham to enjoy the marvellous amenities and beaches.

Low season per week: £260.00
High season per week: £570.00
Short breaks: From £169.00–£370.00
1 cottage
Cards accepted: Mastercard, Delta, Switch, Visa, Diners, American Express

Directions: From A38 Westbound, leave at Totnes exit. At Totnes take A381 to Halwell. A3122 to Dartmouth, turn left at Sportman's Arms signed Dittisham.

The South West Coast Path

Experience some of the magnificent coastal scenery in England with a hike on the South West Coast Path. Start in a dramatic fashion in the Exmoor national park, then continue the walk as it hugs the steep, wooded slopes that drop precipitously to the sea, with stupendous views of the Welsh coast. Further on, the section of Devon coastline from Westward Ho! to the Cornish border is equally lovely as it passes the lovely village of Clovelly and the heights of Hartland Point, with fine views of Lundy Island (pictured).

Rocky promontories and soaring cliffs, interspersed with superb sandy beaches and fishing villages nestling in tiny coves – the Cornish coast is spectacular stuff. The path re-enters Devon and, almost immediately, Plymouth. After the wild terrain of Bolt Head and Prawle Point, it meanders through the gentler landscape of the Devon Riviera and the seaside resorts of Paignton, Torquay, Teignmouth and Dawlish. In Dorset, chalk cliffs run from Lyme Regis to Lulworth, interrupted by the long finger of shingle, Chesil Bank. The walk ends on a scenic high point as it negotiates the limestone heights of the Isle of Purbeck, an island in name only.

As well as offering stunning scenery, the walk is rich in historical interest, from prehistoric hill forts in Dorset to the Palmerston Forts in Plymouth, or the abandoned village of Tyneham (Dorset) taken over by the army in 1943. In Cornwall, defunct engine houses and empty pilchard 'palaces' are relics of a rich industrial past.

Fauna and flora is abundant. The protruding coastline provides a landfall for migrating birds, while sub-tropical species of plants flourish in the mild climes of the south west. The Lizard, in particular, supports a unique flora, while army ranges at Lulworth, untouched by modern farming practices, have preserved a rare botanical habitat.

www.southwestcoastpath.com

England's West Country — Self-Catering

159 : Dartmouth, South Devon

Harbourside ★★★★★

Harbourside, South Town, Dartmouth, Devon
Contact: Coast and Country Cottages,
14 Mayors Avenue, Dartmouth, Devon TQ6 9NG
Tel: 01803 839499 • **Fax:** 01803 835744
Web: www.coastandcountry.co.uk
E-mail: dartmouth@coastandcountry.co.uk

Harbourside is just one of 300 properties in and around Dartmouth and Salcombe and throughout the beautiful South Devon coast and countryside available through Coast and Country Cottages, who have offices in Dartmouth, Salcombe and Kingsbridge. Our local teams will help you select the ideal property and location. We have stylish apartments, seaside family houses, beautifully converted barns and cosy cottages with prices to suit all budgets . All Coast and Country properties are VisitBritain inspected and/or personally inspected by the agency. As an example, Harbourside is stylishly furnished and well-equipped with spectacular river views.

Low season per week: £320.00
High season per week: £822.00
Short breaks: from £230.00
Over 300 properties
Cards accepted: Mastercard, Switch, Visa, Delta

Directions: M4/M5 or M25/M3/A303/A30 to Exeter, then A38 to Buckfastleigh. A384 to Totnes. A381 to Kingsbridge and Salcombe. B3207 to Dartmouth.

160 : Dartmouth, Devon

Sixes 'n' Sevens ★★★★

67 South Ford Road,
Dartmouth, Devon TQ6 9QT
Contact: Liz Harvey
Tel: (day) 01684 896325 (eve) 01531 631718
Web: www.no-67.co.uk
E-mail: enquiries@no-67.co.uk

Sixes 'n' Sevens is a stylish town house in the centre of Dartmouth. Beech, oak, stainless steel and leather finishes are combined in the spacious open plan kitchen, dining and living space. There is a separate first floor sitting room with coal-effect gas fire, DVD and video. There is also a luxury bathroom with separate bath and shower. Both bedrooms have king-sized beds, and the second bedroom also contains a full-size single bed. Sixes 'n' Sevens is within five minutes' level walk of the waterfront and is an ideal base from which to explore this beautiful part of Devon. High chair and travel cot available.

Low season per week: £365
Mid season per week: £440
High season: £575
1 house (sleeps 5)
Cards accepted: Mastercard, Switch, Visa, Delta

Directions: Southbound, take M5 to Exeter, exit A380, take Torbay Ring Road and ferry crossing. Coming from Plymouth, take A379 via Kingsbridge or A38 via Totnes.

South and South East England

Top: Grand Parade at night, Eastbourne, East Sussex

Middle: The Shakespeare Cliff, Dover, Kent

Bottom: Round Table in the great hall at the castle, Winchester, Hampshire

South and South East England

Buildings steeped in history. Magnificent gardens nurtured over the centuries. A vibrant and renowned arts scene. Breathtaking walks from the heights of the chalky Downs to the sandy and shingle shores of the south coast. **Experience** the best of all worlds in England's South and South East. **Discover** the stories and secrets hidden away in the fairytale castles of Leeds and Hever. **Explore** the historic backstreets of Canterbury, Winchester and Rye. Savour the hurly-burly of London, one of the world's most dynamic cities. **Relax** with a pint of real ale in an atmospheric country pub or savour the delights of world-class cuisine.

Rich in heritage from Roman times to the present day, England's South and South East is a fascinating melting pot of history, nature and culture. Whether you want to experience the buzz of the big city or the serenity of the countryside, you'll find your desires not just fulfilled, but exceeded.

Right: Bluebirds or not, the White Cliffs of Dover mean home to travellers returning to England's shores

Below: 1066 and all that – where William conquered at Hastings and poor Harold, sadly, got one in the eye

A place in history

Explore a region that has witnessed some of the most momentous events of British history, from the Battle of Hastings in 1066 to the air raids of the Second World War, the Gunpowder Plot of 1605 and the Great of Fire of London in 1666. Delight in seeing some of the country's most familiar landmarks. The gleaming White Cliffs of Dover, the magnificent cathedral at Canterbury, the spires of Oxford and, of course, the tower of Big Ben. Step back in time with the help of East Sussex's Saxon churches and Lullingstone's glorious Roman villa. It's pure chocolate box territory in the villages of Chiddingstone and Ightham Mote. There are modern masterpieces, too. The British Airways London Eye, the Thames Barrier at Greenwich and the Channel Tunnel. All examples of modern engineering at its most innovative and spectacular.

A shore thing

Leave the hurly-burly behind and head instead to

Southern
comforts

South and South East England

the beaches of the south coast. Eastbourne, Bournemouth, Brighton and Margate were all popular playgrounds for the Victorians. Queen Victoria herself frequently stayed at her Isle of Wight home, Osborne House. Today, the south coast is just as hip. Tourists and city dwellers flock here to sample the shopping and cultural scene. If you're looking for something a bit more peaceful, there are still many gems on this stretch of coastline. Try West Wittering, just down the Sussex coast from Brighton, Pevensey Bay, tucked in between Bexhill and Eastbourne, and Lepe in Hampshire, an area of outstanding beauty.

Live like a lord

Discover a life of privilege when you explore the South and South East's many awe-inspiring castles and palaces. Be enraptured by the dreamy Leeds Castle in Kent, called 'the loveliest castle in the world'. In the ultimate romantic gesture, Henry VIII restored it for his first queen, Catherine of Aragon. Other castles waiting to be fallen in love with are those of Hever, Bodiam, Scotney and Windsor. Henry VIII also lived in the magnificent Hampton Court Palace. Will you find your way out of the ingenious garden maze?

At one with nature

You'll be amazed at how little the region's economic power has affected the beauty of the countryside. It's not for nothing that Kent is called the Garden of England. Commune with nature with a ramble up and down dale or take in the more gentle delights of a country garden – it's a nature lovers' paradise. Take the paths and

South and South East England

bridleways of the New Forest – watching out for wild ponies as they gently graze. Walkers can follow the ancient tracks of the South Downs Way or the Ridgeway that eventually meets the Thames Path. Feeling full of beans? Hop over to the Isle of Wight and circumnavigate the island in 69 glorious miles. Or sample the beauty of country gardens such as Sissinghurst Castle Garden near Tunbridge Wells, the loving creation of Vita Sackville-West and her husband.

Other garden gems include Emmetts at Kent, Polesden Lacey in Surrey and Stowe, near Buckingham. Spend hours in the Royal Botanic Gardens at Kew, the jewel in the crown of English gardens. Explore the garden's incredible 300 acres or wonder at the exotic plants in the world-famous Palm House. All without even leaving London.

Get in the festive spirit

Catch the buzz of a festival or event, whatever the time of year. From rock 'n' pop to hops, from rowing to sailing, from Dickens to dancing round a maypole – the rich tapestry of life. In London, there's the Notting Hill Carnival or the Lord Mayor's Show. The Brighton Festival comes to the hip seaside town every May – a true celebration of the arts. If you're looking for the epitome of elegance, dress up for Glyndebourne's season of opera. Witness sedan chair races in The Pantiles of Tunbridge Wells, or see the streets of Broadstairs thronged with Victorian costumes during the Dickens Festival. There's rock, pop and hip hop mixed with a liberal dose of mud at August's Reading Festival. Don't forget the Henley Regatta or Cowes Week – two internationally famous spectacles.

Tempt your tastebuds

Embark on an epicurean journey through the vineyards, breweries, orchards, oyster houses and fine restaurants of the South East. Stock up with juicy strawberries, raspberries and gooseberries at a farm shop, and wash them down with Monks Delight, a Kentish cider infused with honey and spices. Sample ales such as Bishops Finger and Spitfire – the occasional oast house reveals the area's brewing heritage. Want to know how beer is produced – visit the Whitbread Hop Farm in Beltring for an insight. Oyster connoisseurs flock to Whitstable to sample these salty fruits of the sea. Dining out in Bray, near Windsor, is a gastronome's dream. The small town has the distinction of not one, but two Michelin three-starred restaurants, the Fat Duck and the Waterside Inn. You'll find a third at TV mega-chef Gordon Ramsey's eponymous restaurant in Chelsea.

Right: One of the most famous skylines in the world – the Palace of Westminster, Mother of Parliaments

Below: Prinny's favourite hiding place – Brighton and the marvellously ornate palace he built for himself

South and South East England

City lights

Exciting, dynamic and cosmopolitan. London has something new and exciting to experience round every corner. Historic Westminster Abbey, the Houses of Parliament and the Tower of London. The new pretenders are Tate Modern, the London Eye and the stunning reconstruction of Shakespeare's Globe. On rainy days, the Natural History Museum, the V&A and the National Gallery cannot be missed – admission is free. The West End is abuzz with theatres, bars, restaurants and nightclubs. Shopaholics head for Oxford Street, Knightsbridge or the more eclectic markets of Camden, Borough and Spitalfields. Discover the excitement of the London Marathon, cricket at Lord's and Wimbledon fortnight. Relax on a riverboat as it cruises along the Thames east to west from Greenwich to Richmond. Spend a perfect Sunday strolling on Hampstead Heath or ice-skating at Somerset House. End with a hearty lunch at one of the city's highly rated gastropubs. It's what Sundays were invented for!

Contact

Visit London
tel: 020 7234 5800
www.visitlondon.com

Tourism South East
tel: 023 8062 5505
www.visitsoutheastengland.com

South and South East England — Hotels and Guest Accommodation

South and South East England — Hotels and Guest Accommodation

161 : Richmond, London

Chalon House ♦♦♦♦♦ Gold Award

Chalon House, 8 Spring Terrace,
Paradise Road, Richmond TW9 1 LW
Contact: Ann Zaina
Tel: 020 8332 1121 • **Fax:** 020 8332 1131
Web: www.chalonhouse-Richmond.co.uk
E-mail: chalonhouse@hotmail.com

A Georgian gem, highly commended in the London Tourism Awards in 2003, this three-bedroom guest house offers delightful accommodation within easy reach of central London. All bedrooms are en suite and tastefully furnished, with all the facilities you need for a comfortable stay. There is a garden for relaxation – that is if the nearby attractions of Kew Gardens and the characterful pubs along the Thames don't lure you away. The large, comfortable beds and splendid breakfasts are sure to call you back, however – as our regular guests will testify.

Bed & Breakfast per night:
Single room from £70.00–£75.00
Double room from £80.00–£85.00

Bedrooms: 1 double/2 twin
Bathrooms: 3 en suite
Parking: Available
Cards accepted: None, Euros.

Directions: At Richmond Circus on A316 follow directions to town centre. Pass the station, at first traffic lights turn left into Sheen Road. Chalon House is at the junction with Paradise Road.

162 : Hook, Hampshire

Tylney Hall Hotel ★★★★ Gold Award

Rotherwick, Hook,
Hampshire RG27 9AZ
Tel: 01256 764881 • **Fax:** 01256 768141
Web: www.tylneyhall.com
E-mail: reservations@tylneyhall.com

Amidst 60 acres of Hampshire countryside lies Tylney Hall, an independently-owned Grade II listed country house hotel. The 112 bedrooms are beautifully decorated and fitted with all modern amenities. The award-winning Oak Room Restaurant offers innovative menus for people dining for business or pleasure, complemented by an extensive wine cellar and attentive, yet discreet, service. Twelve individually designed function suites cater for up to 120 people, while extensive and exclusive leisure facilities allow guests to relax in the luxurious surroundings.

Bed & Breakfast per night:
Single room from £135.00–£420.00
Double room from £165.00–£450.00

Dinner, Bed & Breakfast per person, per night:
£112.50–£245.00 (2 nights minimum)

Bedrooms: 59 double/23 twin/29 suites/1 family
Bathrooms: All en suite
Parking: Available
Cards accepted: American Express, Delta, Diners, Mastercard, Switch, Visa, Euros

Directions: Please see website for maps and directions.

Hotels and Guest Accommodation — **South and South East England**

Stunning walks and wonderful sights in beautiful countryside

163 : Andover, Hampshire

Queen Anne Cottage ◆◆◆◆

Village Street, Goodworth Clatford, Near Andover, Hampshire SP11 7RN
Contact: Michael Russell • **Tel:** 01264 323500
Web: www.queenannecottage.co.uk • **E-mail:** mike@queenannecottage.co.uk

This delightful 17th century thatched cottage is a charming marriage of the very old and the very new. The oak-beamed sitting room opens into the new orangery, with rustic slate floor. This is where our guests enjoy generous full English breakfasts – or more modest fare. There may even be exotic wild mushrooms on the menu, if the proprietor has been lucky enough to find some. Accommodation in our new barn is en suite, with lovely slate-floored shower rooms with waterfall showers. Each bedroom is beautifully co-ordinated and fully equipped, including a little welcoming treat to make you feel very much at home. The garden is a wildlife haven and all round are the fascinating sights and attractions of this lovely part of England.

Bed & Breakfast per night:
Single room from £39.00–£45.00
Double room from £70.00

Dinner, Bed & Breakfast per person, per night: £53.50–£80.00

Bedrooms: 1 double/1 twin/1 single

Bathrooms: 3 en suite

Parking: Available

Cards accepted: American Express, Mastercard, Visa, Switch, Delta, Diner

Directions: From A303 take slip road to Stockbridge, at junction follow road to Stockbridge for about 1.5 miles. Turn right to Goodworth Clatford, at junction turn left to Stockbridge and the cottage is 300 yards on the right, opposite Clatford Arms pub.

South and South East England — Hotels and Guest Accommodation

164 : Farnham, Surrey

Bishop's Table — Silver Award

West Street, Farnham,
Surrey GU9 7DR
Contact: Mariam Verjee
Tel: 01252 710222 • **Fax:** 01252 733494
Web: www.bishopstable.com
E-mail: welcome@bishopstable.com

The Marquis of Lothian lived here, so you can tell the quality of this 18th century hotel and restaurant set in its own secluded, walled garden away from the bustle of the town centre. All bedrooms are individually decorated and equipped to a high standard, with the bridal suite having a Victorian half-tester bed. The Bishop's Table thrives on its reputation for guest service and comfort, and nowhere is this more evident than in the Double AA rosette restaurant – one of the finest in the area for its cuisine and carefully selected cellar from the Old and New Worlds.

Bed & Breakfast per night:
Single room from £95.00–£115.00
Double room from £105.00–£165.00

Bedrooms: 8 double/6 single/1 twin
Bathrooms: 15 en suite
Cards accepted: Mastercard, Visa, Switch, American Express

Directions: Convenient to both the M3 and M25 motorways. A3 and A331.

165 : Fordingbridge, Hampshire

The Three Lions ♦♦♦♦♦ Gold Award

Stuckton, near Fordingbridge, Hampshire SP6 2HF
Contact: Maike and Jayne Womersley
Tel: 01452 652489 • **Fax:** 01425 656144
Web: www.thethreelionsrestaurant.co.uk
E-mail: thethreelions@btinternet.com

Built in 1863, The Three Lions nestles on the edge of the New Forest and is owned by Mike and Jayne Womersley. All rooms are en suite, airy and very peaceful and overlooking well-manicured gardens with the forest beyond. Good food is a keystone of The Three Lions and the restaurant, with its 150-bin wine list, is highly rated in all major UK food guides. It has won numerous awards and holds three AA Rosettes. There is an open-air whirlpool therapy spa and sauna for residents to enjoy. Also available are pony-trekking, cycling and golf.

Bed & Breakfast per night:
Single room from £65.00–£85.00
Double room from £75.90–£96.00

Dinner, Bed & Breakfast per person, per night:
£220.50–£270.00 (2 day break)

Bedrooms: 17 double/10 twin/2 four poster
Bathrooms: 31 en suite
Parking: Available
Cards accepted: Mastercard, Visa, Switch, Delta

Directions: 1 mile south east of Fordingbridge, look for Q8 garage and follow brown tourist signs located opposite garage.

Hotels and Guest Accommodation | **South and South East England**

The Landmarks of White Horse Hill

Settlers first came to the Lambourn Downs of South Oxfordshire around 5,000 years ago – the area is liberally sprinkled with traces of their existence.

But it is the stuff of myth and legend that provides the best explanation for a series of mysterious landmarks to be found here.

The Vale of the White Horse, near Uffington, is dominated by the strange, elongated chalk carving from which it takes its name. Believed to have been carved in the image of the horse goddess, Epona, in about 50BC by the Iron Age tribes who lived in the nearby hill fort, it is possibly the oldest chalk carving in the country, and the only one that faces right.

Just below the horse is a mound known as Dragon's Hill – asserted by local legend to be the place where St George killed the dragon. The bare chalk on its top and sides, the story goes, were caused by hot streams of dragon's blood, over which the grass can never grow.

Running along the ridge of the Downs, just south of the White Horse, is the Ridgeway, used by people of the New Stone Age and one of the oldest roads in Britain. It leads south west past Wayland's Smithy, a neolithic burial chamber dating from around 3500BC.

This remote spot is one of many places throughout Europe (usually either caves or burial mounds) imagined as the home of Wayland, the fearsome Saxon blacksmith-god.

The figure of the smith is also associated with another curiosity: a strangely-shaped stone beside the road leading south from Kingston Lisle, just east of the White Horse.

The 'Blowing Stone' was supposedly brought here by a blacksmith living nearby who blew into its many holes to create a gruesome, moaning roar. Another legend tells that King Alfred summoned his troops to battle by blowing through the stone.

www.mysteriousbritain.co.uk

---

166 : New Forest, Hampshire

Cloud Hotel   Silver Award

Meerut Road, Brockenhurst,
New Forest, Hampshire SO42 7TD
Contact: Avril Owton
Tel: 01590 622165 • **Fax:** 01590 622818
Web: www.cloudhotel.co.uk
E-mail: enquiries@cloudhotel.co.uk

The Cloud is a small, popular country hotel perfectly located on the edge of Brockenhurst in the New Forest. It enjoys superb views of the open forest and is an ideal base for riding, cycling and exploring the New Forest. The tastefully-furnished bedrooms are well appointed, with bathrooms en suite and most have forest views. The charming restaurant specialises in traditional English food, with a vegetarian menu available. The Tiller bar has a theatrical theme, with memorabilia of the proprietor Avril Owton's days as a Tiller Girl. Log fires in winter and an attractive garden make the Cloud a hotel for all seasons.

Bed & Breakfast per night:
Single room from £68.00–£72.00;
Double room from £110.00–£144.00

Dinner, Bed & Breakfast per person, per night:
£74.00–£95.00

Bedrooms: 10 double/4 twin/3 single/1 family

Bathrooms: 18 en suite

Parking: Available

Cards accepted: Mastercard, Switch, Visa

Directions: From M27 junction 1, take the A337 to Lyndhurst New Forest. On entering Brockenhurst take first right into Meerut Road. Hotel is 300 yards on right.

South and South East England — **Hotels and Guest Accommodation**

Acclaimed as one of the premier guest accommodations in Southern England

167 : Lymington, Hampshire

The Nurse's Cottage

♦♦♦♦♦ Gold Award

Station Road, Sway, Lymington, Hampshire SO41 6BA
Tony Barnfield, Chef/Proprietor • **Tel:** 01590 683402 • **Fax:** 01590 683402
Web: www.nursescottage.co.uk • **E-mail:** nurses.cottage@lineone.net

There's nowhere quite like The Nurse's Cottage! The former home to a succession of district nurses, this charming little cottage is now widely acclaimed as one of Southern England's premier guest accommodations. A typical Dinner of House Specialities might include mushroom millefeuille followed by guinea fowl in a white wine, tarragon and cream sauce, plus a medley of miniature desserts or West Country cheeses. Local produce is used wherever possible – from Sway sausages at breakfast, to Beaulieu chocolates with tea or coffee after dinner. On the wine list nearly 70 choices from around the world, including wines from Sway and Brockenhurst, offer a selection worthy of much grander establishments. Situated four miles from the coast at Lymington, Sway is a quiet, but thriving village surrounded by the unique open countryside of the New Forest and giving easy access to places of interest like Exbury Gardens and the National Motor Museum at Beaulieu.

Directions: Off B3055 in the centre of Sway village, close to the shops. Easy walking distance from Sway railway station.

Dinner, Bed & Breakfast per person, per night: £75.00

Nurse's Cottage bargain break packages are available: Three nights half board: £210.00 Seven nights £420.00

Bedrooms: 2 double/1 single/1 twin
Bathrooms: 4 en suite
Parking: Available
Cards accepted: American Express, Delta, Mastercard, Switch, Visa

Hotels and Guest Accommodation   **South and South East England**

168 : Milford-on-Sea, Hampshire

Alma Mater   Silver Award

4 Knowland Drive, Milford-on-Sea,
Hampshire SO41 0RH
Tel: 01590 642811 • **Fax:** 01590 642811
Web: www.newforestalmamater.co.uk
E-mail: bandbalmamater@aol.com

Alma Mater is a large Georgian-style chalet bungalow overlooking a landscaped garden in a quiet residential area. It is set in the unique village of Milford-on-Sea close to Keyhaven, the beach and the clifftops with their views across The Solent. Comfortable en suite, centrally-heated bedrooms are tastefully decorated and fully-equipped, with fitted furniture to create space. Breakfasts are superb – four courses, ranging from full English to Continental or Vegetarian – with free range produce. Alma Mater is ideally placed for the New Forest, Beaulieu, Hurst Castle and Lymington with its renowned yachting facilities.

Directions: From Lymington follow signs for New Milton and the west. Continue for 2 miles and bear left on B3058 to Milford-on-Sea. After passing South Lawn Hotel turn right into Manor Road and then first left into Knowland Drive. Third bungalow on right with AA and ETC sign on the gate.

Bed & Breakfast per night:
Single room from £35.00–£40.00
Double room from £56.00–£70.00

Dinner, Bed & Breakfast per person, per night:
£42.00–£45.00

Bedrooms: 2 double/1 twin
Bathrooms: 2 and 1 shower room
Parking: Off road, secure
Cards accepted: None

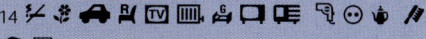

Visitor Attraction Quality Assurance

VisitBritain operates a Visitor Attraction Quality Assurance Service. Participating attractions are visited annually by trained, impartial assessors who look at all aspects of the visit, from initial telephone enquiries to departure, customer service to catering, as well as all facilities and activities. Only those attractions which have been assessed by VisitBritain and meet the standard receive the quality marque, your sign of a 'Quality Assured Visitor Attraction'.

Look out for the quality marque and visit with confidence.

South and South East England — Hotels and Guest Accommodation

169 : Chichester, West Sussex

The Horse & Groom   ◆◆◆◆

The Horse & Groom, East Ashling,
Chichester, West Sussex PO18 9AX
Contact: Michael Martell
Tel: 01243 575339 • **Fax:** 01243 575560
Web: www.thehorseandgroomchichester.com
E-mail: bookings@thehorseandgroomchichester.com

Mike and Michelle Martell welcome you to the Horse & Groom, a unique 17th century country pub, restaurant and bed and breakfast. During their ten years as hosts, Mike and Michelle have carried out substantial renovations throughout the building, including the cellar and the flint barn which houses the guests in stylish and cosy comfort. They have also built the reputation of the Horse & Groom as a hospitable and pleasant place to have a drink or a meal and enjoy a pleasant break, offering excellent value for money. East Ashling is near Chichester and the Horse & Groom is ideal as a base to explore the beauties of the South Downs and the southern coast.

Bed & Breakfast per night:
Single room from £35.00–£45.00
Double room from £55.00–£70.00

Bedrooms: 11 twin/single
Bathrooms: 11 en suite
Cards accepted: Mastercard, Visa, Switch, American Express, Delta

Directions: Head west on the B2178 from Chichester for 3 miles to East Ashling. The Horse & Groom is in the centre of the village.

170 : Chichester, West Sussex

Royal Oak Inn   ◆◆◆◆◆ Gold Award

Pook Lane, East Lavant,
Chichester, West Sussex PO18 0AX
Contact: Nick or Hayley
Tel: 01243 527434
Web: www.sussexlive.co.uk/royaloakinn
E-mail: nickroyaloak@aol.com

Just two miles north of Chichester and set amidst rolling countryside, the Royal Oak Inn is in the picturesque village of East Lavant close to a whole host of attractions, including shopping in Chichester and the renowned Festival Theatre. All bedrooms are individually styled with every modern facility, including plasma audio/video system, CD, direct dialling and internet access. Dining at the Royal Oak is a real experience – with our cuisine earning a widespread and growing reputation and our imaginative wine list adding to the pleasure. When you stay at the Royal Oak, you dine and sleep in style.

Bed & Breakfast per night:
Single room from £60.00–£70.00
Double room from £80.00–£120.00

Bedrooms: 6
Bathrooms: All en suite
Parking: Available
Cards accepted: American Express, Mastercard, Visa, Switch, Delta

Directions: Take the A3 from London to Milford Junction. Take A286 via Midhurst to Lavant. Take left turn signposted East Lavant. Go over the humped-back bridge and we are on the left hand side.

Hotels and Guest Accommodation **South and South East England**

Acclaimed carvery and comfort of this haven in beautiful West Sussex

171 : Steyning, West Sussex

The Old Tollgate

★★★ Silver Award

The Street, Bramber, Steyning, West Sussex BN44 3WE
Contact: Reina Alston • **Tel:** 01903 879394 • **Fax:** : 01903 813399
Web: www.oldtollgatehotel.com • **E-mail:** info@oldtollgatehotel.com

The award-winning carvery – often described as unrivalled in the region – is a key attraction of this outstanding hotel set in the lovely old village of Bramber at the foot of the South Downs. There are 31 bedrooms, beautifully designed in four distinctive styles and all en suite and fully equipped with telephones, toiletries and mini bars. Two rooms have four-poster beds. The lounges and bars are ideal for relaxation – as, indeed, is the scrumptious carvery – after a day exploring the nearby historical sites, or, not much farther afield, the south coast from Brighton to Bournemouth and the glorious Sussex countryside.

Bed & Breakfast per night: Single room from £86.95–£137.95; Double room from £95.90–£146.90

Dinner, Bed & Breakfast per person, per night: £59.50–£85.00 (min 2 nights)

Bedrooms: 17 double/10 twin/2 four poster

Bathrooms: 31 en suite

Parking: Available

Cards accepted: Mastercard, Visa, Switch, Delta, American Express, Diners

Directions: From A24 or A27, take A283 signposted to Steyning then follow signs to Bramber. Brown tourist signs advertise hotel.

At-a-glance symbols are explained on the flap inside the back cover

South and South East England | **Hotels and Guest Accommodation**

Charming English country hotel set in picturesque quayside Bosham

172 : Bosham, Chichester, West Sussex

The Millstream Hotel, Bosham

★★★ Gold Award

Bosham Lane, Bosham, Chichester, West Sussex PO18 8HL
Contact: Antony Wallace • **Tel:** 01234 573234 • **Fax:** 01234 575459
Web: www.millstream-hotel.co.uk • **E-mail:** info@millstream-hotel.co.uk

The Millstream Hotel consists of an 18th century malthouse and adjoining cottages, which have been tastefully restored and seamlessly joined. Period furniture, a grand piano, and freshly-cut flowers make the drawing room a delightful place in which to relax. The bedrooms are immaculately kept and individually decorated with pretty, well co-ordinated colours. The eponymous Millstream runs through colourful beds and manicured lawns to the front of the hotel, before flowing into the harbour a few hundred yards away. What makes The Millstream so special is its relaxed ambience, the superb quality of the food and the disarming blend of friendliness and efficiency of the staff.

Bed & Breakfast per night:
Single room from £85.00–£95.00;
Double room from £135.00–£155.00
Dinner, Bed & Breakfast per person, per night: £73.00–£95.00
Bedrooms: 18 double/8 twin/4 single/2 family/3 suites
Bathrooms: 35 en suite
Parking: Available
Cards accepted: American Express, Delta, Diners, Mastercard, Switch, Visa

Directions: From Chichester or Havant take the A259 to Bosham. At Swan roundabout follow brown signs to hotel which is 1 mile away.

173 : Chichester, West Sussex

Friary Close

♦♦♦♦ Silver Award

Friary Close, Friary Lane, Chichester,
West Sussex PO19 1UF
Tel: 01243 527194 • **Fax:** 01243 533876
E-mail: b&b@friaryclose.co.uk
Web: www.friaryclose.co.uk

Friary Close, a Grade II listed house bestrides the ancient city wall of Chichester, secluded from the bustle of the city by its own large grounds and walled garden, but within easy reach of all the attractions like the cathedral, theatre and Roman palace. All rooms are tastefully furnished and fully-equipped and the gardens are a restful oasis. Breakfasts are buffet-style and are an ideal foundation for a day exploring this fascinating corner of the south coast. Chichester Harbour, Pagham Harbour, Arundel Castle and glorious Goodwood are all easy to get to. The bus and mainline stations are both near to Friary Close, making a convenient venue for your stay.

Directions: Via St Johns Street or Market Avenue. At south end of St Johns Street look for Stride's estate agents, go towards Chichester District Council office and public car park. Turn left into Friary Lane just before entrance to car park. Friary Close is at south end of Friary Lane.

Bed & Breakfast per night:
Double room from £58.00–£70.00

Bedrooms: 3 twin
Bathrooms: 3 en suite
Parking: Available
Cards accepted: Mastercard, Switch, Visa, Delta

174 : Ventnor, Isle of Wight

Under Rock

♦♦♦♦

Shore Road, Bonchurch,
Ventnor, Isle of Wight
Contact: James Pritchett
Tel: 01983 855274
Web: www.under-rock.co.uk

There's nothing like a sea crossing to make a holiday or a weekend break a little bit special. The Isle of Wight is quite different from the mainland and the "away from it all" atmosphere of its south coast even more so. The carriage drive winds through a sub-tropical acre of rocks and foliage to the unusual stone house, once the home of Robert Peel's poet nephew, Edmund. Furnished in a period way, pretty textiles, interesting lamps and paintings all achieve a relaxed atmosphere and provide a pleasant and homely stay. Under Rock is for people wishing to be off the beaten track in a period setting, but with nearby eating places and amenities – not just a bed for the night.

Bed & Breakfast per night:
Double room from £56.00–£60.00

Bedrooms: 2 double/1 twin
Bathrooms: 1/2 en suite
Parking: Available
Cards accepted: None

Directions: 45 minutes' drive from ferry. Between Shanklin and Ventnor turn off A3055 to Bonchurch.

South and South East England — Hotels and Guest Accommodation

175 : Crystal Palace, London

Melrose House ★★★★

89 Lennard Road, Crystal Palace, London SE20 7LY
Tel: 020 8776 8884 • **Fax:** 020 8325 7737
Web: www.uk-bedandbreakfast.com
E-mail: melrose.hotel@virgin.net

A family run guest house in a substantial Victorian town house, Melrose House offers an escape from the hustle and bustle of London, while being in easy reach of the capital's amenities and amusements. All rooms are fully-equipped and en suite. Breakfasts, which are inclusive, are served in the dining room, which leads on to the garden room and pretty garden. We are in easy reach of main airports, including Gatwick, Heathrow and City, and Waterloo is a short train ride away, giving Eurostar access to Paris in only three hours.

Bed & Breakfast per night:
Single room from £40.00–£55.00
Double room from £55.00–£70.00

Bedrooms: 3 double/2 twin/1 suite
Bathrooms: 6 en suite
Parking: Available
Cards accepted: Mastercard, Visa, Switch

Directions: By train from Victoria Station to Penge East, or to New Beckenham from Charing Cross, Waterloo and London Bridge. By car off the South Circular at Streatham to Crystal Palace.

176 : Canterbury, Kent

Magnolia House ◆◆◆◆◆ Gold Award

36 St Dunstan's Terrace,
Canterbury, Kent CT2 8AX
Tel: 01227 765121 • **Fax:** 01227 765121
Web: www.magnoliahousecanterbury.co.uk
E-mail: magnolia_house_canterbury@yahoo.com

This charming late Georgian home offers a warm and friendly welcome and first-class accommodation just ten minutes' walk from the city centre and the magnificent cathedral. The immaculate en suite rooms are beautifully furnished and are fully equipped with TV, fridge, and tea and coffee making facilities to make your stay as comfortable as possible. Breakfasts are a key point of the day and cater for all tastes, setting guests up in style for a day exploring the city, coast or countryside. Magnolia House has its own walled garden and the guest sitting room is a relaxing oasis, well-furnished with books, magazines and games.

Bed & Breakfast per night:
Single room from £55.00–£55.00
Double room from £85.00–£125.00

Bedrooms: 6 double/2 twin/1 single/
Bathrooms: 7 en suite
Cards accepted: Mastercard, Visa, Switch/Delta, American Express

Directions: M2/A2 to Canterbury. At first roundabout, take the left fork signposted to the university. We are in the third turning on the right.

The Eastern Cotswolds

Mirroring the geography of the whole country, the Cotswolds slope gently down from west to east. Oxfordshire and the Eastern Cotswolds may not have great blustery tops and panoramic vistas, but the towns and villages – the true beauty of the area – still invite superlatives from visitors.

To discover some of these gems, follow the Thames Path, which takes the route of the river (known in these parts as the Isis). Buscot, west of the attractive market town of Faringdon, is perhaps the highlight of the upper Thames. An unspoilt estate village, it has a riverside church and two 18th century properties belonging to the National Trust: the Old Parsonage (open by appointment only) and the larger Buscot Park, containing an important collection of paintings and set within fine parkland. Five miles downstream are Pusey House Gardens.

The evocatively named river Windrush flows over grey stone which has been used for St Paul's Cathedral, many Oxford colleges and – on a more modest scale – the houses of Burford, a real Cotswold gem. Between Burford and Witney, an appealing town whose prosperity derived from blanket-making, is Minster Lovell, a charming, tucked-away village with a dark secret. Desperate to escape capture after involvement in a failed insurrection, a 15th-century Lord Lovell had himself walled up by a servant, who suddenly died. The lord's remains were supposedly discovered in 1718. The ruined hall is open to the public.

The Evenlode makes its meandering way through remnants of the ancient Wychwood Forest towards Charlbury, where the quaint museum presents the history of this peaceful, former weaving town. The Glyme, a tributary of the Evenlode, feeds the lakes of the magnificent Blenheim Palace (pictured), given to the Duke of Marlborough by a grateful nation in the early 18th century after his victory in the War of the Spanish Succession. Nearby Woodstock is another picture postcard village, perfect for a dawdle and a traditional cream tea.

www.nationaltrust.org.uk
Minster Lovell, www.english-heritage.com
Charlbury Museum, Tel: 01608 810060
Blenheim Palace, Tel: 08700 602080,
www.blenheimpalace.com

South and South East England — Hotels and Guest Accommodation

177 : Near Dover, Kent

Alkham Court ◆◆◆◆ Gold Award

Meggett Lane, South Alkham,
near Dover, Kent CT15 7DG.
Tel: 01303 892056
Contact: Wendy Burrows
Web: www.alkhamcourt.co.uk
E-mail: wendy.burrows@alkhamcourt.co.uk

Our family farm set in the heart of the Alkham Valley, with spectacular views over the Kent Downs, an area of outstanding natural beauty, offers guests a chance to unwind and enjoy high quality food and accommodation. Our rooms are pretty and individually decorated, with antique furniture. Kingsize, twin beds and ground floor rooms are available with their own separate entrance. We have the perfect base for walking, biking, riding and touring our beautiful countryside, with Canterbury, the White Cliffs of Dover, Leeds Castle and Sissinghurst Gardens all nearby. Enjoy our hospitality and delicious farmhouse breakfast in the conservatory, with special views over the countryside.

Directions: Exit M20/A20 Canterbury A260. Turn left towards Alkham, take second turning on right into Meggett Lane, Alkham Court is nearly at the top of the hill on the right.

Bed & Breakfast per night:
Single room from £35.00–£45.00
Double room from £55.00–£65.00

Bedrooms: 1 double/1 twin/1 double/family
Bathrooms: 2 en suite/1 private
Parking: On site
Cards accepted: Mastercard, Visa, Switch/Delta, American Express, Euros

178 : Forest Row, East Sussex

Ashdown Park Hotel ★★★★

Wych Cross, Forest Row,
East Sussex RH18 5JR
Contact: Dominic Osborne
Tel: 01342 824988 • **Fax:** 01342 826206
Web: www.ashdownpark.com
E-mail: reservations@ashdownpark.com

Ashdown Park is an impressive Victorian mansion set in the heart of Ashdown Forest – home to Pooh Bear – yet within easy reach of London, Gatwick Airport and the South Coast. Each of the bedrooms and suites is beautifully decorated, many enjoying breathtaking views of the surrounding gardens and parklands. There are excellent leisure facilities at Ashdown, with an indoor pool, sauna and steam room, gym, games room, his and her spa treatments riding and golf. To relax in the evenings, the award-winning Anderida Restaurant offers an unforgettable dining experience, complemented by an extensive wine collection.

Directions: See website for maps and directions.

Bed & Breakfast per night:
Single room from £135.00–£335.00
Double room from £165.00–£365.00

Dinner, Bed & Breakfast per person, per night:
£112.50–£210.00 (2 nights minimum)

Bedrooms: 106
Bathrooms: 106 en suite
Parking: Available
Cards accepted: American Express, Visa, Mastercard, Diners Club, JCB

Hotels and Guest Accommodation | **South and South East England**

Ten minutes' walk to Dymchurch blue flag beach. Ten minutes' drive to Port Lympne

179 : Romney Marsh, Kent

Haguelands Farm

◆◆◆◆◆ Gold Award

Burmarsh, Romney Marsh, Kent TN29 0JR
Contact: Anne Clifton-Holt • **Tel:** 01303 872273 • **Fax:** 01303 873266
Web: www.haguelandsfarm.co.uk • **E-mail:** anne@aaclifton.ltd.uk

Haguelands Farm offers guests a warm welcome to the beautiful Romney Marsh area of Kent. The bedrooms are tastefully furnished and fully-equipped and the guests' sitting room with log fire is a joy to relax in. This is a working farm and all produce is locally sourced – you can even gather your own eggs for breakfast! Beauty and health treatments are available from our trained therapists and the garden offers tranquillity with many quiet spots to sit and enjoy yourself. There is also lots to do – nearby are the blue flag sands of Dymchurch, while Canterbury, Rye, Leeds Castle, Port Lympne Zoo and Chartwell are just some of the places to visit, just half an hour's drive away.

Bed & Breakfast per night:
Single room from £55.00–£60.00
Double room from £65.00–£70.00

Dinner, Bed & Breakfast per person, per night: £27.50–£35.00

Bedrooms: 2 double
Bathrooms: 2 en suite
Parking: Available
Cards accepted: None

Directions: 65 Miles from London. M20 exit junction 11. Follow signs to Hythe. Join A259 towards Hastings for about 3 miles. On reaching the Dymchurch sign, turn right into Burmarsh Road. We are 1/4 mile on the right-hand side.

Epsom Derby

First run in 1780, the Derby is arguably the most famous horserace in the world. So great was the race's popularity in the second half of the 19th century, that Parliament was suspended. Today crowds of some 100,000 or so attend the race, held on the first Saturday in June.

The Derby is named after the 12th Earl of Derby, Edward Smith-Stanley, who, together with his colourful uncle, General John Burgoyne, organised the first contest for three-year-old fillies in 1779. The race over Epsom Downs was named The Oaks after Burgoyne's rambling house, near Epsom, and was won by Derby's filly, Bridget. At the celebration dinner that followed, Derby planned a second race for three-year-old colts and fillies, which would take his name. On 4 May 1780, the first Derby took place – and a great English tradition was born. Both races continue to run, with The Oaks taking place the day before the Derby.

The race has had its fair share of drama. In 1913, the suffragette Emily Davison was killed when she threw herself in front of the King's horse, an act of martyrdom which generated maximum publicity, though many thought she was deranged. More recently, in 1981, the crowds witnessed the most dramatic Derby win ever, when the legendary colt Shergar, ridden by Walter Swinburn won effortlessly by a clear ten lengths. Two years later, Shergar was kidnapped from the Aga Khan's stud in Ireland and, to this day, his fate remains a mystery.

For runners and riders, the course over the Epsom Downs is supremely challenging. Run early in the season when the going can be heavy, the undulating and twisting $1^1/_2$ mile (2.4km) course requires great stamina. Rising 150ft (46m) in the first four furlongs, it then falls 100ft (30.5m) in varying gradients to the famous Tattenham Corner, before rising again towards the finishing post – making it a true test of equine greatness.

www.epsomderby.co.uk

Hotels and Guest Accommodation | **South and South East England**

Ideally situated for visiting castles and gardens. Woodland and seaside walks

180 : Rye, East Sussex

Flackley Ash Hotel

★★★ Silver Award

Peasmarsh, near Rye, East Sussex TN31 6YH
Contact: Emma Betteridge • **Tel:** 01797 230651 • **Fax:** 01797 230510
Web: www.flackleyashhotel.co.uk • **E-mail:** enquiries@flackleyashhotel.co.uk

This Georgian country house hotel stands in its own beautiful gardens, with croquet and putting lawns to enjoy. There is an indoor swimming pool and leisure centre, with gym, saunas, whirlpool spa and steam room. There is also a beauty salon offering an aromatherapy massage. Flackley Ash has a warm and friendly atmosphere with fine wines and good food. It is well-situated for visiting the castles and gardens of East Sussex and Kent and the ancient Cinque Port of Rye. Golf, bird-watching, country and seaside walks, steam trains and potteries are all available in the area.

Bed & Breakfast per night:
Single room from £85.00–£95.00;
Double room from £135.00–£155.00

Dinner, Bed & Breakfast per person, per night: £73.00–£95.00

Bedrooms: 45

Bathrooms: 45 en suite

Parking: Available

Cards accepted: American Express, Delta, Diners, Mastercard, Switch, Visa, Euros

Directions: From junction 5 on M25 turn on to A21 signposted Tunbridge Wells/Hastings. At traffic lights turn left on to A268. At Newenden take A268 towards Rye. Flackley Ash Hotel is on the left.

South and South East England — Hotels and Guest Accommodation

An award-winning little gem of an hotel in the ancient Cinque Port of Rye

181 : Rye, East Sussex

Rye Lodge Hotel

★★★ Silver Award

Hilder's Cliff, Rye, East Sussex TN31 7LD
Tel: 01797 223838 • **Fax:** : 01797 223585
Web: www.ryelodge.co.uk • **E-mail:** info@ryelodge.co.uk

Rye Lodge Hotel sits in a premier position on East Cliff, close to the historic 14th century Landgate, High Street restaurants, teashops, antique and art shops of this charming medieval Cinque Port with its cobbled streets and picturesque period buildings. Luxury bedrooms are all en suite. There is room service – with the bonus of breakfast in bed. The elegant marble-floored Terrace Room serves superb cuisine and fine wines – and there is an indoor pool, sauna and aromatherapy steam cabinet to complete your enjoyment of this elegant and charming hotel. Rye Lodge is ideally placed for you to enjoy the historic and beautiful places of East Sussex and the eye-catching coastline of this lovely part of England.

Bed & Breakfast per night:
Single room from £69.50–£105.00
Double room from £95.00–£190.00

Dinner, Bed & Breakfast per person, per night: £69.50–£109.50 (min 2 nights)

Bedrooms: 12 double/6 twin

Bathrooms: 18 en suite

Parking: Private car park

Cards accepted: Mastercard, Visa, Switch, Delta, American Express, Diners, Maestro, plus Euros, US dollars

Directions: On entering Rye follow town centre signs after going through Landgate Arch (historical monument) and Rye Lodge is 100 metres on the right.

Hotels and Guest Accommodation — **South and South East England**

Lovingly restored listed building with galleried dining room

182 : Rye, East Sussex

Jeake's House Hotel

♦♦♦♦♦ Silver Award

Mermaid Street, Rye, East Sussex TN31 7ET
Contact: Jenny Hadfield • **Tel:** 01797 222828 • **Fax:** 01797 222623
Web: www.jeakeshouse.com • **E-mail:** stay@jeakeshouse.co

Open any door in Jeake's House and you will open a door to yet another delight – a further sign that this hotel prides itself on old fashioned, friendly and efficient hospitality and service. Each bedroom has been individually restored to combine traditional elegance and luxury with modern amenities. There are brass or mahogany bedsteads, antique four-poster beds and roll-top baths. On chilly mornings a roaring fire greets guests in the oak-beamed parlour. Delicious breakfasts, including devilled kidneys, vegetarian and fish dishes, are served in the elegant galleried hall of what was a Quaker meeting house. Pre-dinner drinks are sipped in the comfort of the book-lined bar, while guests peruse the menus of the restaurants they are about to visit. All this amid the beauty and fascination of the ancient Cinque Port, an ideal base from which to explore this historic part of the south east. There is a private car park nearby – a great bonus in Rye.

Bed & Breakfast per night:
Single room from £39.00
Double room from £86.00–£118.00
Bedrooms: 8 double/3 twin/1 single/3 family/3 suites
Bathrooms: 10 en suite
Parking: Available
Cards accepted: Mastercard, Visa, Switch, Delta

Directions: Road: take M20 towards Dover. Exit M20 at j 10 (Ashford). Take A2070 then A259 into Rye. Rail: from Charing Cross, change at Ashford for services to Rye.

South and South East England — **Hotels and Guest Accommodation**

Rudyard Kipling and Bateman's

When Rudyard Kipling first set eyes upon Bateman's in 1902, he knew he wanted it as his home: 'That's her! The only she!' he exclaimed, 'Make an honest woman of her – quick!'

A perfect example of the English Jacobean manor house, Bateman's is almost unaltered since its completion in 1634. Situated near Burwash in Sussex, it was built from warm local sandstone and its rooms are fashioned from dark panelling and polished old wood. A large, rambling place with an asymmetrical frontage, it is surrounded by large trees and the beautiful gardens the Kiplings created there.

For Kipling, literary acclaim came early and by his late twenties he was already well known in London's intellectual circles. In 1892, he married Caroline Balestier and spent the next four years at her family's estates in America, where he wrote his famous *Jungle Book*. Kipling then returned to England and settled at Rottingdean, a village not far from Burwash. The years there, however, were clouded by the death of his six-year-old daughter from pneumonia and, after only a year or so, the hunt began for a new house. After years of searching, Bateman's became his next, and final, home. It was also where he wrote, amongst others, *Puck of Pooks Hill* and the poems *If* and *The Glory of the Garden*.

After his death in 1936, Caroline Kipling lived on at Bateman's for three years, finally bequeathing the house to the National Trust as a memorial to her husband. Many of their furnishings are still on display. Most evocative of all is the author's study, barely touched since the day of his death. The table where he wrote, in front of the window, still bears his writing implements, and the view is of a little grassy knoll, immortalised in his writings as Pooks Hill.

Bateman's
Tel: 01435 882302, www.nationaltrust.org.uk

183 : Eastbourne, East Sussex

Brayscroft House ◆◆◆◆

13 South Cliff Avenue, Eastbourne BN20 7AH.
Contact: Susan Carter
Tel: 01323 647005
Web: www.brayscrofthotel.co.uk
E-mail: Brayscroft@hotmail.com

This award-winning delightful small hotel is commended for lovely accommodation and thoughtful hospitality and selected by Which? Hotel Guide 2005. Artistic flair and antique furniture add eclectic style. The fresh restful bedrooms are all en suite with TV and refreshments. The hotel is licensed and the food is excellent, using fresh local produce including home-made jams. The hotel is in a superb position at the western end of the seafront and is within easy walking distance of Devonshire Park Tennis Lawns, Western Lawns, the Bandstand and the town centre.

Bed & Breakfast per night:
Single room from £32.00–£35.00
Double room from £64.00–£70.00

Dinner, Bed & Breakfast per person, per night:
£46.00–£49.00

Bedrooms: 3 double/2 twin/1 family

Bathrooms: 6 en suite

Parking: Available

Cards accepted: Mastercard, Visa, Switch/Delta, American Express

Directions: At Eastbourne take King Edward's Parade and pass the Grand Hotel on your right. Take the slip road marked South Cliff and turn right almost immediately into South Cliff Avenue.

184 : Eastbourne, East Sussex

The Grand ★★★★★

King Edward's Parade,
Eastbourne, East Sussex
Contact: Tina Miller
Tel: 01323 412345 • **Fax:** 01323 412233
Web: www.grandeastbourne.com
E-mail: sales@grandeastbourne.com

Benefiting from a complete restoration and spectacular improvement, The Grand takes pride of place as one of England's premier resort hotels. The atmosphere is restfully opulent, but certainly not stuffy, with a wonderful location overlooking the sea in the elegant coastal town of Eastbourne. Boasting fine bedrooms and suites, two award-winning restaurants and comprehensive health and beauty facilities including two pools, The Grand offers genuine service to match its elegant surroundings.

Bed & Breakfast per night:
Single room from £135.00–£420.00
Double room from £165.00–£450.00

Bedrooms: 68 double/60 twin/24 suites

Bathrooms: 152 en suite

Parking: Available

Cards accepted: American Express, Delta, Diners, Mastercard, Switch, Visa, Euros

Directions: Please see website for maps and directions.

South and South East England — Self-Catering

SELF-CATERING South and South East England

South and South East England : Self-Catering

185 : Naphill, Buckinghamshire

High Gables ★★★★★

Stocking Lane, Naphill,
Buckinghamshire HP14 4RE
Contact: Patricia Zachary
Tel: 01494 562591 • **Fax:** 01494 562592
Web: www.high-gables.com
E-mail: zacharydesign@btconnect.com

This a completely private, spacious, self-contained professionally designed, contemporary luxury apartment annexed to a large country house. Located in an area of outstanding natural beauty in the heart of the Chilterns, there are wonderful views and walks all round and High Gables is within easy reach of Speen, Amersham, Marlow and Henley. Nearby are Hughenden Manor, West Wycombe Park and the Hell Fire Caves. Heathrow and Luton airports are short distances away. The apartment, which is fully-equipped, has an en suite double bedroom, comfortable lounge, kitchen and entrance hall.

Low season per week: £500.00
High season per week: £500.00
Short breaks: From £100.00
1 apartment
Cards accepted: None

Directions: From High Wycombe take A4128. Follow signs for Speen, then left for Naphill. Go past The Wheel pub and the take next right into Stocking Lane. Enter Little Moseley House on right to collect keys.

186 : Taplow, Berkshire

The Studio Boathouse
★★★★/★★★★★ Pending

Mill Lane, Taplow, Berkshire SL6 0AA
Contact: Heather Lindsey
Tel: 01628 630249 • **Fax:** 07801 985936
Web: www.studioboathouse.co.uk
E-mail: heather@jfaexport.com

The Studio Boathouse on the River Thames is an idyllic hideaway for honeymooners and incurable romantics. It has been beautifully restored, with top quality flooring, beams and vaulted ceiling – a tribute to the boatbuilders' craft. It provides exceptional accommodation for one or two people, with a private balcony and terrace with barbecue overlooking the river. A stone path leads from the balcony to gardens and the boats below, and a wooden bridge leads to a private island where willow trees frame views of Boulter's Lock. The Studio is a haven of tranquillity, but within easy reach of London and the major centres of the South East.

Low season per week: £295.00–£340.00
High season per week: £455.00–£590.00
Short breaks: From £180.00–£270.00
1 boathouse
Cards accepted: Mastercard, Switch, Visa

Directions: At M4 junction 9, take A4 to Maidenhead. Turn right into Mill Lane at the foot of Maidenhead Bridge and proceed 600 yards up Mill Lane.

Self-Catering | **South and South East England**

Isle of Wight geology

For some of the most spectacular coastal scenery in southern England, and some of its most complex geology, created by the ebb and flow of the sea, it is hard to beat the Isle of Wight.

The island is bisected by a high chalk ridge running east–west and rising to a height of some 650ft (198m). At its western end this chalk band forms a narrow headland pointing out to sea, shaped by the waves into the spectacular snow-white cliffs of Freshwater Bay – and, at its furthest extremity, eroded into a series of jagged, white teeth poking from the sea, are the famous Needles.

The character of the landscape north and south of the band of chalk differs markedly. The soils of the northern half of the island were laid down about 60 million years ago, in sedimentary layers of sand (crushed quartz) and clay. At Alum Bay, just north of the Needles, some of these layers have been exposed by the sea, to reveal an amazing variety of coloured sands; white, black, green, red and yellow, created by impurities in the usually white quartz.

On the south side, ancient earth movements have exposed sedimentary layers laid down between 120 million and 65 million years ago. Of these, the Wealden group, Wight's oldest rocks, meet the sea in just two places. They also yield some of the richest sources of dinosaur bones in Europe. On the beach at Hanover Point is Pine Raft, the fossilised remains of tree-trunks, some beautifully preserved, with annual growth rings still visible.

For more explanation of the island's geology and to see a display of some spectacular fossil remains, visit the Dinosaur Isle Museum at Sandown.

Dinosaur Isle Museum
Tel: 01983 404344, www.dinosaurisle.com

At-a-glance symbols are explained on the flap inside the back cover

South and South East England — Self-Catering

187 : Rochester, Kent

Stable Cottages ★★★★ Gold Award

Fenn Croft, Newlands Farm Road,
St Mary Hoo, Rochester, Kent ME5 8QS
Contact: Debbie Symonds
Tel: 01634 272439
Web: www.stable-cottages.com
E-mail: stablecottages@btinternet.com

There are four cottages set in 20 acres of secluded farm land, with a panoramic view of the Thames and open countryside. Each cottage, with its oak beams, comprises two bedrooms – one with a double bed, the other with bunk beds. The kitchens are fully-fitted and equipped and the lounge/diners have three-piece suites and dining space for six guests. The cottages are maintained in spotless condition. The shared utility room has every appliance you are likely to need. Stable Cottages have their own garden with furniture and barbecue, and children can play in safety. Close by are several attractive walks and bird reserves, while nearby Rochester has every amenity, together with the cathedral and castle.

Low season per week: £250.00–£400.00
High season per week: £400.00
Short breaks: From £175.00–£250.00
4 cottages
Cards accepted: None

Directions: Take A289 junction off the A2, follow signs to Grain (A228). Get on new bypass, turn left at roundabout up Four Elms Hill, turn left into Fenn Street then first left.

188 : Gravesend, Kent

Russell Quay ★★★★

27 Russell Quay, West Street,
Gravesend, Kent DA11 0BP
Contact: Mr TM Dickety, Laharna,
Brimstone Hill, Meopham, Kent DA13 0BN
Tel: 01474 573045 • **Fax:** 01474 573049
Web: www.halcyon-gifts.co.uk/holidaylet.htm
E-mail: mikedickety@beeb.net

A modern first floor, tastefully furnished flat, overlooking the Thames near the Gravesend/Tilbury ferry. Accommodation comprises entrance hall, living room and dining area, separate kitchen, one double bedroom with en suite shower room with toilet, and a single bedroom. The flat is tastefully furnished and fully-equipped throughout. Central London is 40 minutes away by train, while Bluewater, Europe's largest shopping centre, Leeds Castle, Chartwell and the National Maritime Museum at Greenwich, are all easily accessible from this charming base with its splendid views. Town centre location, with easy access to M25, buses and trains.

Low season per week: £225.00–£275.00
High season per week: £350.00–£400.00
Short breaks: From £140.00–£250.00
1 flat
Cards accepted: Delta, Mastercard, Switch, Visa

Directions: Town centre location within easy access of the M25, and a short walk from train and bus stations.

Self-Catering | **South and South East England**

189 : Tonbridge, Kent

The Oast Barn ★★★★

5 Bourne Lane, Tonbridge, Kent TN9 1LG,
Contact: Mr Trevor Bartle
Tel: 01732 353298 • **Fax:** 01732 353298
Web: www.kentcottage.co.uk
E-mail: trevor@kentcottage.co.uk

Character detached converted barn next to owner's oast house, located in quiet lane within ten minutes' walk of central Tonbridge. Attractively furnished, fully-equipped, spacious accommodation on two levels. Sleeps four, plus child's cot. Private garden, with barbecue and furniture. Welcome pack included. Every effort is made to ensure your holiday is as comfortable and relaxing as possible. Tonbridge Castle and Park have indoor and outdoor swimming pools, health suite, tennis courts, boat trips and play area for children. There are fast and frequent trains to London (35 mins). The south coast is about an hour away. An ideal location for touring Kent and Sussex, with many places of historical interest nearby.

Low season per week: £285.00–£370.00
High season per week: £420.00–£475.00
Short breaks: From £215.00–£355.00
1 cottage – 4 people, plus cot

freezer compartment   tumble dryer   MW video

Directions: Take Hildenborough exit from A21. through Hildenborough towards Tonbridge, then left into Dry Hill Park Road. Over roundabout into Yardley Park Road. Turn right at end of the road and first right again.

Tourist Information Centres

When it comes to your next English break, the first stage of your journey could be closer than you think. You've probably got a tourist information centre nearby which is there to serve the local community – as well as visitors. Knowledgeable staff will be happy to help you, wherever you're heading.

Many tourist information centres can provide you with maps and guides, and often it's possible to book accommodation and travel tickets too.

Across the country there are more than 550 TICs. You'll find the address of your nearest centre in your local phone book.

Flemings and Huguenots

The distinctive Flemish flavour of the streets of Sandwich, one of Southern England's most pleasant small towns (pictured), is difficult to miss. Firstly, there's the prevalence of Dutch gables – there are some on the corner of the church of St Peter and others on Manwood Court, built in 1564 as a grammar school. Another clue is the use of the Dutch word 'polder' to describe the low-lying marshes between Sandwich and Canterbury.

The Flemings – as the immigrants from the Low Countries were known – were first invited by Edward III in the 14th century for their skill in weaving – an important part of the area's economy. The silting up of the harbour over many years (Sandwich is now some two miles from the sea) and the inefficiency of the old cloth-manufacturing techniques meant that the new arrivals were particularly welcome. Business boomed, and Sandwich's density of substantial timbered houses (Strand Street boasts some of the finest) reflects the town's newfound prosperity.

The immigrants also brought other trades with them, such as hop-growing and commercial market gardening; skills which are still synonymous with Kent.

The European influence in Sandwich was further bolstered by another influx, this time in the 17th century. Following the revoking of the Edict of Nantes in 1685, which had allowed a degree of religious freedom, nearly half a million French Protestants abandoned their homeland, many crossing the Channel. Many of these new immigrants, known as Huguenots, remained in Kent. Echoing the achievements of their earlier Flemish counterparts, the Huguenots established the silk-weaving industry in England. At the industry's peak, around 2,000 people were employed in the silk business in Canterbury alone. Indeed the contribution of the Huguenot community to the city was such that they were granted their own chapel within the cathedral.

Sandwich Tourist Office
Tel: 01304 613565

Canterbury Cathedral
Tel: 01227 762862

Self-Catering — South and South East England

190 : Ashford, Kent

Arundel Oast ★★★★★

Woodchurch Road, High Halden,
Ashford, Kent TN26 3JQ
Contact: Serena Maundrell
Tel: 01233 850871 • **Tel:** 01233 850248
Web: www.vintage-years.co.uk
E-mail: serena@vintageyears.demon.co.uk

A superb, newly refurbished 19th century oast house, located in its own private gardens and surrounded by fields and mature ponds. This delightful character property offers four comfortable bedrooms, generously sized living rooms and all modern conveniences. It is ideally located for visiting Kent's famous gardens and buildings of historical interest, or for a quick day trip to France. Nearby Tenterden is an ancient Cinque Port and is packed with antique shops and tea rooms, while Ashford has more modern shopping centres. Arundel Oast is just one of our three self-catering country properties which have been thoughtfully equipped to provide a homely atmosphere with maximum comfort and convenience.

Low season per week: £560.00–£670.00
High season per week: £712.00–£785.00
Short breaks: From £420.00–£500.00
1 oast house, 1 stable. 1 barn, 3 in all.
Cards accepted: None

Directions: From M25 join M20 to Folkestone. At junction 9 take the A28 to Ashford/Tenterden. At High Halden turn left at Chequers pub, we are one mile on the left.

191 : Brighton, East Sussex

Best of Brighton Cottages ★★★★★

19A Metropole Court,
Kings Road, Brighton, Sussex BN1 2FA
Contact: RTS Harris, Best of Brighton Cottages,
Laureens Walk, Nevill Road,
Rottingdean, East Sussex
Tel: 01273 308779 • **Fax:** 01273 390211
Web: www.bestofbrighton.co.uk
E-mail: enquiries@bestofbrighton,cop,uk

This is a magnificent five-star penthouse balcony apartment set on top of the famous Hilton Metropole Hotel on Brighton seafront. The accommodation comprises three bedrooms, two bathrooms, lounge and fully-equipped kitchen. There is a free car parking space in the underground car park and the penthouse is reached by lift. The penthouse is one of many other properties, rated four and five star, in Metropole Court and nearby Bedford Towers. Ideal for all the amenities of this famous and popular resort. There are excellent sea views from all our five-star properties.

Low season per week: £650.00–£800.00
High season per week: £800–£1000.00
Short breaks: From £400.00–£600.00/£500.00–£700.00
25 Houses, 24 cottages, 3 bungalows, 50 apartments
Cards accepted: American Express, Mastercard, Switch, Visa, Delta, Euros

Directions: Take A23 right into the heart of Brighton to Brighton Pier. Turn right at roundabout. The Metropole Hotel is about 1 mile on the right hand side.

Dickens's Kent

For eight days in late June, visitors to Broadstairs, on Kent's eastern coast, may be forgiven for thinking they have stepped into a time warp. The streets are filled with people in Victorian dress, participating in period cricket matches, bathing parties and other amusements. What they are encountering is in fact the Dickens Festival, a literary event first staged in 1937 to mark the centenary of the author's first visit, and held annually ever since.

Dickens first came to Broadstairs aged 25 and on the point of achieving nationwide fame with *The Pickwick Papers*. For 14 years he frequently spent summer and autumn months in the town, eventually leasing Fort House, a fine residence overlooking Viking Bay. Now called Bleak House and open to the public as a museum, it is thought to have been the inspiration for its namesake in Dickens's famous novel, for it stands, tall and solitary, on the cliffs far above Broadstairs. Also in Broadstairs is the Dickens House Museum, once the home of Miss Mary Strong, an eccentric woman who was probably the inspiration for one of Dickens's most colourful creations, Miss Betsey Trotwood, David Copperfield's aunt.

In 1856, Dickens purchased Gad's Hill Place, near Rochester, which he had admired as a boy, and had always dreamed of owning. This substantial house, now a private school, is occasionally open to the public (details from Rochester's Tourist Information Centre). The town also provided inspiration for many places in Dickens' works. Eastgate House was both Nun's House School in *The Mystery of Edwin Drood* and Westgate House in *The Pickwick Papers*. Now the Rochester Dickens Centre, it recreates scenes and characters from the author's best-known works. Further Dickensian associations may be found using The Dickens Trail, available from local tourist information centres.

Bleak House
Tel: 01843 862224, www.bleakhouse.ndo.co.uk

Dickens House Museum
Tel: 01843 861232, www.dickenshouse.co.uk

Rochester Tourist Information Centre, tel: 01634 843666

Further information

General advice and information
    Booking checklist   184
    Prices   184
    Deposits and advance payments   185
    Credit/charge cards   185
    Cancellations   185

Hotels and guest accommodation
    Service charges and tipping   186
    Telephone call charges   186
    Security of valuables   186
    Code of conduct and
        conditions of participation   187
    Feedback   187

Index   188

Left, from top: St Christopher's Village, Borough, London; Whatley Manor, Malmesbury, Wiltshire

General advice and information

Booking checklist

When enquiring about accommodation make sure you check prices and other important details. You will also need to state your requirements clearly and precisely – for example:

- Your intended arrival and departure dates, with acceptable alternatives if appropriate.
- The type of accommodation you require.
- The number of people in your party and the ages of any children.
- Any particular requirements, such as a special diet or a ground-floor room.
- If you think you are likely to arrive late in the evening, mention this when you book. Similarly, if you are delayed on your journey a telephone call to inform the management may well help avoid any problems on your arrival.
- If you are asked for a deposit or the number of your credit card, find out what the proprietor's policy is if, for whatever reason, you can't turn up as planned – see 'cancellations' opposite.
- Exactly how the establishment's charges are levied – see opposite.

Misunderstandings can easily occur over the telephone, so it is advisable to confirm in writing all bookings, together with special requirements. Please mention that you learnt of the establishment through Somewhere Special. Remember to include your name and address, and please enclose a stamped, addressed envelope – or an international reply coupon if writing from outside Britain. Please note that VisitBritain does not make reservations; you should address your enquiry directly to the establishment.

Prices

The prices given throughout this publication will serve as a general guide, but you should always check them at the time of booking.

- Prices were supplied during the autumn of 2004 and changes may have occurred since publication.
- Prices include VAT where applicable.
- Prices are often much cheaper for off-peak holidays; check to see whether special off-season packages are available.

For hotels and guest accommodation the following information may also prove useful when determining how much a trip may cost:

- You should check whether or not a service charge is included in the published price.
- Prices for double rooms assume occupancy by two people; you will need to check whether there is a single person supplement if a single occupancy rate is not shown.
- A full English breakfast may not always be included in the quoted price; you may be given a continental breakfast unless you are prepared to pay more.
- Establishments with at least four bedrooms or eight beds are obliged to display overnight accommodation charges in the reception area or at the entrance.
- Reduced prices may apply for children; check exactly how these reductions are calculated, including the maximum age for the child.

Deposits and advance payments

When booking a hotel or guest accommodation, reservations made weeks or months ahead will usually require a deposit that will be deducted from the total bill at the end of your stay.

Some establishments, particularly the larger hotels in big towns, will require payment for the room upon arrival if a prior reservation has not been made. This is especially likely to happen if you arrive late and have little or no luggage. If you are asked to pay in advance, it is sensible to see your room before payment is made to ensure that it meets your requirements.

When booking self-catering accommodation, the proprietor will normally ask you to pay a deposit immediately and then to pay the full balance before your holiday date. This is to safeguard the proprietor in case you decide to cancel at a later stage, or simply do not turn up. He or she may have turned down other bookings on the strength of yours and may find it hard to re-let.

If you book by telephone and are asked for your credit card number, you should note that the proprietor may charge your credit card account even if you subsequently cancel the booking. Ask the owner what his or her usual practice is.

Credit/charge cards

Any credit/charge cards that are accepted by the establishment are indicated at the end of the written description. If you intend to pay by either credit or charge card you are advised to confirm this at the time of booking.

Please note that when paying by credit card, you may sometimes be charged a higher rate for your accommodation in order to cover the percentage paid by the proprietor to the credit card company. Again find this out in advance.

When making a booking, you may be asked for your credit card number as 'confirmation'. The proprietor may then charge your credit card account if you have to cancel the booking, but if this is the policy, it must be made clear to you at the time of booking – see opposite.

Cancellations

When you accept offered accommodation, including over the telephone, you are entering into a legally binding contract with the proprietor. This means that if you cancel a reservation or fail to take up all or part of the accommodation booked, the proprietor may be entitled to compensation if the accommodation cannot be re-let for all or a good part of the booked period. If you have paid a deposit, you will probably forfeit this, and further payment may well be asked for. You should be advised at the time of booking of what charges would be made in the event of cancelling the accommodation or leaving early. If this does not happen, you should ask, to avoid any future disputes.

No claim can be made by the proprietor until after the booked period, during which time every effort should be made to re-let the accommodation. It is therefore in your interests to advise the management immediately in writing if you have to cancel or curtail a booking. Travel or holiday insurance, available quite cheaply from travel agents and some hotels, will safeguard you if you have to cancel or curtail your stay.

And remember, if you book by telephone and are asked for your credit card number, you should check whether the proprietor intends charging your account should you later cancel your reservation. A proprietor should not be able to charge for a cancellation unless he or she has made this clear at the time of your booking and you have agreed. However, to avoid later disputes, we suggest you check whether he or she intends to make such a charge.

Left: Bath Spa Hotel, Avon
Right: Manor House hotel, Castle Combe, Wiltshire

Hotels and guest accommodation

Service charges and tipping

Some establishments levy a service charge automatically, and, if so, must state this clearly in the offer of accommodation at the time of booking. If the offer is accepted by you, the service charge becomes part of the contract. If service is included in your bill, there is no need for you to give tips to the staff unless some particular or exceptional service has been rendered. In the case of meals, the usual tip is 10% of the total bill.

Telephone call charges

There is no restriction on the charges that can be made by hotels for calls made from their premises. Unit charges are often considerably higher than telephone companies' standard charges to defray the costs of providing the service. It is a condition of the National Rating Standard that unit charges are displayed by the telephone or with the room information. In practice it is not always easy to compare these charges with standard rates. Before using a hotel telephone, particularly for long-distance calls, it is advisable to ask how the charges compare.

Security of valuables

It is advisable to deposit valuables for safe-keeping with the management of the establishment in which you are staying. If the management accept custody of your property they become wholly liable for its loss or damage. They can, however, restrict their liability for items brought on to the premises and not placed in their special custody to the minimum amounts imposed by the Hotel Proprietors Act, 1956. These are the sum of £50 in respect of one article and a total of £100 in the case of one guest. To restrict their liability the management must display a notice in the form required by the Act in a prominent position in the reception area or main entrance. Without this notice, the proprietor is liable for the full value of the loss or damage to any property (other than a motor car or its contents) of a guest who has booked overnight accommodation.

Code of Conduct and Conditions of Participation

The operator/manager is required to observe the following Code of Conduct:

- To maintain standards of guest care, cleanliness, and service appropriate to the type of establishment;
- To describe accurately in any advertisement, brochure, or other printed or electronic media, the facilities and services provided;
- To make clear to visitors exactly what is included in all prices quoted for accommodation, including taxes, and any other surcharges. Details of Charges for additional services/ facilities should also be made clear;
- To give a clear statement of the policy on cancellations to guests at the time of booking i.e. by telephone, fax, email as well as information given in a printed format;
- To adhere to, and not to exceed prices quoted at the time of booking for accommodation and other services;
- To advise visitors at the time of booking, and subsequently of any change, if the accommodation offered is in an unconnected annexe or similar, and to indicate the location of such accommodation and any difference in comfort and/or amenities from accommodation in the establishment;
- To give each visitor, on request, details of payments due and a receipt, if required;
- To deal promptly and courteously with all enquiries, requests, bookings and correspondence from visitors;
- Ensure complaint handling procedures are in place and that complaints received are investigated promptly and courteously and that the outcome is communicated to the visitor;
- To give due consideration to the requirements of visitors with special needs, and to make suitable provision where applicable;
- To provide public liability insurance or comparable arrangement and to comply with applicable planning, safety and other statutory requirements;
- To allow a VisitBritain representative reasonable access to the establishment, on request, to confirm the Code of Conduct is being observed.

Feedback

Let us know about your break or holiday. We welcome suggestions about how the guide itself may be enhanced or improved and you will find our addresses on page 4 of the guide.

Details listed were believed correct at time of going to press (December 2004), but we advise telephoning in advance to check that details have not altered and to discuss any specific requirements.

Most establishments welcome feedback. Please let the proprietor know if you particularly enjoyed your stay. We sincerely hope that you have no cause for complaint, but should you be dissatisfied or have any problems, make your complaint to the management at the time of the incident so that immediate action may be taken.

In certain circumstances VisitBritain may look into complaints. However, we have no statutory control over establishments or their methods of operating. We cannot become involved in legal or contractual matters, nor can we get involved in seeking financial recompense.

If you do have problems that have not been resolved by the proprietor and which you would like to bring to our attention, please write to:

Quality Standards Department
VisitBritain
Thames Tower
Blacks Road
Hammersmith
London W6 9EL

Left, from top: Malmaison Hotel, Birmingham; Bath Spa Hotel, Avon
Right: Seaham Hall, County Durham

Index

Alkham Court, Dover, Kent	166
Alma Mater, Milford-on-Sea, Hampshire	159
April Cottage, Wadebridge, North Cornwall	132
Arundel Oast, Ashford, Kent	181
Ashdown Park, Forest Row, East Sussex	166
Ayrlington Hotel, Bath, Somerset	116
Bamham Farm Cottages, Launceston, Cornwall	130
The Bantam Tea Rooms, Chipping Camden, Gloucestershire	111
Barbican House, York, North Yorkshire	30
Beach Court, Beadnell, Northumberland	21
The Beach House, Blackpool, Lancashire	50
Beryl, Wells, Somerset	118
Best of Brighton Cottages, Brighton, East Sussex	181
Bishops Table Hotel, Farnham, Surrey	156
Blaize Cottages, Lavenham, Suffolk	91
Blue Hayes Private Hotel, St Ives, Cornwall	108
Bluebell, Bonny, Buttercup & Bertie, Saxmundham, Suffolk	88
Bowling Green Hotel, Plymouth, Devon	108
Bowood Farm, Abbotsham, North Devon	130
Brayscroft House, Eastbourne, West Sussex	173
Brittannia House, Teignmouth, Devon	122
Budock Vean, Falmouth, Cornwall	109
Buxton's Victorian Guest House, Buxton, Derbyshire	65
Canfield Moat, Dunmow, Essex	77
Cardwen Farm, Looe, Cornwall	107
Cardynham House, Painswick, Gloucestershire	112
Cary Court Hotel, Torquay, South Devon	125
Castle of Comfort, Bridgwater, Somerset	119
Castle Road Cottages 6, 17 & 64, Colchester, Essex	93
Chalon House, Richmond, London	154
Chestnuts, Penrith, Cumbria	52
Clare House, Grange-over-Sands, Cumbria	41
Cloud Hotel, Brockenhurst, Hampshire	157
Combe House Hotel, Honiton, Devon	120
Corston Fields Farm, Bath, Somerset	114
Cottage in the Wood Hotel, Malvern Wells, Worcestershire	69
Cragside, Aldeburgh, Suffolk	93
Cransley Hotel, Bournemouth, Hampshire	121
Cressbrook Hall, Buxton, Derbyshire	64
Cuckoo's Nest, Ambleside, Cumbria	53
Cumbrian Lodge Hotel, Seascale, Cumbria	39
Daisy Cottage, Middleton-in-Teesdale, County Durham	45
Dales Holiday Cottages, Skipton, North Yorkshire	48
De Vere Slaley Hall, Hexham, Northumberland	22
Derwent Cottage Mews, Keswick, Cumbria	51
Domineys Cottages, Dorchester, Dorset	143
Druid House, Christchurch, Dorset	120
The Durdans, Mundesley, North Norfolk	73
Eastleigh Farm, Warminster, Wiltshire	140
Edgemoor Cottage, Tavistock, Devon	133
Far Nook, Ambleside, Cumbria	36
Fieldhead Hotel, West Looe, Cornwall	107
The Firs, Bath, Somerset	115
Flackley Ash Hotel, Rye, East Sussex	169
The Foredeck, Falmouth, Cornwall	139
Francis Farm Cottages, Bury St Edmunds, Suffolk	91
Friary Close, Chichester, West Sussex	163
Froyz Hall Barn, Halstead, Essex	94
Gallon House, Harrogate, North Yorkshire	28
Gilpin Lodge Hotel, Windermere, Cumbria	40
Glebe Cottage, Hardwick, Cambridgeshire	90

Glebe Farm, York, North Yorkshire	31		Laneside, Forest-in-Teesdale, County Durham	45
Glebe House, Chippenham, Wiltshire	117		Langley Castle Hotel, Hexham, Northumberland	34
Glen Cottage, Cullompton, Devon	142			
Glencot House, Wells, Somerset	117		Lilac Cottage, Stow-on-the-Wold, Gloucestershire	137
Glenview, Bodmin, Cornwall	103			
The Grand Hotel, Eastbourne, East Sussex	173		Lindeth Howe, Bowness-on-Windemere, Cumbria	40
Great Bodieve Farm Barns, Wadebridge, North Cornwall	131		Linthwaite House, Windermere, Cumbria	41
Haguelands Farm, Romney Marsh, Kent	167		Little Holtby, Northallerton, North Yorkshire	25
Haldon Priors, Torquay, South Devon	124		Lucknam Park, Chippenham, Wiltshire	113
Harbourside, Dartmouth, Devon	146		Magnolia House, Canterbury, Kent	164
Harefield Cottage, Bude, Cornwall	104		Manor House Farm, Uttoxeter, Staffordshire	67
Harrabeer Country House Hotel, Yelverton, Devon	133		Marlborough House, Bath, Somerset	116
Hartpiece, Barnstaple, Devon	129			
Headlam Hall, Darlington, County Durham	24		Martinhoe Cleave Cottages, Barnstaple, Devon	128
Heatherly Cottage, Corsham, Wiltshire	114		The Meadow House, Bunwell, Cambridgeshire	75
High Gables, Naphill, Buckinghamshire	176			
High Oxnop, Richmond, North Yorkshire	46		Melrose House, Crystal Palace, London	164
Higher Laity Farm, Redruth, Cornwall	136		The Mill House, Delabole, Cornwall	132
Higher Trezion, Camelford, Cornwall	103		The Millstream Hotel Bosham, Chichester, West Sussex	162
Highleadon Holiday Cottages, Newent, Gloucestershire	136		Milton Farm, Fairford, Gloucestershire	112
The Hillcroft, Torquay, South Devon	125		Monket Cottage, Kirbymoorside, North Yorkshire	47
Holdfast Cottage Hotel, Malvern, Worcestershire	69		Moreton Cottage, Much Wenlock, Shropshire	85
Holkham Cottage, Dersingham, Norfolk	73		The Mount, Sedbergh, Cumbria	55
Holly Lodge, Thursford Green, North Norfolk	72		Mounts Bay House, Marazion, Cornwall	109
Holmwood House, York, North Yorkshire	31		Neighbrook Manor, Moreton-in-Marsh, Gloucestershire	111
Homefinders Holidays, York, North Yorkshire	49		Neptune Inn, Old Hunstanton, Norfolk	72
Horse and Groom, Chichester, West Sussex	160		Newton House, Knaresborough, North Yorkshire	29
Hotel Riviera, Sidmouth, Devon	122		No 54, Helmsley, North Yorkshire	26
Hotels-apart, Cheltenham, Gloucestershire	137		Norman's Barn, Ashby-de-la-Zouch, Leicestershire	84
Ingleby Manor, Great Ayton, North Yorkshire	46		Northam Mill, Taunton, West Somerset	119
Ivy House Farm, Diss, Norfolk	88		The Nurse's Cottage, Lymington, Hampshire	158
Jeake's House Hotel, Rye, East Sussex	171			
Kirkstead Old Mill Cottage, Woodhall Spa, Lincolnshire	70		The Oast Barn, Tonbridge, Kent	179
Lakelovers, Windermere, Cumbria	55		Old Bridge Hotel, Huntingdon, Cambridgeshire	75
Lakeside Country House, Keswick, Cumbria	36		Old Quarry Cottage, Much Wenlock, Shropshire	68
Lampen Farm, Liskeard, Cornwall	104			

The Old School House, Collaton St Mary, Devon	123
The Old Stables, Devizes, Wiltshire	139
The Old Tollgate, Steyning, West Sussex	161
The Old Vicarage, Easingwood, North Yorkshire	27
Omnia Somia, Ashbourne, Derbyshire	66
Orchard Cottage, Near Stilton, Peterborough, Cambridgeshire	87
Oswald Cottage, Corbridge, Northumberland	44
Outchester and Ross Farm, Belford, Northumberland	44
Peak Weavers, Leek, Staffordshire	65
The Plough Inn, Hope Valley, Derbyshire	64
Ponsbourne Park Hotel, Hertford, Hertfordshire	78
Pound House, Barnard Castle, Northumberland	23
The Priory Hotel, Preston, Lancashire	33
Pudding Cottage, Nr Ambleside, Cumbria	54
Queen Anne Cottage, Andover, Hampshire	155
3 Randle How, Holmrook, Cumbria	54
Ravenscourt Manor, Ludlow, Shropshire	68
Red House Farm, Great Eversden, Cambridgeshire	90
River Cottage, Dorchester, Dorset	144
River Lodge, Southburgh, Norfolk	87
Riverdale Court, Bellingham, Northumberland	51
Rothay Manor, Ambleside, Cumbria	37
Royal Oak, Chichester, West Sussex	160
Russell Quay, Gravesend, Kent	178
Rye Lodge Hotel, Rye, East Sussex	170
Sarah Elliott's Cottage, Dartmouth, Devon	145
Scalebeck Holiday Cottages, Appleby, Cumbria	53
Sea Tree House, Lyme Regis, Dorset	144
Seabreeze Guest House, Blackpool, Lancashire	32
Seckford Hall, Woodbridge, Suffolk	77
Shallowdale House, Ampleforth, North Yorkshire	27
Shoreline Cottages, Whitby, North Yorkshire	50
Sixes 'n' Sevens, Dartmouth, Devon	146
Smallwood House Hotel, Ambleside, Cumbria	38
Spanhoe Lodge, Corby, Northamptonshire	74
The Spinney, Barnstaple, Devon	102
Stable Cottage, Dorchester, Dorset	143
Stable Cottages, Rochester, Kent	178
Staveley Grange, Harrogate, North Yorkshire	29
The Studio Boathouse, Taplow, Berkshire	176
Sunflower Lodge, Bridlington, East Yorkshire	30
Swallow Court Cottage, Wadebridge, North Cornwall	130
The Swan Hotel, Lavenham, Suffolk	76
Swinton Park, Masham, North Yorkshire	25
Three Gates Farm, Tiverton, Devon	140
The Three Lions, Fordingbridge, Hampshire	156
Throwley Moore Farmhouse, Throwley Cottage and Lathem Hall Farmhouse, Ashbourne, Derbyshire	82
Tides Reach, Salcombe, Devon	110
Tiverton Castle, Tiverton, Devon	141
Tom's Barn, Ashbourne, Derbyshire	82
Tor Cottage, Lifton, Devon	102
Townsend House, Corfe Castle, Dorset	121
Tregondale Farm, Liskeard, Cornwall	105
Tregongeeves Farm, St Austell, Cornwall	135
Treworgey Cottages, Liskeard, Cornwall	134
Tylney Hall Hotel, Hook, Hampshire	154
Under Rock, Ventor, Isle of Wight	163
Waren House Hotel, Belford, Northumberland	20
The Watermark Club, South Cerney, Gloucestershire	138
West Acre House, Alnwick, Northumberland	21
Westwood Lodge, Ilkley, West Yorkshire	49
Wisteria Lodge Country House, St Austell, Cornwall	105
Woodview Cottages, Owthorpe, Nottinghamshire	84
Wrea Head Country Cottages, Scarborough, North Yorkshire	58

Ratings you can trust

When you're looking for a place to stay, you need a rating system you can trust. VisitBritain's ratings are your clear guide to what to expect, in an easy-to-understand form. Properties are visited annually by our trained, impartial assessors, so you can be confident that your accommodation has been thoroughly checked and rated for quality before you make a booking.

Based on the internationally recognised rating of one to five stars, the system puts great emphasis on quality and is based on research which shows exactly what consumers are looking for when choosing an hotel.

Ratings are awarded from one to five stars – the more stars, the higher the quality and the greater the range of facilities and level of services provided.

Look out, too, for VisitBritain's Gold and Silver Awards, which are awarded to properties achieving the highest levels of quality within their star rating. While the overall rating is based on a combination of facilities and quality, the Gold and Silver Awards are based solely on quality.

The ratings are your sign of quality assurance, giving you the confidence to book the accommodation that meets your expectations.

enjoyEngland™
official guides to quality

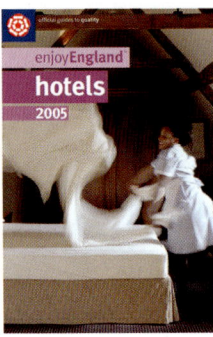

Hotels, Townhouses, Travel Accommodation and Restaurants with Rooms in England 2005
£10.99

Guesthouses, Small Hotels, Bed & Breakfast, Farmhouses, Inns, Campus Accommodation and Hostels in England 2005
£11.99

Self-Catering Holiday Homes and Boat Accommodation in England 2005
£11.99

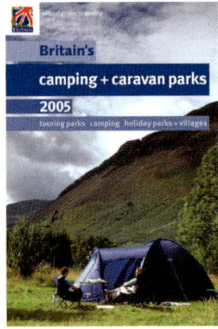

Touring Parks, Camping, Holiday Parks and Holiday Villages in Britain 2005
£8.99

Somewhere Special in England 2005
£8.99

Families and Pets Welcome in England 2005
£11.99

INFORMATIVE • EASY TO USE • GREAT VALUE FOR MONEY

The guides include:
- **Accommodation entries packed with information**
- **Full colour maps**
- **Places to visit**
- **Tourist Information Centres**

From all good bookshops or by mail order from the:

VisitBritain Fulfilment Centre,
c/o Westex Ltd, 7 St Andrews Way,
Devons Road, Bromley-by-Bow, London E3 3PA
Tel: 0870 606 7204
Fax: (020) 7987 6505
Email: fulfilment@visitbritain.org